John Malcolm Forbes Ludlow

The War of American Independence, 1775-1783

John Malcolm Forbes Ludlow

The War of American Independence, 1775-1783

ISBN/EAN: 9783337115708

Printed in Europe, USA, Canada, Australia, Japan

Cover: Foto ©ninafisch / pixelio.de

More available books at **www.hansebooks.com**

Epochs of Modern History

EDITED BY

EDWARD E. MORRIS, M.A. & J. SURTEES PHILLPOTTS, B.C.L.

THE WAR OF AMERICAN INDEPENDENCE

J. M. LUDLOW

LONDON PRINTED BY
SPOTTISWOODE AND CO., NEW-STREET SQUARE
AND PARLIAMENT STREET

OF

AMERICAN INDEPENDENCE

1775–1783

BY

JOHN MALCOLM LUDLOW

AUTHOR OF 'A SKETCH OF THE HISTORY OF THE UNITED STATES
FROM INDEPENDENCE TO SECESSION' 'PRESIDENT LINCOLN SELF-POURTRAYED'
ETC.

WITH FOUR MAPS

LONDON
LONGMANS, GREEN, AND CO.
1876

All rights reserved

CONTENTS.

CHAPTER I.
INTRODUCTORY.
                                                                                       PAGE

Why the war of American independence forms an epoch in history 1

CHAPTER II.
THE AMERICAN COLONIES (TO 1763).

Races inhabiting the colonies 2
I. THE RED MAN 3
    What the Indian is 3
    What he was; towns, agriculture 4
    Arts; written language; observation of nature . . 4
    Languages 6
    Forms of government 6
    Inferiority of women 7
    Beliefs 7
    Mode of warfare 8
    Absence of the pastoral element 8
    Code of morals 9
    Capacity for endurance 9
    Influence of the Indian element on the colonists . . 10
    General character of relations between the red and white man 11

Contents.

	PAGE
Distinctions between the **Latin and** Teutonic races in relation to the red man	12
Roman Catholic nations most successful in Christianising the red man	12
Most powerful tribes, Iroquois, Cherokees, and Creeks	13

II. THE WHITE MEN 14

   1. *The Spaniards* 14

      1. The Spaniards. England and Spain the only Continental powers in North America 14
      Early Spanish discoveries 14
      Settlement of Florida 15
      Occasional warfare **with** England 16
      Spain's **position in America** after the treaty of Paris, 1763 16

   2. *The French* 16
      Importance of the French element 16
      Early discoveries and settlements 17
      Heroic missionaries and heroic adventurers; Cavalier de la Salle 18
      Progress of France in the Mississippi valley . . 19
      Cape Breton colonised; extension of French colonisation in the west; New Orleans 20
      What France had done: scanty population of her colonies 21
      In the coming war, the French **colonists** will side with the English 22
      The Indians will do the same 22

   3. *The English* 22
      The North American continent discovered by England 23
      The English colonies 23
      The northern and southern groups 23
      Southern group: the thirteen colonies and their limits 24
      Distinctions between the colonies of the southern group 25
      Three sub-groups 26

      1. *Virginia* 26
         The name formerly wider than now . . 26
         Early attempts at colonisation by Gilbert and Raleigh 26
         The London Company; a colony established; House of Burgesses 27

	PAGE
John Smith; Pocahontas	28
Indian wars; the Stuart kings	28
Submission to the Commonwealth; growth of landed aristocracy	29
The Restoration; Bacon's Rebellion	30
Distress of the colony	31
Return of prosperity	31
2. *Maryland*	32
Liberal charter: Lord Baltimore.	32
Early prosperity: troubles with Clayborne	33
Commonwealth; Restoration; Maryland after 1683 a royal government	34
Similarity to Virginia	34
3 & 4. *The Carolinas*	34
Early charters; Shaftesbury and Locke's 'grand model'	35
Turbulent early history of these colonies. Slavery	35
The colonists break up Indian civilization in Florida	36
Indian wars; the Carolinas become colonies, 1729	37
5. *Georgia*	37
The last founded colony	37
Oglethorpe; his charter and his government	37
Hostilities with Spain	38
Failure of Oglethorpe's plans	38
6 & 7. *New York and New Jersey*	39
New York the centre of a sub-group	39
Hudson at Manhattan Island; the New Netherlands; New Amsterdam	39
New Sweden; eventually annexed to the New Netherlands	40
The Dutch territory conquered by England, and divided into New York and New Jersey	41
History of New Jersey soon connected with that of Pennsylvania	41
8 & 9. *Pennsylvania and Delaware*	42
Pennsylvania the last founded of the religious colonies	42
The Quakers in America; Penn; Philadelphia; Delaware	42
The Pennsylvania constitution; Penn's proprietary rights confiscated in 1688	43

viii   Contents.

PAGE

10, 11, 12, 13. **New England: Massachusetts, Connecticut, New Hampshire, and Rhode Island** 43

    Early attempts at settlement 43
    The 'Pilgrim Fathers' 43
    Their compact before landing 44
    Early difficulties 45
    Relations with the Indians; Massasoit; Canonicus . 46
    The Indians degenerate 47
    Settlement of New Hampshire, Massachusetts Bay, Rhode Island; Roger Williams 48
    Rapid **growth** of Massachusetts; Vane and Mrs. Hutchinson 48
    Settlement of Connecticut; the Pequod war . . 49
    Cruel fate of Miantonomo the Narragansett . . 50
    The 'United Colonies' **of** New England . . . 50
    The oppressive conduct **of** Charles I leads to a federation 50
    Massachusetts during the Commonwealth . . . 51
    The **Restoration** 52
    King Philip's war 52
    Struggle of Massachusetts against **the** Restoration Government. The Revolution of 1688 54
    Warfare with the French till 1748 54

III. **THE BLACK MAN** 55

    Growth of slavery 56
    Royal slave traders; the Asiento 56
    Support of slavery and the slave trade by the mother country 57

    General Colonial History 1748–63 58
    Connexion of King George's War with Franklin . 58
    Benjamin Franklin; the author of the first military organization in the colonies 58
    The 'French and Indian War', George Washington . 59
    Franklin's proposed congress 60
    General Braddock's defeat 61
    Conquest of New Brunswick, expulsion of the Acadians 62
    French successes 62

	PAGE
The French defeated; Canada conquered; Peace of Paris	62
Pontiac's war	63
The colonies in 1763	64

CHAPTER III.

CAUSES OF DISCONTENT. STRUGGLE BEFORE THE WAR (1763-75).

Montcalm's prediction	64
Mingled loyalty and disaffection of colonies	64
The Navigation Laws	65
Struggle against the Navigation Laws, in New England especially	65
The coming contest prefigured	66
Other causes of discontent	67
Mutual complaints between the mother country and the colonies	68
The attempt to raise a revenue from the colonies; George Grenville	68
The colonial Revenue Act	69
Protests of the colonists; Otis; Samuel Adams	69
The Stamp Act, 1765	69
Patrick Henry's resolutions	70
A congress convened; riots at Boston and elsewhere	71
Independence already spoken of; New York Congress and its proceedings	71
The Stamp Act cannot be carried into effect	72
The Rockingham Cabinet; Pitt rejoices that America has resisted	73
The Stamp Act repealed, 1766; the Declaratory Act	73
Rejoicings in the colonies	74
Further obnoxious measures	74
The Quartering Act. Suspension of the New York Assembly	75
The Chatham Cabinet, 1766-8	76
Renewed agitation in the colonies; non-importation agreements; French intrigues	76
The Boston Convention	78

Troops sent to the colonies; Hillsborough's and North's policy;
  feelings of Washington (1768–9) 78
Spread of non-importation agreements; the Boston massacre . 79
Lord North attempts a compromise; the Tea Act (1770) . . 79
The burning of the 'Gaspee,' 1772 80
The committees of correspondence; destruction of tea at Boston (1772–3) 80
Indignation of parliament; the Boston Port Act 81
Other repressive measures 82
Protests of Virginia and Massachusetts; a Congress called . . 83
The Continental Congress at Philadelphia (Sept. 1734) . . 84
Washington still disclaims the idea of colonial independence . 85
The Massachusetts provincial congress; raising of troops . 86
Large majorities in parliament against concession; Chatham's warnings 87
Lord North's new measures; the prohibition of trade extended 88
Massachusetts prepares for war; a collision barely averted . 89
Virginia prepares for war; Washington ready to devote his life to the cause 89
The train ready for the spark 90

CHAPTER IV.
1775.

The colonial powers 90
Europe 91
France and Spain the only powers directly interested in the American struggle 94
France the intellectual centre of Europe; Voltaire, Rousseau . 94
Sense of a coming revolution 95
The new reign in France a hopeful one; Turgot and Malesherbes. The corn riots of 1775 96
French sympathy with America preceded the American Revolution 97
Special grounds for such sympathy; admiration for England . 97
America for France an ideal England 98
Influence of the partition of Poland 99

	PAGE
England	99
The Jacobite party extinct	99
George III.	100
Wilkes, Junius, Chatham, Burke, Fox	100
Literature and art : Johnson, Hume, Gibbon, Cowper, Macpherson, Walpole, Sheridan, Reynolds, Gainsborough	101
Industry: the inventors — Strutt, Hargreaves, Arkwright, Watt, Wedgwood, Flaxman	101
Chemistry and Priestley ; engineering — Brindley, Smeaton	102
Growth of population ; improved agriculture ; Arthur Young	103
Two boys of six, Napoleon Bonaparte and Arthur Wellesley	103

CHAPTER V.

THE WAR : FIRST PERIOD ; TILL THE FRENCH ALLIANCE (1775-8).

	PAGE
The war : divided into two periods by the French alliance	104
The first shot ; battle of Lexington, April 18-19, 1775	104
The whole country astir ; Boston invested	105
Surprise of Ticonderoga, May 10	105
Second Continental Congress ; a Continental army voted	106
General Gage proclaims martial law ; Washington commander-in-chief	106
Washington	106
Battle of Bunker's Hill, June 17, 1775	107
Washington in command ; his difficulties	108
Proceedings in the south ; the governors on board ship	110
Last attempts at conciliation by Congress ; Richard Penn and the 'Olive Branch'	111
Proclamation against rebellion ; application to German princes for troops	111
The English people do not appreciate the crisis	112
Debates in parliament ; Lord George Germain ; the ministry supported	112
The General Prohibition of Trade Act ; votes for German troops	113
America receives with divided feelings the proclamation against rebellion	114
The invasion of Canada by Montgomery	114

Contents.

	PAGE
Arnold; the failure before Quebec (Dec. 31, 1775)	115
Lord Dunmore in Virginia; Norfolk burnt (Jan. 1, 1776); the American flag	116
Washington's difficulties continue	116
Boston evacuated, March 1776	117
Measures of Congress; resolution against the slave trade; free trade	118
America **secretly aided by France and Spain**	118
Dissolution **of the old** colonial **governments**; Declaration of Independence proposed	119
British attack on Fort Moultrie; American disasters in Canada; the retreat	120
Washington at New York; miserable state of the army	121
Arrival of a British fleet, and **of** royal commissioners	122
The Declaration of Independence, July 4, 1776	122
A paragraph relating to slavery and the slave trade struck out	123
Declamatory character of the Declaration; **its** unfairness	124
The Declaration in fact one of war	126
Its influence on foreign countries	126
Its enthusiastic reception in America	126
The need of union still scarcely felt. Postponement of the plan of confederation	127
The royal commissioners and Washington; New **York** threatened	127
Battle of Long Island, August 27, 1776	128
Discouragement of the troops; Washington's position desperate	129
Fruitless peace conference; New York evacuated (Sept. 15)	130
Congress raises a new army to serve during the war	131
General Howe's advance; Fort Washington taken (Nov. 16)	131
Washington's retreat through New Jersey; Rhode Island recovered by the British; results of the campaign	132
Indignation caused in England by the Declaration of Independence; Franklin in Paris; John the Painter	133
Outcry in America against Washington. Reed and Lee; Lee's capture	133
Disaffection in Pennsylvania; Washington's temporary military dictatorship	134
The surprise of Trenton, Dec. 25, 1776	135
The battle of Princeton, January 1777; New Jersey nearly recovered	136

	PAGE
Washington's winter difficulties; smallpox disastrous	136
The ravages of the British alienate the people	137
Foreign volunteers; they become a difficulty	137
The Marquis de la Fayette; Kosciusko	138
Lord Chatham's reappearance; expedition from Canada decided on	139
Burgoyne's advance; at first successful	140
Battle of Bennington, August 16, 1777	140
Battle of Brandywine, Sept. 11, 1777	141
Philadelphia occupied by the British, Sept. 26; battle of Germantown, Oct. 4	141
Renewed outcry against Washington	142
The battles of Stillwater, Sept. 19, Oct. 7	142
Burgoyne's surrender at Saratoga, Oct. 16	143
Gates and Washington	144
Rejoicings in England over the occupation of Philadelphia; Chatham's inconsistency	144
Gloomy impressions produced by the Saratoga surrender; France ready to treat with America	145
Sense of an impending crisis; the king has forebodings	146
The scheme of Confederation adopted by Congress, Nov. 15, 1777	147
Impotency of Congress	147
Washington's miserable winter at Valley Forge	147
Inaction of the English	148
The treaty between France and America, February 6, 1778	149
The theatre of the war enlarged	149

CHAPTER VI.

THE WAR: SECOND PERIOD; FROM THE ALLIANCE WITH FRANCE TILL THE END OF THE WAR (1778-83).

France and the treaty	149
Lord North's conciliatory bills	150
The king will not have Lord Chatham as premier	151
Death of Chatham, May 11, 1778	152
Preparations for war with France	153

	PAGE
Rejoicings over the treaty in America	153
Reception of the Conciliatory Bills	154
Arrival of the royal commissioners (June 4, 1778)	154
The evacuation of Philadelphia ordered	155
Philadelphia evacuated; battle of Monmouth (June 28); Lee and Washington	156
Articles of Confederation signed by several States	157
D'Estaing and the French investment of Newport	157
Indian massacres	158
Failure of the peace commission	158
The war in other quarters; Keppel; Paul Jones; Hyder Ali	158
Increasing impotency of Congress; it solicits French 'protection'	159
British operations in the South. Savannah taken (December 29), and Georgia recovered	161
South Carolina invaded, and Charleston threatened (May 1779)	161
Washington's army during the winter of **1778–9**. Defensive campaign	162
General Sullivan devastates the Iroquois **country**	164
The British in Penobscot Bay	164
Congress appoints peace commissioners	165
The war in Europe **uneventful**	165
Spain's backwardness in going to war	165
War convention between France and Spain, April 12, 1779	166
The north-western territory coveted by Spain, but occupied by the backwoodsmen	167
England **ready for** war **with** Spain, but impatient of that with America. **The** king's obstinacy	168
Siege **of** Gibraltar; the combined fleets in the Channel	168
Paul Jones's sea-fight; vast scale of the war	169
Failure of the **French** and Americans before Savannah, October 9, 1779	170
Rhode Island evacuated by the British; Charleston taken (May 12, 1780), and South Carolina subdued	171
Another gloomy winter for Washington, 1779–80. Supineness of the Americans	172
The war at sea; Rodney	174
Nelson in Central America. England's quarrel with Holland	175
The armed neutrality	176

	PAGE
Ireland; the Yorkshire Committee; the Protestant Association and Lord George Gordon	177
Burke's plan of Economic Reform; Dunning's resolution	178
The London No-popery riots, June 2-8, 1780	179
Spanish negotiations stopped by the riots	180
The war in South Carolina; battle of Camden (August 16, 1780)	180
Cornwallis's march into North Carolina checked. American partisans. Greene in command	181
Little doing in the North	183
Arnold's treason, Sept. 1780	183
The war in India and at sea, 1780	185
The new Parliament; war with Holland declared, Dec. 20, 1780	185
The war in Europe, 1781	185
Seizure of St. Eustace, Feb. 3, 1781; the war in the West Indies, Florida, and India, 1781	186
France anxious for peace. Mediation of Austria	187
Washington's army during the winter of 1780-1. Mutinies	188
The crisis tided over; the Articles of Confederation finally signed, March 1, 1781	189
Greene in the South. Battle of the Cowpens, Jan. 17, 1781	190
Lord Cornwallis advances again into North Carolina, Greene retreating	190
Battle of Guilford Court House, March 15, 1781; Cornwallis falls back to the coast	191
La Fayette and Arnold in Virginia. Cornwallis leaves Wilmington (April)	192
Greene recovers the greater part of South Carolina	192
Proceedings in parliament; Fox and the younger Pitt	194
Weakness of America; subserviency to France	194
Cornwallis in Virginia. He withdraws to Yorktown (August 1781)	194
Battle of Eutaw Springs, September 8, 1781; the war at an end in the South	195
Arnold in Connecticut (September)	196
Junction of Washington and the French; operations on the Chesapeake decided on	196
The march to Virginia, August 1781	196
Yorktown invested, September 28; Cornwallis surrenders, October 19	197

Contents.

	PAGE
Rejoicings in America	198
Proceedings in parliament; the ministers fiercely attacked; meetings against the war	198
The war almost everywhere disastrous to England. Minorca lost (Feb. 7, 1782)	199
Weakness and fall of Lord North's ministry (March 20, 1782)	200
The second Rockingham ministry; Shelburne treats with Franklin	201
America so reduced that she cannot believe in peace	202
The crown offered to Washington	202
Rodney's victory in the West Indies (April 12, 1782)	203
The Shelburne ministry; evacuation of Savannah (July 12)	**203**
Active warfare confined to the siege of Gibraltar	**204**
Progress of negotiations; preliminary articles of peace between **England** and America, Nov. 30, 1782	204
Opening **of** parliament, Nov. 5; the king's speech	205
The French troops return to Europe	206
Preliminaries of peace with France and Spain, **Jan.** 20, 1783	206
Peace with Holland and with Tippoo Sultan	207
Fall of Shelburne; the coalition ministry (April 2, 1783)	**207**
Discontent of Washington's officers. Cessation of hostilities (April 17, 1783)	208
Congress threatened by mutineers	**208**
Ratification of the treaties, Sept. 3, **1783**; the slave question	**208**
Evacuation of New York, Nov. 25, 1783	209
Washington's farewell to his officers; he is thanked by Congress	210
Cost of the war	210
What England had done	211
Results of the war for the different races	211
(1) The Red man driven back	211
(2) Advance of the White man	212
(3) The Black man; what he got from the Americans	212
The Black men badly treated by the English	214
How the Black man's wrongs will avenge themselves	214

CHAPTER VII.

THE PARADOXES OF THE WAR, AND ITS TRUE CHARACTER.

	PAGE
England's success seemingly impossible	215
England was often on the verge of triumph	215
Puzzles to be explained	217
Reliance of the English on the loyalists	217
Inadequate support really afforded by the loyalists	219
Incapacity of the American politicians	220
Supineness and want of patriotism of the people	221
Why did England fail	223
Incompetency of British generals no sufficient reason	223
Ministerial incapacity no sufficient reason	224
Importance of the foreign aid supplied to America	226
The war ceased when the English nation thoroughly understood its character	227
Early popularity of the war the result of ignorance	227
The popularity of the war never but skin-deep	228
Contrast with feelings called out by war with France and Spain	228
The war in fact a duel between Washington and George III.	229
American success impossible without Washington	229
George III. the centre of English resistance to American independence	230
In such a duel, Washington must win	231
Character of Washington's greatness	232
Washington and Wellington compared	233
Washington a thorough Englishman	234

CHAPTER VIII.

1783.

State of the world	234
The balance of power but slightly affected by the war	234
New political events since 1775 outside of the war	234
Other events	235

	PAGE
Voltaire's return to Paris (Feb. 1778)	235
Voltaire's death, May 30, 1778	236
Rousseau's death, July 1, 1778	236
Financial ruin of France	236
The heroes of the day in France, and the coming men of the future	236
Germany; sympathy with America	237
England; the literary world	237
The political world	237
America	238

Quotations for which no source is quoted are derived from Mr. Bancroft's 'History of the United States.'

LIST OF MAPS.

♦

The World .... *To face Title*

British Colonies in North America .... *page* 24

North America before the War .... ,, ,, 66

   ,,   After the War .... ,, ,, 210

THE WAR OF AMERICAN INDEPENDENCE.

CHAPTER I.

INTRODUCTORY.

THE war of American Independence deserves on several grounds to be deemed an epoch in history. Why the war of American independence forms an epoch in history.

It was the first instance in modern times of the successful revolt of a colony against the mother-country.

It was followed by a series of more or less similar revolts, which stripped France of her largest remaining colony in the western world, deprived Spain of the whole of her possessions on both continents of America, and have probably not yet been brought to a close, as the pending Cuban insurrection seems to show.

It created the first independent state on either American continent which had existed since the downfall of the great Indian kingdoms of Mexico and Peru in the sixteenth century.

By depriving England of her most important colonies in America, it shifted the centre of gravity of her colonial empire from the western to the eastern hemisphere.

Through the share taken by France in the struggle,

and its influence on public opinion in that country, it contributed largely to the French Revolution, and thereby to the complete transformation of the political and social state of Europe, which has resulted therefrom, and which is still going on.

It laid the foundation of a polity which is the first realisation in history of a federal republic on a large scale; which exhibits features previously unprecedented in the records of political experience; but which has in turn been largely followed.

It has virtually altered the whole theory of the relations of colonies to the mother-country.

By splitting the English race into two nations, it has doubled its influence on the destinies of mankind.

CHAPTER II.

THE AMERICAN COLONIES (TO 1763).

We think, and think rightly of the war of American independence as of a struggle between thirteen English colonies, and England their mother-country. Yet, besides the English, several other races had contributed to build up the English colonies; Dutch in New York, Swedes and Fins in Delaware and New Jersey; French on almost every outskirt; Spaniards to the far south; a scattering of Germans in Georgia, Pennsylvania, and New Jersey. Among all these, the Dutch is the only race that has shown any persistent force, giving for instance a President to the Republic in the person of Mr. Van Buren.

Races inhabiting the colonies.

Behind them all lay another element, which can scarcely be said to have entered into the composition of the American people, so slight has been the mixture of blood between the white man and the red, but which must have acted powerfully from without on the formation of the American character. This element is found in the North American Indians, or Red Men, whom European colonists found in the seventeenth century on the shores of the Atlantic Ocean, and whom they are now exterminating from those of the Pacific.

And in the midst, another race foreign to the continent had been introduced by European colonists, destined to grow up and multiply; amongst the white men but not of them; a leaven of discord, a ferment which should some day seethe and bubble into civil war—the black men of Africa, imported as slaves.

Let us consider each type in turn, taking as the starting point of our survey the year 1763, the date of the Peace of Paris. At this period the common danger, arising from the presence of France on the North American continent, which had hitherto united the English colonists and the mother-country, had, as will hereafter be seen, passed away; and their jarring interests began to come out more distinctly. We will begin with

I. THE RED MAN.

The North American Indian is for most persons now-a-days, and not unjustly so, the embodiment of the untameable, irreclaimable savage. Under his highest aspects, we scarcely see him but as a *What the Indian is.* wandering robber; under his lowest, as a lazy, filthy, drunken vagabond, crawling about like vermin on the outskirts of civilisation. From what he is, would-be philosophers spin theories as to why he is so, and invariably conclude that it is, and always must have been, his manifest destiny to be swept away before the white man, his superior. It is probable, indeed, that no influence now in the world can stop the extermination of the

Indian race—a few tribes acknowledged as 'civilised' perhaps excepted—within the Great Republic. But justice is due to the dead, to the dying, to the dumb, still more than to the living and the healthy, who can speak for themselves. And history shows us the red man in a very different light from that in which we see him now.

When the European first met with the North American Indian, he was no irreclaimable savage. He had settled abodes, villages, towns; a Franciscan monk speaks of a village of seven or eight thousand souls in what is now Illinois. So far from being mere wandering hunters, Mr. Bancroft expressly says that 'all the tribes south of the St. Lawrence, except remote ones on the north-east and the north-west, cultivated the earth. The Iroquois or Five Nations, who long defied the power of France, dwelt in fixed places of abode, surrounded by fields of beans and of maize.' Strachey, in his 'Historie of Travaile into Virginia,' tells of the Indians of the coast, how about their houses they have commonly square plots of cleared ground, which serve them for gardens, some 100, some 200 foote square.' The knowledge of two of the main products of American agriculture at the present day, maize and tobacco,—products which have overspread the world,—is due to these irreclaimable savages.

What he was: towns, agriculture.

Without the use of iron, they built huts, boats, palisades for fortification, wove mats and embroidered them, drew thread from the wild hemp and the nettle, wrought feather mantles, nets, baskets, fish-weirs, dressed skins to exquisite suppleness, made pottery, prepared various brilliant pigments. The snow-shoe, the vapour bath, and, above all, the pipe, appear to be of their invention. They stored for the winter, fruits, maize, dried buffalo meat, smoked fish. They had a kind of written language, consisting of

Arts, written language: observation of Nature.

strings of shells known by the name of wampum. The office of the herald, bearer of the peace-pipe, was sacred among them. They were careful observers of Nature; their power of interpreting her phenomena has been described as almost miraculous. In striking contrast with the Australian black, whose skill as a path-finder, equally wonderful at first sight, has been found to depend so completely on the retentiveness of his memory that, when taken into a strange district, he is utterly helpless, the expertness of the Red Indian rests upon generalisations of a truly scientific character, enabling him to make his way through a perfectly unknown country with almost the same accuracy as through one with which he is familiar. He is a geographer by instinct, not only understanding maps when shown to him, but tracing them rudely for himself. Thus, the latest writer who has had opportunities of observing the Indian whilst yet undegraded, Mr. Joaquin Miller, says : 'All Indians are great travellers. . . . A traveller with them is always a guest. He repays the hospitality he receives by relating his travels, and telling of the various tribes he has visited, their extent, location, and strength. . . . Telling stories, their history, traditions, travels, and giving and receiving lessons in geography, are their great diversions around their camp and wigwam fires at night. . . . Geography is taught by making maps in the sand or ashes with a stick. For example, the sea a hundred miles away is taken as a base. A long line is drawn there, and rivers are led into the sea by little crooked marks in the sand. Then sand or ashes are heaped or thrown in ridges to show the ranges of mountains. This tribe is defined as having possessions of such and such an extent on the sea. Another tribe reaches up this river so far to the east of that tribe ; and so on, till a thousand miles of the coast are mapped out with tolerable accuracy.' Hence those raids which, in the days when the red men were numerous on the eastern coast, used to terrify the colonists, when parties of two or three braves only would travel hundreds of miles to carry back a few scalps.

If we look to language alone as a basis of nationality, they formed nations rather than tribes. Although the Algonquin language spread from the Atlantic to the Mississippi, and from Cape Fear to the Esquimaux country, over sixty degrees of longitude and over twenty of latitude, still within this vast region the Huron-Iroquois occupied a large tract of country, about Lake Erie and Lake Ontario, besides a smaller one in North Carolina. To the south, the Mobilian language extended from the Atlantic to the Southern Mississippi. Cherokees and others, among whom may be mentioned the Natchez, a tribe of Mexican origin, towards the mouth of the Mississippi, formed subordinate families or branches of more westerly races.

{.sidenote}
Languages.

Their forms of government were various. When the white men came in contact with them, they had republican confederacies like that of the Five Nations (Mohawks, Oneidas, Onondaguas, Cayugas, and Senecas), extending from the St. Lawrence to what is now Virginia; or that of the Creeks which almost joined the limits of the former, extending from the Gulf of Mexico to Cape Fear. They had despotisms, as among the Natchez, or again, such as that of Powhatan, described by William Strachey as the 'great emperor of Virginia,' at 'the least froun' of whose brow the greatest would tremble, and whose majesty would sometimes strike 'awe and sufficient wonder in our people.' Chieftainship was generally hereditary in the female line. Among the Natchez and Hurons the chiefs formed a caste, as being descended from the sun. But the council,

{.sidenote}
Forms of government.

to which all grown men were admitted, with right of speech, must have formed everywhere a strong counterpoise to any hereditary or caste rights.

The rights of the sexes were not equal; the woman was little more than a beast of burthen, generally a slave. She was the sole tiller of the ground, and ingatherer of the harvest; all household work was hers; she carried the game, the wood, the hut and its contents on a journey. 'The greatest toils of the men were to perfect the palisades of the forts, to manufacture a boat out of a tree by means of fire and a stone hatchet, to repair their cabins, to get ready instruments of war or the chase,' and, it must be added, the toils of the chase itself, and of war. *Inferiority of women.*

They had a universally diffused faith in the immortality, if it may be so termed, of life in every living thing, and in the existence for every kind of animal of some typical exemplar, larger and more powerful than all other creatures of the same kind, called the manitou. These manitous became chief objects of worship, one man chiefly venerating the manitou of the buffalo, another the manitou of the bear, etc. Besides these, however, all nature was filled for them with spiritual presences, and one Great Spirit was generally acknowledged as ruling above all, though too high for worship. As usual with savage nations, the deities really worshipped were those whose malevolence was most to be feared. The war god, in particular, was appeased by human sacrifices; and the frightful tortures usually inflicted on prisoners taken in war seem to have been more or less of a sacrificial nature. They had medicine-men, or sorcerers, who claimed to be familiar with the secrets of the unseen world. The Natchez kept up a sacred fire. *Beliefs.*

Revenge was a leading Indian virtue, and was, indeed,

an hereditary duty. That which, perhaps, most alienated
the white man from the Indian was the
character of his warfare, turning mainly upon
surprises. The Red Indian's glory consists not in fighting his enemy, but in killing him, and carrying off his
scalp as a trophy. Hence he will never meet him in
open fight if he has a chance of slaughtering him unawares
or asleep; nor would he shrink from carrying off the
scalp of the woman and the child, if it be not worth his
while to carry the women or children themselves off as
prisoners. Still, he was not guilty of indiscriminate
scalp-hunting like the head-hunting of the Dyak of Borneo who cannot marry till he has cut off a head, it
matters not whose if not of his own tribe.

 One great cause which seems to have retarded the
development of the Indian races of North America was
the absence of the pastoral element, and of
tamed animals larger than the dog. Yet even
in this respect they have given the lie to those
who treat them as unteachable. Since the European
has introduced the horse into America, whole tribes
of Indians have become as thorough horsemen as the
wandering Arab or Tartar. Again, when in the beginning
of the eighteenth century the settlers of South Carolina
invaded Florida, they found the Indians round St. Mark's
in possession of cattle. Anyone who chooses to read
that black page of American history which records the
driving of the Creeks and Cherokees out of Georgia will
find that the latter at least were, as indeed they are still,
to all intents and purposes a civilised people, engaged in
agriculture and trade, and with a written language of
their own—an irrefragable proof that the Red Indian is
no irreclaimable savage, but has only been forced by the
white man to become so. Indeed, even in their least
advanced condition the Indians have never been slow in

Mode of warfare.

Absence of the pastoral element.

availing themselves of those resources of civilisation which suit the condition of a race hunted out wherever it is not hunted down, and compelled always to stand in an attitude of self-defence. They have exchanged the stone tomahawk for the steel one, the bow and arrows for the musket or rifle, the ignition of wood by friction for the lucifer-match.

Their code of morals, says a writer whom I have already quoted, Joaquin Miller, 'consists chiefly of a contempt of death, a certainty of life after death, temperance in all things, and sincerity. Their fervid natures and vivid imaginations make the spirit-world beautiful beyond description, but it is an Indian's picture... Woods, deep, dark, boundless, with parks of game and running rivers; and above all and beyond all, not a white man there.' Code of morals.

In the courage of endurance, no race of men, except the Northmen of Europe, seem ever to have equalled them. In nothing was this more shown than in the tortures inflicted upon captives when they were not adopted into their captors' tribe. These were expected, whilst fastened to the stake, lacerated, mutilated in every way, not only to give way to no groan or sign of pain, but to chant their war-song and boast of their exploits and those of their tribe against their enemies. On a large scale, the same endurance has been exhibited by the whole race in its struggles against the white man. If it be true, as American writers are of opinion, that at the time of the discovery of North America the Indians south of the St. Lawrence and east of the Mississippi were not more than 200,000 in number, the stubbornness of their resistance has been something incredible. A mere fragment of the old Creek confederacy, the Seminoles of Florida, maintained as late as 1835-39 a harassing war against the United States. In our Capacity for endurance.

own days a Modoc war has been carried on in the west against the American people by literally a score or two of Indian warriors. Cheered by no hope of ultimate triumph, the red man has never counted the odds against him, and at ten to one, at a hundred to one, has fought on a fight which after-ages will perhaps recognise as the most heroic of which history bears record, if his courage rather than his manner of waging it be considered.

It will easily be seen how strong an influence upon the colonists of North America must have been exercised by the presence of the Indian element, through the necessities of constant watchfulness, and almost constant warfare, against such enemies. The Indians were always too few to overpower a settlement, except in its very beginnings; but a few raiders were enough to keep hundreds of miles of settlements in a state of disquietude. The Red Indian was, as it were, the whetstone on which the courage, the wits, and alas! too often the ferocity of the white man were sharpened for two centuries. The Spaniard found in Hispaniola a population which seems to have been one of the gentlest the world has ever seen, and which perished off the face of the earth almost without striking a blow. In Mexico he found one not devoid of bravery, but accustomed to obey, which accepted his sway after a few sharp struggles. But further north, the Englishman, Dutchman, Frenchman found himself confronted by a race of the most stubborn tenacity, for the most part passionately fond of their freedom, full of individual hardihood, each man a host in himself, having to be quelled or killed one by one. White weaklings, white cowards, were no match for them. The discipline of the soldier was of small avail against them. The only colonists that could prosper in their neighbourhood must be such as could fight and win their own battles.

Influence of the Indian element on the colonists.

The history of the relations of the Indian tribes with the European settlers varies little. As a rule, the newcomers are well received at first by the natives, except where distrust has been excited by the previous visits of white kidnappers. Contracts and treaties are entered into before each party thoroughly understands the other's meaning, and sooner or later these treaties are sure to be differently interpreted by them. Quarrels ensue, almost universally provoked by the white man; massacres are perpetrated, seldom on one side alone; perhaps what the white man calls a war breaks out, which seldom lasts more than a campaign, ending in the white man's victory, and in some fresh treaty, which the red man understands a little better than the first, and hates all the more. The Indian is pressed back and back; perhaps allows himself to be driven into some angle of land, with the sea in his rear. Now he feels himself doomed; but almost invariably another fierce struggle has to be gone through, in which he attempts to use the white man's all-powerful weapon, organisation; but it is too late, and he is finally crushed, either into slavery or death. The story indeed changes a little when white men of different races or faiths settle in each other's neighbourhood, and gradually come into contact. Here the Indian becomes valuable as an ally, and his aid is contended for by both parties; he is kept in leash as it were, to be let loose, when the day of conflict comes, in all his savagery upon the white enemy, and upon his own red kinsmen who may side with the latter. But if this state of things may protract for a time the existence of the tribe as a power, it does not the less hasten the extermination of the race through the white man's wars. Sooner or later the one white race triumphs finally over the other, and from that day the fate of the red man is sealed.

General character of relations between the red and white man.

Still, a difference is to be observed between the colonisation of the Latin races on the one hand, and of the Teutonic races on the other. The former, as a rule, enslave rather than exterminate the native races; the latter exterminate far more than they enslave. Again, as a consequence of preserving the native races by slavery, the former easily amalgamate with them; the latter, because they exterminate, have none to amalgamate with. Thus, although the first madness of ferocious cupidity in the Spaniard may have swept away the natives of the West India islands, and led to many a massacre by the hands of the early 'Conquistadores,' it is certain that throughout the whole of the Spanish possessions, both in North and South America, the Indian population has subsisted to this day, mingling more and more in blood with its conquerors. Even without such admixture it has risen gradually once more in the social scale, till, as now, the whole-blood Indian race is found constantly at its very summit, especially in Central America and Mexico, to which it has given one who may perhaps be her last hero Juarez. In North America, again, the French mingled freely with the natives; and thus one of the most adventurous classes of the population in what is now British, and was French, America is that of the Canadian *voyageurs*, largely composed of half-breeds.

This result has been no doubt owing in great part to the Roman Catholic Church. It must be admitted that, however heroic, and even temporarily successful, may have been the efforts of individual Protestant missions among the red men, they have in most cases been either spasmodic and intermittent, or their results have been annihilated by some selfish act of the civil power, such as the displacement of the whole Indian population. There is nothing similar to the wholesale Christianising—whatever may have been the means employed, and however low the grade of Christianity imparted—of the Indians in the Spanish colonies, or to the vast network of French missions in Northern America, and to their wide-spreading influence over the natives. It is impossible to read without horror the story of the massacre of Sébastien Rasles, the last of the French missionaries in New England, who had gathered round him a flourishing village of Abenakis, with a church and two chapels. Hounded on to their bloody work by a Government reward of 100*l*. for each Indian scalp, a party of New Englanders, after pillaging and setting fire to village and church, left him, mangled by many blows, scalped, his skull broken in several places, his mouth and eyes filled with dirt. (1724.)

In 1763, the time of which we are speaking, the only Indian power deserving the name was that of the Five Nations. These had become Six Nations, since the migration of the Tuscaroras from Carolina in 1715, and their adoption into the Confederacy. They were spread on both sides of the St. Lawrence, from the region near Lake Champlain to Lakes Erie and Huron. The Cherokees were, however, strong in the valley of the Tennessee, and the Creeks further south. In the basin of the Mississippi the Indian tribes subsisted still, with the exception of the Natchez, who had been exterminated by the French, as will be related in the next section.

Most powerful tribes, Iroquois, Cherokees, and Creeks.

II. THE WHITE MEN.

1. The Spaniards.

Of the various European nations named above as having contributed to people the North American colonies, only one besides the English retained, in 1763, a position on the continent—Spain. With the exception of the Dutch, the history of the others had merged so soon into that of two or three of the English settlements that it deserves no separate treatment. The original settlement of New York by the Dutch - unique as having grown out of purely commercial motives—has left its stamp to this day on that state, the chief centre of American commerce, and the head-quarters of the commercial spirit within the union.

1. The Spaniards, England and Spain the only Continental powers in North America.

The coast of Florida had been discovered in 1512 by Ponce de Leon, who took possession of it in the name of Spain; but the first attempt to form a colony there cost him his life (1521). Already, the year before, two Spanish slavers had visited the coast of Carolina, and kidnapped a living freight; but here too, when they attempted to conquer, the resistance of the natives defeated their efforts (1525). Other attempts failed equally, though the last, by Ferdinand de Soto, resulted in the exploration of a large tract of country, and in the discovery of the Mississippi nearly as far as its junction with the Missouri (1539-43). These Spanish expeditions, negative as were their results as respects the colonising of the country, should not be overlooked. The wanton cruelty displayed at this early period by the Spaniards may afford the key to much of the opposition afterwards offered by the Indians to colonists of other white races. In his adventurous march up

Early Spanish discoveries.

the valley of the Mississippi, Soto found the Indians, says Bancroft, an agricultural people, with fixed places of abode, subsisting upon the produce of the fields more than on the chase, neither turbulent nor quarrelsome. The Spaniards enslaved them, would cut off the hands of numbers on a slight suspicion, threw to the hounds the unfaithful or unsuccessful guide, set fire to hamlets for any trifling cause, and sometimes burnt a native alive.

After these early discoveries, little more is known of the history of the Spanish colonies in North America, excluding of course Mexico—except at those few points of time when it touches that of the French or English. *Settlement of Florida.* Spain indeed had given up all efforts for colonising Florida, when hatred to French Huguenots made her resume them. An attempt at colonisation by a party of these was made, in the latter half of the sixteenth century, on the coast of what is now Carolina, a name first derived from a fort erected by these settlers in honour of Charles IX. of France. This attempt was made in accordance with the plans of the Admiral Coligny, the great champion of the Huguenots. Two colonies were founded (1562 and 1564) but home-sickness broke up the first, the Spaniards exterminated the second. The Spanish commander professed to hang the Frenchmen, 'not as Frenchmen, but as Lutherans.' When the news of the disaster reached France, a Gascon soldier fitted out three ships with which he sailed for the American coast (1568), and ravaged the Spanish settlements, hanging up in turn his prisoners, 'not as Spaniards, but as traitors, robbers, and murderers.' But this time the Spaniards kept their ground, and the town of St. Augustine, founded by them in 1565, is the oldest in the United States.

Although, under the name of Florida, Spain laid claim to the whole of the coast northwards, Canada included, there is little more to be said of the history of the Spanish settlements on the northern coast of the Gulf of Mexico. In 1686 we find the Spaniards again destroying a Protestant settlement, this time of Scotch Presbyterians, as far north as Port-Royal. Ten years later (1696) Pensacola is founded by three hundred Spaniards from Vera Cruz, to become a border town of West Florida. The rest of the story of Spanish Florida belongs really to the history of the neighbouring English colonies. It is sufficient to say that, in 1763, when the treaty of Paris concluded that wide-spreading Seven Years War whose centre lies in the struggle between Frederick the Great of Prussia and the combined forces of Austria and France, Spain, as the ally of France, gave up Florida to England, receiving in exchange from France Louisiana beyond the Mississippi. Whatever right Spain thereby acquired merged in her own indefinite claims to territory in North America as the sovereign of Mexico. The settled population of Florida is said to have sunk by this time to a few hundreds.

Occasional warfare with England.

Spain's position in America after the treaty of Paris, 1763.

2. *The French.*

Although the French flag had, by 1763, been swept from the mainland of North America, the French element upon it cannot be overlooked, any more than the Indian, with which, indeed, it had shown singular affinity. By far the larger portion of the romance of American colonial history belongs to the French settlements. No other European nation sends forth missionaries so devoted, adventurers so enterprising as the French. France gives a name to the St. Lawrence and to the Mississippi; to Carolina and to Louisiana; to the Iroquois on Lake

Importance of the French element.

Ontario, and to the Grosventres on the eastern slopes of the Rocky Mountains; to the 'portage' and to the 'prairie.' Whilst the English settlers hugged the Atlantic seaboard, French missionaries and traders were establishing communications between the great lakes and the Gulf of Mexico. Always ready to spring to arms on the outbreak of every war between the two mother-countries, always seconded by large numbers of Indian allies, the French colonists kept their English neighbours constantly on their mettle, although never powerful enough to overpower them altogether.

Although France had not been first in the race of discovery, her flag was seen early on the shores of North America. In the first quarter of the fifteenth century, Verrazzani, an Italian in the service of Francis I. of France, reaching the coast about the latitude of Wilmington, followed it northwards to Nova Scotia (1524). A few years later, hardy Jacques Cartier of St. Malo discovered the St. Lawrence (1534), and settlements were soon attempted in the north of the continent, though they only began to succeed in the early years of the seventeenth century. With the colonisation of Canada, Nova Scotia, and Cape Breton by the French this work has no concern; but it must be remembered that the southern limits of Acadia or New France (the present Nova Scotia) extended to the latitude of Philadelphia, thus covering the whole of what became the New England Colonies, and that, in particular, what is now the State of Maine, as well as north-western New York, was first settled by the French. Moreover, notwithstanding one or two attempts at colonisation in the south—such as that ill-fated one of French Huguenots in the latter half of the sixteenth century—it was from the north that French influence in North America was destined to spread. But this influence

Early discoveries and settlements.

was no true measure of French power. In 1679, the European population of New France amounted only to 8,515 souls, and throughout nearly the whole of the seventeenth century the Indian confederacy of the Iroquois balanced the whole power of France in America. They were allies of the English, and to their valour, as Mr. Bancroft admits, the State of New York 'owes its present northern boundary.'

Substantially, Canada was almost as truly colonised through religious enthusiasm as the New England States themselves. Following the Franciscans, the Jesuits (1632), encouraged by the eminent governor, Champlain (whose name has clung to a beautiful lake in the State of New York), attempted first the conversion of the Hurons hereditary foes of the Iroquois, then of the Chippeways, then of the Abenakis of Maine, then of the Iroquois themselves. They crept from shore to shore along the whole line of the great lakes, frequent martyrdom begetting only fresh enthusiasts. They carried the French name to what are now the States of Michigan, Ohio, Wisconsin, Illinois, and reached the Mississippi in 1673, floating down the great river in Indian canoes, beyond the limit reached by De Soto long before, to a point below the mouth of the Arkansas. Close on their steps followed adventurers of the heroic type, such as Cavalier de la Salle, who in 1682 descended the Mississippi to the sea, planted the flag of France on the shores of the Gulf of Mexico, named the territory Louisiana in honour of him whom men then called Louis the Great, and then returned to France to press the establishment of a colony in the vast and fertile region which he had explored. He was listened to with favour, and sailed once more for America with 280 colonists, but was shipwrecked on the coast of Texas, which he took possession of in the name of France (1685),

Heroic missionaries and heroic adventurers Cavalier de la Salle.

building a fort which he named St. Louis. From this point he endeavoured in vain to find the Mississippi in canoes, made an excursion into northern Mexico, from whence he brought back five horses (those animals having already gone wild, and been tamed afresh by the Indians, since the Spanish conquest of Mexico). Finally, with sixteen men, he determined to travel back on foot to Canada, but was murdered on the way by his companions (1687).

The events of the various wars between England and France in America belong rather to the history of our own colonies. Towards the end of the seven- *Progress of* teenth century France held possession of the *France in the Missis-* whole American coast and islands, from *sippi valley.* Hudson's Bay and Labrador to Maine, of Canada and the Mississippi valley, the eastern half of Newfoundland being alone excepted. To Illinois, which seems to have been occupied by the French since the time of La Salle, was soon added a fort at Detroit, in what is now Michigan (1701.) Kaskaskia was the first permanent European settlement in the Mississippi valley, gathering round a most successful Jesuit mission, where marriages of French emigrants with converted Illinois Indians were solemnised according to Roman Catholic rites. On the other hand the gallant Canadian, d'Iberville, sought in France for emigrants to Louisiana, and, more fortunate than La Salle, reached safely the southern coast (1699), and began at Biloxi the European settlement of the present State of Mississippi. Missionaries and others soon descended the Mississippi from the north; the new comers in turn ascended part of it; exploring parties, mostly in search of minerals, rambled through western Louisiana, and to what is now Iowa. The chief settlement was ere long transferred from the arid shore of Biloxi to the western bank of the Mobile river, and what is now Alabama began to be colonised. The possessions of Spain on the mainland were henceforth regarded as commencing only on the eastern shore of the last-named river, and running westward till they bordered on the English settlements in the debateable land of Carolina.

At the Peace of Utrecht in 1713, France ceded to England Hudson's Bay, Acadia or Nova Scotia, and Newfoundland, **and agreed** never to 'molest the Five Nations subject to the dominion of Great Britain;' but she retained **Louisiana, as** well as Canada. Cape Breton was colonised by French refugees from Acadia and Newfoundland; and, thanks in great **measure to her** far-spread influence over the Indian tribes, **France not only** held her ground, but her colonists advanced their settlements, occupying western New York, establishing themselves along the banks of the Alleghany to the Ohio, beginning the settlement of what is now Indiana, and possessing themselves of all the great lines of communication between the St. Lawrence and the Mississippi. They claimed the shore of the Gulf of Mexico to the west, as far as the Rio del Norte; they pushed up the Red River (of the south), till they reached the Spanish borders. Louisiana, it was asserted, extended to the head-springs of the Alleghany, the Monongahela, the Kenawha, and the Tennessee. New Orleans was founded by Law's famous Mississippi Company (1718), and Arkansas began to be settled. An Indian war followed some years later, in which the chief actors **were**, on the one side, the Natchez and Chickasaw Indians—the latter allies of the English—on the other, **the** French and **the** Choctaws. The Natchez, after a massacre of French settlers, were destroyed, their chief (named the Great Sun) **and more** than four hundred prisoners being shipped for sale to St. Domingo (1732). Peace was made with **the** Chickasaws (1740); but the

Cape Breton colonised: extension of French colonisation in the west; New Orleans.

French retained their country, and thereby the command of the middle course of the Mississippi, between Lower Louisiana and Illinois. Another war with England left the ever-unsettled boundary as it was. The French sought to win favour with the Iroquois by separately treating with them, established a new mission south of the St. Lawrence, and occupied the valley of the Ohio, whilst border conflicts broke out first on the Acadian (now Nova Scotian) frontier (1748-50), and then in the Miamis and Ohio valley (1752-54). But the fall of the French power in North America was at hand. What follows is so mixed up with the history of the great hero of American independence that it need not be here dwelt upon. It is enough to say, that the Peace of Paris left nothing to France in North America but a couple of islets off Newfoundland.

Thus, although the adventurous spirit of her sons had girdled round the English settlements to the north, to the west, and partly to the south, and had laid the foundations of almost every one of the present inland States of the American republic east of the Mississippi, still France had only worked for England. South of the St. Lawrence (New Brunswick and Nova Scotia excepted), the French population was a mere scattering, not capable even of estimation ; and even of the colonies of the St. Lawrence basin, the population was insignificant in comparison with that of the region originally settled by the English. Canada is estimated to have had, in 1760, 65,000 inhabitants; in 1784, after a considerable influx of loyalists through the war, 113,000. Nova Scotia, including New Brunswick, is reckoned to have had 13,000 in 1764 ; the population of Cape Breton was over-estimated in 1758 at 10,000. In the year 1763 the whole group together, including Newfoundland, cannot have

What France had done: scanty population of her colonies.

reached 100,000; not a twelfth, as will soon be seen, of the population of the English colonies proper.

One consequence of this entire disproportion in population between the English-speaking and the French-speaking colonies in North America was, that the sympathies of the latter were sure to be in the long run in favour of any cause which would hinder their absorption in the former.

In the coming war, the French colonists will side with the English.

And since their struggles had after all been not so much with Englishmen, as such, as with their neighbours the English colonists, it followed that if any rupture should occur between the latter and their mother-country, the sympathies of the French colonists would easily be enlisted on behalf of that mother-country. Hence the curious result, that whilst continental France was marked out by every feature as the destined ally of the revolted English colonies, the French colonists of what had been New France were carried by the force of circumstances into the opposite camp, and were to be made loyal subjects of England by the very events which deprived the latter of her English colonies.

And what was true of the French was equally so of the Indians, their old allies. The red man's foe too was not the Englishman, but the English colonist. It was not the British parliament, but the colonial governments, which had many a time offered rewards for his scalp. When the hour of battle came, the redskin was the destined auxiliary of King George's pale-faces against his revolted American subjects.

The Indians will do the same.

3. *The English.*

The discovery of the North American continent belongs, if not to an Englishman, yet to England. Under a patent which already contemplated occupation, it was first touched, far away to the north, by John Cabot in 1497.

The eastern shore of part of the present United States was first coasted, at least as far as the southern border of Maryland, by his son Sebastian Cabot in 1498. Yet it was not till eighty years later that the first heroically ludicrous attempt at English colonisation on the American shore was made, when Martin Frobisher, believing that he had found an Eldorado near the pole, tried with a fleet of fifteen sail to found a settlement north of Hudson's Straits (1578). Several subsequent attempts were also failures, and it is only from the first expedition sent by the 'London Company' to Virginia in 1606, that the permanent settlement of North America by Englishmen must be dated. Yet at the period we are treating of (1763) —little more than a century and a half later—we must think of British North America as extending in latitude from the Gulf of Mexico to the far north, in longitude from the Atlantic to the Mississippi, and in the northern part of the Mississippi basin stretching away indefinitely into the unexplored west. *The North American continent discovered by England. The English colonies.*

A line of moral demarcation, substantially the same which now separates geographically British North America from the United States, divided the northern colonies conquered from France from the southern ones settled by England. *The northern and southern groups.*
This line was formed by the St. Lawrence and the chain of the Great Lakes, except that the northern group of colonies threw out a spur on the right bank of the great river, comprising Nova Scotia and New Brunswick. It has already been stated that of the northern group the population cannot in 1763 have reached 100,000. That of the southern group, on the contrary, has been variously estimated at from 1,216,000 to 1,700,000.

The settled country proper extended from 32° to 44°

north latitude. But it was as yet only a mere fringe on the Atlantic coast. In Virginia, the oldest colony, it did not extend further west than the Blue Ridge. Yet these colonists were profitable customers for the mother country. They consumed one-sixth of the woollen manufactures of Great Britain, besides linen, cotton, iron, and other goods. In 1760 their imports were reckoned to be 2,611,766*l*. 16*s*. 10*d*., or over 2*l*. a head. A much lower figure is given for their exports—761,101*l*. 11*s*. 6*d*.; but this probably does not include exports to foreign countries, in breach of the navigation laws. Lord Chatham estimated the profits of their trade at two millions a year.

Thirteen colonies composed the group: Massachusetts, Connecticut, New Hampshire, Rhode Island, known together as the New England Colonies; New York and New Jersey, Pennsylvania, Maryland and Delaware, Virginia, North and South Carolina, and Georgia; names many of them of far larger import then than now, when State after State has been carved out of either the original settlements themselves as Vermont out of New York, Maine out of Massachusetts, Western Virginia out of Virginia), or out of the then unsettled territory claimed by them, and including all the present central states of the Union east of the Mississippi. Mr. Thackeray falls almost short of the truth when he says, in his 'Virginians': 'The maxim was, that whoever possessed the coast had a right to all the territory inland as far as the Pacific; so that the British charters only laid down the limits of the colonies from north to south, leaving them quite free from east to west.' Such was the case in the first charter for Virginia. But the Plymouth charter for New England expressly extended to the Pacific (1620); so did that of Connecticut (1662); so did that of Carolina

<small>Southern group: the thirteen colonies and their limits.</small>

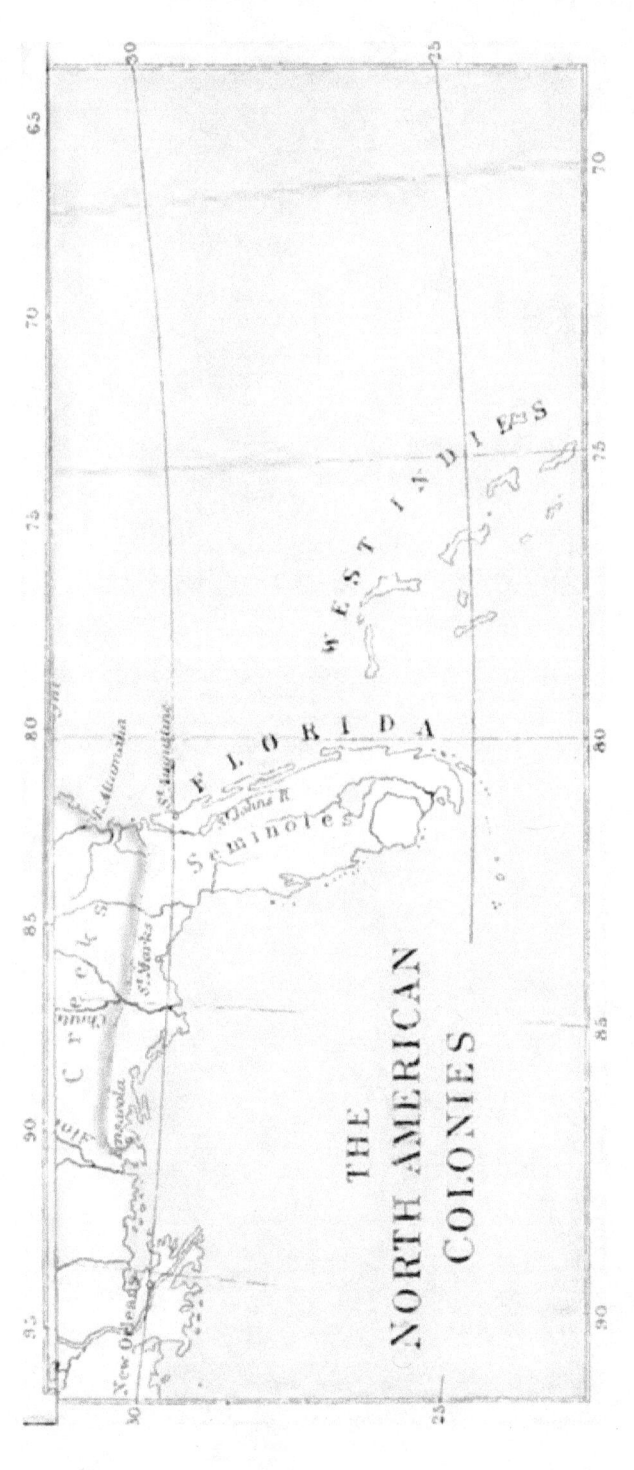

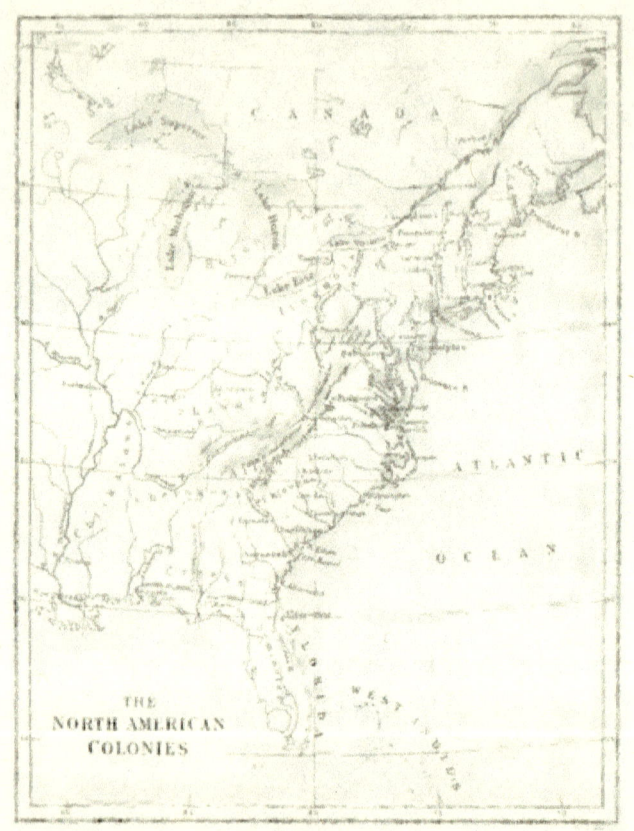

(1665); so did that of Georgia (1732). New York, under its original name of New Netherlands, and New Sweden, which became Delaware and New Jersey, had virtually no boundaries at all, having been founded by companies with unlimited rights of settlement on the American continent. On the other hand, Pennsylvania and Maryland were limited to the westward from the first. So were also necessarily those colonies which were carved out of others during the colonial period itself, as New Hampshire and Rhode Island.

Without any actual line of division, there was again a moral distinction between the colonies of the north (New York only excepted) and those of the south, with perhaps the exception of Georgia. Religious principle had founded the northern colonies, the spirit of adventure the southern. Other characteristics distinguishing the two elements may be noted hereafter, but all, perhaps, flow from that one. Otherwise, as has been well observed by a recent German writer, Professor von Holst, the thirteen colonies varied in some respects 'so widely from each other that almost more essential differences were to be found between them than points of comparison and resemblances.' Their only geographical tie was their separation from all the civilised world besides; their only moral tie, their relation to a common mother-country. The sense of unity which has sprung up so rapidly in our Australian colonies, while as yet no political ties unite them formally, did not exist. There were no 'Americans,' as there are now 'Australians,' or if the term was used it was by Englishmen at home in speaking of the colonists, not by the colonists in speaking of themselves. Each colonist, as the writer I have just quoted justly remarks, was first a child of his own colony, then an Englishman. At the same time it must be said that, from about the middle of

Distinctions between the colonies of the southern group.

the 18th century, owing partly to the growth of population in the English settlements, still more, perhaps, to the spread of French influence along the whole rear of them, there begins to be a general colonial history in place of that of separate colonies.

Let us now briefly sketch the growth of the thirteen colonies. Historically, it will be found that they *Three sub-* resolve themselves into three sub-groups, of *groups.* which Virginia, New York, and Massachusetts are the centres.

1. *Virginia.*—Precedence of course belongs to Virginia, the first founded of all, the 'Old Dominion' of the *The name* planter, the 'Ole Virginny' of his slave. The *formerly wider than* name is indeed now much narrower than it *now.* was at first, since the first attempts to colonise the Virginia of the sixteenth century were made on one of the islands of what is now North Carolina.

It is not improbable that the abortive attempts of the French Huguenots in Carolina paved the way to the English colonisation of America. It has been no-
Early attempts at ticed that our Raleigh reached France the year
colonisation by Gilbert after De Gourgues' return (1569), and learnt the
and Raleigh. art of war under the great Huguenot, Coligny, the planner of French colonisation in Florida, for the benefit of his co-religionists. Nine years later (1578) Sir Humphrey Gilbert, Raleigh's step-brother, obtained a colonisation patent, to be of perpetual validity, if a plantation were established within six years. Two expeditions (1579 and 1583) failed; Gilbert perished in the second. Raleigh took up his step-brother's work, under a new patent, and an actual settlement was formed (1585) on Roanoke Island, now in North Carolina. Treachery and cruelty, however, marked the brief existence of even this first English colony; a leading Indian chief and his principal followers were massacred by preconcert at an audience,

at which no sign of hostility was shown by the Indians, and the island had to be deserted next year. A second attempt on the same spot (1587) was an equal failure; the very fate of the colonists was never known, though Raleigh is said to have five times sent vessels in search of them. The next attempt at colonisation was on the shores of New England (1602), and was equally abortive.

The hour of success was, however, at hand. There was a strong feeling in England in favour of colonisation. Two companies were formed for the purpose; one only succeeded, the London Company, the real founders of Virginia, whose first expedition set sail December 19, 1606, and landed on the shores of a river flowing into Chesapeake Bay. *The London Company; a colony established; House of Burgesses.* Yet the composition of the colony was absurd. There were four carpenters to forty-eight gentlemen; only twelve labourers, and very few mechanics, out of 105 emigrants. The early years of the colony were disastrous, but it was reinforced from time to time by fresh batches of emigrants. Men of high position were sent out as governors. The introduction of tobacco into Europe became a source of wealth; even the streets of Jamestown, the Virginian capital, were planted with it; it was the usual medium of exchange. The first colonial assembly in the New World, the Virginian 'House of Burgesses,' sat for the first time in Jamestown in the year 1619. In 1622, the white population amounted to about 4,000, and spread nearly 150 miles up the James River. But a canker had already been introduced, which was some day to eat almost into the vitals of the American people. The first negroes were sold as slaves in the James River by a Dutch man of war in August 1620. By 1650 Virginia held fifty whites to one black.

Two names must be mentioned in connexion with

the early history of Virginia. One is that of John
Smith, an adventurer of genius, who had
fought the Spaniards in the Low Countries,
the Turks in Hungary, had wandered as far as Egypt
and Morocco, had been taken in battle in Wallachia,
sent as a slave to Constantinople, then to the Crimea,
and had escaped through Russia and Transylvania. This
man is treated by most historians (but chiefly, it would
seem, on the strength of his own narratives) as the hero
of Virginian story—'the Father of Virginia, the true
leader who first planted the Saxon race within the borders of the United States.' A still more romantic personage is Pocahontas, daughter of the chief Powhatan,
who married an Englishman named John Rolfe, was
brought to England and received by King James, but
died at Gravesend on her way back (1617), having given
birth to a son, Thomas Rolfe, from whom the 'first
families of Virginia' are proud to claim descent.

An Indian massacre, planned by Powhatan's successor, Opechancanough, stopped the growth of Virginian prosperity. In one hour 347 colonists were killed, and the war which ensued,
followed by sickness and the return of many
emigrants, reduced the population by 1624 to 1,800. In
the same year James I. cancelled the patents of the
London Company; but the framework of the colonial
constitution remained on foot, and to protect the growth
of Virginian, the import of foreign tobacco into England
was prohibited. Charles I., who succeeded the next year
to the throne, confirmed by proclamation the monopoly
of the import of tobacco to Virginia and the Somers
Islands, but sought by another proclamation to constitute himself the sole factor of the planters. The Virginians were thankful for their own monopoly, but steadily
repudiated that of the king. Under the governorship of

Sir William Berkeley (1641-5) the colony, reduced indeed in extent through the Maryland charter, began again to flourish, although his administration was marked by its second and last great Indian war. In 1643 the Assembly enacted, says Bancroft, that 'no terms of peace should be entertained with the Indians, whom it was usual to distress by sudden marches against their settlements.' The Indians retorted by another massacre, in which 300 whites perished. In the warfare which followed, the old chief Opechancanough was taken prisoner, and died from a wound inflicted on him after his capture. His successor made peace (1646) on the terms of submission and large cessions of land. Henceforth any hostilities with the Indians in Virginia were considered to be not with enemies, but with rebels.

On the outbreak of the English civil war, Virginia, true to the aristocratic character of its original settlement, remained at first faithful to the crown. Fugitive Cavaliers flocked to its shores, and after the execution of Charles I., Sir George Berkeley, the governor, received a new commission from Charles II. A fleet, however, was sent out by Cromwell, which received the submission of the West Indian colonies, and on the arrival of a single frigate in the Chesapeake, Virginia in turn acknowledged the Commonwealth, receiving in exchange practical independence. Its people were to have all the liberties of the freeborn people of England; no taxes or customs were to be levied except through their representatives, nor any forts erected or garrisons maintained without their consent (1652). Till the end of the Commonwealth, Virginia elected her own governors. On the other hand, a law which gave fifty acres of land to planters for every person whom they should import at their own cost, tended rapidly to build up a landed aristocracy of large

Submission to the Commonwealth; growth of landed aristocracy.

proprietors. Add to this, that for many years Virginia, like other colonies, was for the mother-country a place of transportation for offenders, and that there was no provision for education, so that in 1671 Sir George Berkeley (who had been re-elected governor at the Restoration) could 'thank God there are no free schools nor printing, and I hope we shall not have, these hundred years.' So Virginia grew up to be what it has been till within our own days, a land of great gentlemen and of 'mean whites.'

During the latter years of the Commonwealth the northern portion of Carolina had begun to be explored from Virginia, and in the early years of the Restoration her colonists began to settle there. In this direction, however, also, the expansion of her territory was stopped by the Carolina patents (1663, 1665). The era of the Restoration was indeed a dark one for Virginia. A strong partisan Assembly had been elected, which acted with great oppressiveness. Severe penalties were enacted against nonconformists; the suffrage was restricted. On the other hand, trade was crippled by Charles II.'s Navigation Acts; the colony was irritated by a royal grant to Lord Culpeper, including lands already settled, and at last by one of 'all the dominion of land and water called Virginia,' for thirty-one years, to Lords Culpeper and Arlington (1673). Some hostilities with the Indians on the Maryland frontier kindled discontent into a flame, and gave rise to the most remarkable event, perhaps, in Virginian colonial history—a civil war known as 'Bacon's Rebellion,' from the name of Nathaniel Bacon, its leader, which assumed a republican character, and was for a time triumphant, but was eventually stamped out with ruthless severity by Sir George Berkeley (1675-7). The executions were continued even after a royal proclamation

The Restoration; Bacon's Rebellion.

had arrived, promising pardon to all but the leader, Bacon. 'The old fool has taken away more lives in that naked country than I for the murder of my father' was Charles II.'s characteristic comment on Berkeley's proceedings.

The effects of the insurrection were disastrous. Lord Culpeper was made governor for life (1677), and the government became thus a proprietary one. A perpetual export duty of 2s. a hogshead was laid on tobacco for the support of the government, and was to be accounted for only to the crown. The Navigation Law pressed with even sorer weight. Virginia had in vain endeavoured to procure its mitigation, and, when foiled, had proposed repeatedly to Carolina and Maryland to stop the growing of tobacco for a year, in order to enhance the price to the English consumer. At last she solicited the crown itself to prohibit the growth of the plant for a year by proclamation, and when this was refused, mobs began to root up the tobacco in the fields. Between the crippling of her trade, the effects of the insurrection, the suppression of many of her liberties, and the madness of her own people, Virginia was, by the end of Charles II.'s reign, in a state of extreme distress, and the inauguration of that of James II. by an additional arbitrary duty on tobacco (1685), was not of a nature to mitigate such distress. Voluntary emigration ceased, and the only additions from England to the white population were by means of transportation and kidnapping, the latter practised chiefly from Bristol.

Distress of the colony.

Still, with no foreign neighbours except the French in what was then the Far West, and at peace with the Indians, Virginia began to recover her prosperity. Peace with the Indians had been secured by the conclusion of a treaty at Albany in 1684 between herself, New York, and Massachusetts on the one side, and the Five

Return of prosperity.

Nations on the other. The second in age of the educational foundations of the United States, William and Mary College, was established under the sovereigns whose names it bears (1692); though the proposal for so doing, on the plea that Virginians had souls as well as Englishmen, was at first met by Attorney-General Seymour with the reply, 'Souls! d——n your souls! make tobacco.' The Indian title to land in Virginia was extinguished by a further treaty with the Five Nations, now the Six Nations, at Lancaster, in Pennsylvania, in 1744. The Assemblies continued to be in a state of chronic opposition to the governors, but virtually the real governor and king of Virginia was tobacco, in which taxes were paid, and which was wealth to whoever chose to plant it. Thanks to tobacco, ' alone of all the colonies' Virginia 'had no debts, no banks, no bills of credit, no paper money;' but it had also no towns to speak of, no villages, no trade, no manufactures, nothing but scattered plantations, in which every man not a slave did very much that which was right in his own eyes. In 1748 it was believed that the population had nearly doubled itself in twenty-one years.

2. *Maryland.*—With the history of Virginia is closely connected that of Maryland. Under a charter of the year 1632 (granted after the cancelling of the Virginian patents), a portion of the territory comprised in the second Virginian charter to the northward, and partly settled by Virginian colonists, extending as far as the 40th parallel of latitude, was formed into a new colony under the name of Maryland, so called from Henrietta Maria, Charles I.'s queen. With the formation of Maryland is linked the memory of a remarkable man—Sir George Calvert, Lord Baltimore, who, in an age of growing alienation from the Romish Church in England, resigned the secretaryship of state, to become a Roman Catholic. He was a zealous promoter of coloni-

Liberal charter. Lord Baltimore

sation, had been a member of the Virginia Company, and had endeavoured to colonise the southern promontory of Newfoundland. By the Maryland charter Lord Baltimore was constituted owner of the soil, with power to create manors and courts baron, on payment of a yearly rent of two Indian arrows and a fifth of all gold and silver discovered. But he could only legislate with the consent of the majority of the freemen; his authority was not to extend to the life, freehold, or estate of any emigrant; Christianity was made the law of the land, but religious equality was granted, all liege subjects, present and future, being allowed to emigrate to the new colony. Last, not least, the crown reserved to itself no control, and expressly stipulated that it would never lay imposition, custom, or tax on the inhabitants of the province. In conformity with this singularly liberal charter, the governor of Maryland had to swear that he would not, by himself or any other, 'directly or indirectly molest any person professing to believe in Jesus Christ, for or in respect of religion,' and a colonial act of 1649 enacted provisions to the same effect. Lord Baltimore had invited the Puritans of Massachusetts (who will be presently spoken of) to emigrate to Maryland; he welcomed those from Virginia, and at the same time the Anglicans whom Massachusetts disfranchised.

The early beginnings of the colony were exceedingly prosperous. The first emigrants, headed by Lord Baltimore's younger son, had been carefully selected, and they were well received by the natives. It is specially recorded that 'the Indian women taught the wives of the new-comers to make bread of maize.' Within six months the colony 'had advanced more than Virginia had done in as many years' (1634). Soon afterwards, however, troubles arose with a man of the name of Clayborne, one of the early Vir-

Early prosperity; troubles with Clayborne.

ginian settlers, who claimed some jurisdiction under a royal license of earlier **date than the** Maryland charter, and it was not till **1647,** after hostilities with the Indians, and an insurrection which was **for a time** triumphant, that peace was eventually restored.

During the English civil war and commonwealth, the government of Maryland was disputed between the representatives of the 'proprietary,' **Lord** Baltimore, and the republican party, in which Clayborne was now a leader; but at the Restoration, **Lord** Baltimore's **authority was** generally recognised. Under his son, the **second** Lord Baltimore, troubles, more or less connected with Bacon's rebellion in Virginia, again broke **out.** A restriction of the suffrage **by proclamation of the proprietary** gave one ground for **discontent ; the creed of Lord Baltimore was** another. **With the** Revolution **of** 1688 the proprietary government was swept away, Maryland **was** declared **a** royal government (1691), and **the Church of** England that of the State. Toleration was **continued only** to dissenters, and the exercise of the Roman Catholic worship was made illegal. About a quarter **of a** century **later,** however, the government **was** restored to the Baltimores, who **had** meanwhile **reverted to** the Protestant faith ; but from henceforth the **authority of** the proprietaries **was** but fretfully borne with.

<small>Commonwealth ; Restoration : Maryland after 1688 a royal government.</small>

Like Virginia, Maryland's chief staple was tobacco, and her social condition was very similar ; she **had** large scattered plantations, but few large towns.

<small>Similarity to Virginia.</small>

3 & 4. *The Carolinas.* Geography would lead us to connect Delaware with Maryland; but its history binds it rather to the more Northern States. **On** the other hand, **Carolina** occupies much the same position towards Virginia to the south **as** Maryland to the north.

The name, it will be recollected, was originally French,

though revived at first under Charles I. as Carolana, eventually as Carolina under Charles II. That Raleigh's early attempts at Virginian civilisation were made on what became eventually North Carolinian soil will also be recollected. The Carolana charter came to nothing. A different charter, of the year 1663, granted the province of Carolina, from the 36th degree of north latitude to the river San Matheo, to seven proprietaries, the first two named of whom were the Lords Clarendon and Albemarle. But the whole coast was claimed by Spain. There was a previous patent of the year 1630; there were settlers from New England and Virginia, and others came from Barbadoes. A second and vastly more extended charter was granted in 1665 to the proprietaries, which embraced eight whole States of the present Union, parts of three others, and much of Mexico. The powers given were as extensive as the territory itself, and gave actual sovereignty, including not only the right of legislation, but that of making war. An elaborate constitution or 'grand model,' devised by Shaftesbury and Locke on an exaggeratedly feudal pattern, with ' starosts,' 'landgraves,' 'caciques,' 'leetmen,' the first to be for ever self-elected, the last to be for ever attached to the soil, 'under the jurisdiction of their lord without appeal,' was probably the most absurd that had ever been devised by the stupidity, let alone the philosophy, of mankind. Human nature itself rebelled against it.

Early charters; Shaftesbury and Locke's 'grand model.'

Hence the peculiar characteristic of the foundation of Carolina, which has remained in a manner attached to her whole history. All other of the American colonies were founded under charters; in spite of these charters, the two Carolinas founded themselves. Their history begins with defiance of law, not less real because it was necessary. By the

Turbulent early history of these colonies. Slavery.

force of things the one province of Carolina divided itself into two governments. The proprietaries vainly endeavoured to enforce the 'grand model;' there was no peace till it was given up, and nothing perhaps remained of it beyond a provision that every freeman should have absolute power and authority over his negro slaves. No colonies have a more turbulent early history. Insurgents from Virginia found a refuge in North Carolina, and soon fomented an outbreak against the enforcement of the navigation laws. In South Carolina too there were constant struggles, though with less violence, and both colonies expelled their governors in 1688. South Carolina has the grievous distinction of having been cradled in the practice of slavery, Africans having been imported into its first plantations in 1671. In a few years the blacks in its territory were as 22 to 12 whites. Kidnappers as well as slave-buyers, the colonists broke the treaties with the Indians, harried them with what would be now termed razzias or commandos, and sold them as slaves to the West Indies. A leaven of French Huguenots in South Carolina after the revocation of the Edict of Nantes in 1685, and a later one of exiled German Protestants in North Carolina (1711), seems to have done little to raise the tone of Carolinian society.

When the war of the Spanish succession, arising from the establishment of a French prince on the throne of Spain, broke out, the English colonists of South Carolina threw themselves upon Florida. The Spaniards 'had gathered the natives into towns, built for them churches, and instructed them by missions of Franciscan priests.' The Indians had horses and cattle. Fifty volunteers, with 1,000 Indian allies, swept down on the Indian towns near St. Mark's, burnt a church, made 150 prisoners, including women and children, for the slave market, received the submission

The colonists break up Indian civilisation in Florida.

of town after town, and carried the English flag to the Gulf of Mexico (1705). Most of the people 'abandoned their homes, and were received as free emigrants into the jurisdiction of Carolina.' So perished out of Florida the beginnings of Indian civilisation.

The Peace of Utrecht, which concluded the war, was in turn followed by Indian wars in both colonies, with the Tuscaroras in North Carolina (1711-3), with the Yamassees in South Carolina (1715); the former caused by the parcelling out of the Indians' lands amongst German emigrants; the latter by the exactions of the English traders. The former ended with the migration of the Tuscaroras to the northward, to join their Iroquois kinsmen, who admitted them as the sixth nation in their confederacy (1715); the latter with the driving of the Yamassees into Florida. A few years later (1719-20) South Carolina openly threw off allegiance to the proprietaries, who eventually sold their rights to the crown (1729). Both colonies now became royal ones. *Indian wars; the Carolinas become colonies, 1729.*

5. *Georgia.*—As Carolina had been carved out of Virginia, so was the southernmost and the westernmost of the colonies, Georgia, out of Carolina. The story of this, the last formed of the British colonies of North America, reads like a page of the annals of the early half of the seventeenth century transferred to that of the eighteenth. *The last founded colony.*

James Oglethorpe was a member of an old English family. He had served as a volunteer in the army of Prince Eugene, and had taken part in his campaigns against the Turks on the Danube. He had shown in England his sympathy for the oppressed; for he had, in Parliament, taken up the cause of prisoners for debt, and by obtaining a commission for inquiring into the jails of the kingdom, he had been the means *Oglethorpe: his charter and his government.*

of restoring many hundreds of unfortunates to liberty. He now obtained in 1732 a charter from George II., erecting the country between the Savannah and the Alatamaha, and from their **head-springs as far** as the Pacific, **into the** province of **Georgia.** The vine and the silkworm were **to** be its staples. Ardent spirits were not to be imported; and above **all** there were to be no slaves. Oglethorpe **himself** took out the first party of 120 emigrants, **and** chose the site of **Savannah** for his capital. The Indians **from all** sides—Creeks, Cherokees, Choctaws— **proffered their** friendship. The Moravians of Salzburg, **persecuted in their own** country, sought a home in Georgia, **and were followed by many** other emigrants, amongst whom the most noteworthy **were a party of** Highlanders.

A few years later, when war was declared by England **on** Spain in **1739,** Oglethorpe invaded Florida, but failed
<small>Hostilities with Spain.</small> **to take** St. Augustine. A large Spanish fleet in turn attacked Georgia, but was beaten off; **and thanks, in great** measure, **to** the support of the **Indians, the result of the** war (1739-42) was **to** leave the St. John's river as the practical British boundary, although the exact frontier between the British and Spanish colonies remained unsettled by diplomacy.

Oglethorpe (who **had** made two intermediate voyages **to and from Europe)** finally **left** his colony in **1743.** His
<small>Failure of Oglethorpe's plans.</small> **institutions did not last.** The liquor-traffic **was** allowed to grow up; slaves were hired, first for a short period from Carolina, then for life or **for a hundred years,** then imported direct from Africa. The famous Whitefield, one of the leaders of the Methodist movement, **who** as well as **the two** Wesleys visited America at this period, urged the expediency of allowing slavery. The Moravians remained longer opposed to it, but at last gave in (**1751.**) So failed the first practical attempt to rescue the American soil for freedom.

6 & 7. *New York and New Jersey.*—Georgia completes the sub-group of colonies whose history has its root in that of Virginia. The next sub-group to the northward is that of the former Dutch and Swedish colonies, comprising New York, New Jersey, Delaware, and Pennsylvania. Here New York is the centre, until Pennsylvania rises to substantive importance.

<small>New York the centre of a sub-group.</small>

The first name in the story of Dutch America is an English one. Henry Hudson, sailing in the service of the Dutch East India Company, discovered Delaware Bay, and the river now known by his name (1609). At an interview with the Indians on the southern point of the island now occupied by the city of New York, he offered the chiefs rum. One only took it in the first instance; but on seeing him reel and fall, then recover, and hearing his account of his sensations, the rest followed his example. The place was afterwards called by the natives, Manhattan—'the place of drunkenness.' Ships were sent out to trade for furs with the Indians. A few huts were erected for the summer shelter of the traders, then a few of these remained through the winter, then a rude fort was erected, then a settlement was made at Albany, still the legal capital of the State of New York (1615). But although the Dutch came at first only to trade and not to colonise, the Dutch West India Company in 1621 was constituted for both purposes. By 1623 the coast from the southern shore of Delaware Bay to Cape Cod became known as New Netherlands; and New Amsterdam began to grow up where New York is now. The island of Manhattan was bought of the Indians by the first governor, Peter Minuits, for 24 dollars (1625). To encourage settlement, every man who in four years should plant a colony of 50 souls was to be 'patroon' or

<small>Hudson at Manhattan Island; the New Netherlands; New Amsterdam.</small>

lord of a tract 16 miles in length. The colonists were forbidden to make any woollen, linen, or cotton fabrics; in return the Company undertook to supply negroes if it could do so profitably.

The first relations with the English settlers, whether New Englanders or Virginians, were friendly. But some Dutch settlements in Connecticut were ere long overwhelmed by the increase of English immigration, and the New Netherlands were themselves invaded, whilst a colony of Swedes made its appearance in Delaware Bay (1638). This colony was headed by Peter Minuits himself, for on being deposed he had sold his services to Sweden. The settlement, prospering for a time, extended itself into what is now Pennsylvania, and became known as 'New Sweden.' The Dutch moreover became involved in an all but fatal war with the Indian tribes, aggravated by a treacherous night massacre of Algonquins when they were soliciting the protection of the Dutch against their enemies the Mohawks (1643). At one time the Dutch had to sue for grace, and only obtained a truce through the mediation of Roger Williams, whom we shall presently hear of as the founder of Rhode Island. But under the leadership of John Underhill, a New England fugitive, they recovered the upper hand, and a solemn treaty was concluded (1645). Under an able and mild governor, Stuyvesant, the New Netherlands obtained at last from the mother-country freedom of trade, and New Amsterdam began to prosper (1648). A few years later Stuyvesant annexed New Sweden (1655). Although during his absence New Amsterdam was attacked by the Indians, peace was restored on his return.

This was the most brilliant period of Dutch colonisation in North America; but the end was near at hand. At the Restoration, Charles II. granted the Dutch territory, from the Connecticut to the Delaware, to his brother the Duke

New Sweden; eventually annexed to the New Netherlands.

of York (1664.) A fleet was sent out, and the Dutch settlers, who had in vain demanded of the mother-country greater political freedom, offered no resistance. The colony and its capital both took the name of New York, whilst the territory between the Hudson and the Delaware was granted by the Duke of York to Berkeley, former governor of Jersey. This territory, under the name of New Jersey, became a proprietary government under Berkeley and Sir George Carteret. New York was indeed recovered for a time (1668-74) by Holland through bribery, but passed finally to the English by treaty in 1674. The first English governors, however, allowed the colonists no more liberty than their Dutch predecessors had done, and it was only in 1683 that, by William Penn's advice to the Duke of York, the authority of the provincial assembly was recognised, after the recall of an unpopular governor, Sir Edmund Andros. But on his accession to the throne James II. made Andros governor of New England, to which New York was united until the Revolution of 1688, when all the colonies subject to Andros revolted, New York among the rest, and he himself was sent to England for trial. In New York a committee of safety appointed Jacob Leisler governor, but after two years he was tried for treason and executed under the authority of a new governor appointed from England, and until the accession to the governorship of Lord Bellamont in 1698, New York was harassed by bad governors.

The Dutch territory conquered by England, and divided into New York and New Jersey.

The history of New York, it will be seen, has little to impress the mind. It was from the first above all things a commercial settlement, in which freedom was of late growth. Of New Jersey still less is to be said, although, when separated from New York at the English conquest, it became rapidly peopled, thanks to a liberal constitution which gave

History of New Jersey soon connected with that of Pennsylvania.

freedom of worship and the exclusive right of self-taxation to the colonists. Its history, however, soon became mixed up with that of the next great colony of the sub-group.

<small>Pennsylvania the last founded of the religious colonies.</small>

8 & 9. *Pennsylvania and Delaware.*—Though lying south of New York, Pennsylvania belongs morally rather to the more northern than to the southern colonies, being in fact the latest born of what may be termed the religious colonies.

<small>The Quakers in America; Penn; Philadelphia; Delaware.</small>

There were Quakers in Maryland as early as the middle of the seventeenth century, and they were at first left unmolested. But by the end of 1657 those persecutions of the 'Friends' commenced which in New England were carried as far as death. Quakerism, however, took root in America; and before long the proprietary rights of Lord Berkeley and Sir George Carteret in both West and East New Jersey were bought by Quakers, William Penn, son of Admiral Penn, among the number. In 1682 Penn obtained from Charles II., in exchange for a claim of 16,000*l.* against the State, the grant of a large tract of country west of the Delaware, partly settled already by Swedes and Dutchmen. Emigrants were sent out, Penn himself soon followed, and in 1682 founded the city of Brotherly Love, (Philadelphia). He soon afterwards concluded a celebrated treaty with the Indians, which, strange to say, was never broken, so that the history of the Pennsylvanian colony knows of no Indian wars. The growth of Philadelphia was extremely rapid; it is said to have increased more in three years than New York in half a century. There were, however, boundary disputes with Maryland, which were settled by a grant to Penn of half the territory between Chesapeake Bay and the Delaware. This territory, known at first as the 'three lower counties' of Pennsylvania, was eventually separated from Pennsylvania, and became the colony of Delaware.

The constitution of Pennsylvania was liberal, all sects being tolerated, and the franchise being open to every freeman who believed in God and abstained from work on the Lord's day. But after Penn's departure for Europe, in 1684, discontents arose; his rents were in part appropriated for the public service; and at the Revolution of 1688 his proprietary rights were confiscated. He died involved in debt in 1718. *The Pennsylvania constitution; Penn's proprietary rights confiscated in 1688.*

10, 11, 12, 13. *New England: Massachusetts, Connecticut, New Hampshire, and Rhode Island.* We come now to the colonies of the New England sub-group, which from the first have formed, and still do form, the very backbone of the American nation. Their history goes back to the early years of the seventeenth century. Fruitless attempts at settlement were made on the northern coast in 1607-8, and again in 1615; from the second, under Smith of Virginian fame, the name of New England which he gave to the country remained. A Company established by King James, and known as the Council of Plymouth (1620), received enormous powers, and the ownership of a belt of territory stretching from ocean to ocean, between the 40th and 48th degrees of north latitude. But the colonisation of New England was not to issue from its monopoly. *Early attempts at settlement.*

A congregation of Separatists in the North of England, formed towards the close of the reign of Elizabeth (1602), had, to escape religious persecution, and not without much difficulty, taken refuge in Holland (1608). But the climate, the manners, the language of the country repelled them. Persecuted though they had been by their countrymen, they were Englishmen to the backbone. They durst not return to *The 'Pilgrim Fathers.'*

English soil. But the spirit of enterprise was abroad; they thought they might still live for England, if not in England. They applied to the London Company, the then owners of Virginia, for permission to emigrate thither. 'We are knit together as a body,' they wrote, 'in a most sacred covenant of the Lord, of the violation whereof we make great conscience, and by virtue whereof we hold ourselves strictly tied to all care of each other's good, and of the whole. It is not with us as with men whom small things can discourage.' A patent was granted to them by the Company, though, as events turned out, it never became available (1619). Capital for the enterprise was obtained on onerous terms from London merchants. Of two ships which set sail in the first instance from Southampton, the Mayflower and the Speedwell, the latter refused to proceed, and when the Mayflower finally left Plymouth on September 6, 1620, the little party were reduced to 102 souls. Their destination was the Hudson river; but after 65 days' sail they saw land far to the northward, and two days later came to anchor within the harbour of Cape Cod. Before landing, they entered amongst themselves into the following compact, which was signed by all the forty-one men, gentle and simple, who, with their families, made up the 102:—

'In the name of God, Amen. We whose names are undermentioned, the loyal subjects of our dread sovereign King James, by the grace of God, &c., having undertaken, for the glory of God and advancement of the Christian faith, and honour of our king and country, a voyage to plant the first colony in the northern parts of Virginia, do by these presents solemnly and mutually, in the presence of God, and one of another, covenant and combine ourselves into a civil body politic, for our better ordering and preservation, and furtherance of the ends aforesaid; and by virtue

Their compact before landing.

hereof to enact, constitute, and frame such just and equal laws, ordinances, acts, constitutions, and offices, from time to time, as shall be thought most meet and convenient for the general good of the colony, unto which we promise all due submission and obedience. In witness whereof we have hereunder subscribed our names, at Cape Cod, the 11th of November, in the year of the reign of our Sovereign Lord King James, of England, France, and Ireland the 18th, and of Scotland the fiftie-fourth, Anno Dom. 1620.'

It is not too much to say that all that is highest in the polity of the United States to the present day has its root in this compact, by which freemen bind themselves before God to laws which they have freely adopted. There can be no greater contrast than between New England, cradled thus in law, and the Carolinas, cradled in defiance of law. The whole future history of the States in question is in fact prefigured at their birth.

The season was far advanced, for those northern latitudes, when the Pilgrims arrived. During the month of hardships which was spent in exploration of the coast, the water sometimes freezing on their clothes and making them 'like coats of iron,' many of them took, in the language of one of them, 'the original of their death.' At last they fixed upon Plymouth Bay for a settlement, and on Monday, December 11 (O.S.) or 22nd (N.S.) 1620, now 'Forefathers' Day' in New England, they landed on that which is now 'Forefathers' Rock.' During the winter many of their number died, the women first. By the end of March 1621, they were reduced to about sixty. An arrival of thirty-five new emigrants in the autumn, without provisions of their own, reduced the whole colony for six months to half allowances. Indeed their condition was frequently one of starvation until the harvest of 1623, after which 'there was no general

Early difficulties.

want of food.' Their shipments for England were captured, and their English partners would only supply them with goods at extortionate profits. They failed in all their attempts to obtain a royal charter. At the end of ten years the colony contained no more than 300 souls. But with stubborn heroism they held on.

Space forbids us to linger over the details of the story, the noblest probably in the annals of colonisation. One of its features, however, must not be overlooked. The first relations of the Pilgrims with the Indians had been hostile. A shower of arrows had been discharged on one of the exploring parties at a place afterwards known as 'First Encounter.' But on March 15, 1621, a solitary Indian, it is said, came out from the forest, and advanced towards a party of them, saying the word 'welcome.' He had learnt some English from the fishermen who frequented the coast, and although his tale was one of the usual violence on the part of a white man named Hunt, who, having enticed Indians on board his ships, had carried them off and sold them as slaves, he showed himself friendly, and stayed the night. He left next morning with a few presents, and returned some days afterwards with five other Indians, including one of the men kidnapped by Hunt, who became interpreter to the English. On March 22 they had an interview with the great Indian sachem of the country, Massasoit, and a treaty of alliance offensive and defensive was concluded—'the oldest act of diplomacy recorded in New England.' Massasoit's object seems to have been to obtain allies against his enemies the Narragansetts, and their chief Canonicus, head of 5,000 warriors. Probably as a result of the alliance, a messenger from Canonicus appeared in the autumn of 1622, and left with the English a token of war in the shape of a bundle of arrows tied in a rattlesnake's skin. Governor

Relations with the Indians: Massasoit; Canonicus.

Bradford, the elected chief of the colonists, sent back the skin filled with powder and bullets, and the Indians refrained from war. But the Pilgrims were in the following year involved in hostilities through the misconduct of another colony of mere adventurers, known as Weston's colony, who wasted their stores, hired themselves to the Indians to obtain food, and then robbed them. It will be remembered that this was the period when the Virginian colonists were involved in a fierce war with the Indians, consequent upon the Indian massacre (1622). The facts were known to both races, and a conspiracy similar to the Virginian one was formed for the extermination of the New England pale-faces as well. Massasoit revealed the design, and a colonist named Standish, with four others, 'having got the chiefs of the conspiracy into a wigwam, gave the signal, sprang suddenly upon them, secured the door, and buried his knife in the heart' of one of the fiercest of the chiefs. The other Indians were massacred, except one who was hanged. The Indians took to flight, and eventually sued for peace; but Weston's colonists all perished or disappeared.

Friendly intercourse with the Indians seems afterwards to have been renewed, yet to have itself aided in causing the degeneration of their race. The English, *The Indians* being far superior to the Indians in agriculture, *degenerate.* soon produced more corn than enough for their own consumption, which they sold to the Indians. On the other hand, the only articles in which a profitable trade could be carried on by the colonists with England were beaver and other skins, which the Indians procured for them. Hence it came to pass that the Indians 'abandoned culture,' and betook themselves entirely to the chase, trusting to the colonists for their supply of corn. Their doom was as thoroughly sealed by this step backwards from the position of a semi-agricultural community into that of mere hunters, as it would have been by immediate extermination.

Various other settlements followed those of the Pilgrims. Sir Ferdinando Gorges and John Mason (1622) obtained from the Council of Plymouth an extensive grant of land, which resulted in the settlement of what is now the State of New Hampshire. John Endicott, under another grant from the same Company, made a settlement in Massachusetts Bay (1628), at first at Salem, a town which was soon afterwards eclipsed in importance by Boston. A young preacher, Roger Williams, who had settled in the former town, was sentenced to exile by the Puritans for teaching absolute freedom of conscience. He took to flight; wandered about for fourteen weeks, 'not knowing what bread or bed did mean.' But the Indians, to whom he had always been friendly, received him. From the Narragansett chiefs, Canonicus and Miantonomo, he received an extensive grant of land, which grew eventually into the colony of Rhode Island. It was to be a pure democracy, without any state-worship. All manner of fugitives resorted to him, and the colony increased and prospered, though Cotton Mather, a celebrated New England divine, spoke of Rhode Island as a 'colluvies' of 'everything but Roman Catholics and true Christians.'

Settlement of New Hampshire, Massachusetts Bay, Rhode Island; Roger Williams.

The growth of Massachusetts soon attracted great numbers of emigrants. Three thousand came in 1635, including two men whose names were soon to become celebrated in their mother country, the preacher Hugh Peters, and Henry Vane the younger, better known as Sir Harry Vane, the subject of one of Milton's noble sonnets. Vane was elected governor, but soon got into trouble with the Puritans through favouring Mrs. Hutchinson, another new-comer, a woman of great eloquence but extreme

Rapid growth of Massachusetts. Vane and Mrs. Hutchinson.

religious views, who was eventually excommunicated. Mrs. Hutchinson took refuge in Rhode Island, and having after her husband's death moved into the Dutch territory, was killed with all her family, except one daughter, by the Indians. Vane left for England (1637.)

Vane's departure took place during the first great Indian war of the northern colonies, arising out of the settlement of what is now the State of Connecticut, by emigrants from Massachusetts. Two Englishmen had been killed by the Pequod Indians—the first, it would seem, only in revenge for the kidnapping and murder of an Indian chief. An expedition was sent from Massachusetts which ravaged the Indian country, burning houses and corn. The Pequods tried to gain over the Narragansett Indians, their hereditary foes, into an alliance against the whites. Roger Williams in vain endeavoured to conciliate the red men; but the Narragansetts eventually declined to join the league. Connecticut declared war upon the Pequods; a body of eighty English set out to attack them. The Narragansetts would not join them, deeming them too few; but Uncas, chief of the Mohegans, brought 100 warriors to their aid. The combined body surprised at night the chief village of the Pequods, set it on fire, 'formed a circle round the burning huts, and slew their enemies without mercy as the fire drove them into sight. Six hundred Pequods, men, women, and children, perished in an hour, while but two of the English were lost.' Three hundred more Pequods who arrived the next morning were defeated after a fierce resistance, and the rest of the tribe driven from place to place and butchered, alike by the red-faces and the pale; 200 surrendered, and were either sold into slavery or incorporated among the friendly tribes, and the Pequod people disappeared from the face of the earth.

Settlement of Connecticut ; the Pequod war.

The turn of the Narragansetts came next. Connecticut accused the chief Miantonomo to the Massachusetts magistrates of plotting. Being summoned to Boston, he came, and dared his accusers to meet him face to face, declaring that this was a false accusation of Uncas the Mohegan, and that he would be revenged. He watched for his opportunity, and in 1643 invaded Uncas's territory. But the Mohegans had the best of the fight; Miantonomo was taken prisoner. Uncas feared to kill him, and took him to Hartford to ask leave of the magistrates. He was kept prisoner till the meeting of the commissioners of the United Colonies at Boston, two months later. The commissioners were in doubt, and consulted five ministers. They quoted the fate of Agag, and doomed Miantonomo to death. He was delivered over to Uncas, whose brother, marching behind him, sunk a hatchet into his brain. Such was the end of 'the most potent Indian prince the people of New England ever had to do with,' of whom a governor of Rhode Island declared that he, 'with his uncle Canonicus, were the best friends and greatest benefactors the colony ever had.'

Cruel fate of Miantonomo the Narragansett

Mention has been made just now of the 'United Colonies.' This remarkable union between the four northern colonies, which prefigured the great confederacy of the present day, must now be briefly noticed.

The United Colonies of New England

The New England colonies had almost from the first been treated as step-children by the English state. Ships bound for New England had been detained in the Thames by order of the Council of State (1634, 1638). The letters-patent of the Company had been ordered to be produced in England. Stranger still and more offensive, a special commission had been issued for the American colonies, empowering Archbishop Laud and others to

The oppressive conduct of Charles I. leads to a federation

establish the government, frame the laws, regulate the church, inflict punishments, and even to revoke charters surreptitiously obtained or harmful to the prerogative. When such measures were set at nought, emigration was restrained, no person over the rank of a servant being allowed to leave for the colony without the permission of the commissioners. Only with the growth of parliamentary resistance to Charles I. did a friendlier spirit prevail. The neighbourhood of the Dutch appears to have suggested the idea of federation. But of the four settlements which formed 'the United Colonies of New England' in 1643 only two, Massachusetts and Connecticut, still remain on the list of States, the other two, New Haven and Plymouth, having long since lost any separate existence. Whilst the local self-government of the several colonies was jealously reserved, the conduct of the general affairs of the confederacy was entrusted to commissioners, two from each colony. These not only had charge of the common relations with the Indian tribes, but concluded an actual treaty with the governor of the neighbouring French colony of Acadia.

During the civil war, Massachusetts for a time remained neutral, and claimed a large degree of independence. It refused twice, both before and after the execution of the king, to accept a new charter from the parliament, and through its agent in England publicly denied the jurisdiction of parliament over America; but it acknowledged the Commonwealth, and, on the passing of an ordinance against the royalist colonies, prohibited for a time, by its own enactment, intercourse with Virginia. With Cromwell indeed, who seems to have had a strong sympathy with the New Englanders, the friendliest relations were established, and he even endeavoured to procure settlers for Ireland from among them. His Navigation Act (1651)—far less oppressive than that of

Massachusetts during the Commonwealth.

The War of American Independence.

the Restoration—was favourably received by the colonies, and indeed its provisions against foreign commerce were scarcely enforced. The American colonies remained in profound peace until the Restoration, and acknowledged in turn without demur Richard Cromwell as Protector and Charles II. as king.

Some important events in New England history belong to the period of the Restoration (1660-88). The **The Restoration.** enlargement of Connecticut by the incorporation with it of New Haven (1665) may be dismissed in a line. 'King Philip's war' deserves a longer notice.

Some sincere attempts had been made in New England for the conversion of the Indians. John Eliot, known as 'the Apostle of the Indians,' devoted himself to those of Massachusetts, and translated the Bible into Algonquin. Villages of 'praying Indians' **King Philip's war.** were established; an Indian became a Bachelor of Arts. But other tribes were jealous alike of the white man and of his faith. The new-comers were about two to one of the red men. The Wampanoags, the old allies of the English, found themselves crowded into two peninsulas, and almost driven into the sea. Old Massasoit was dead. Of his two sons, one had died of a fever 'brought on by mortification at being arrested and imprisoned by the English.' His other son, who remained in sole possession of the chieftainship, was Philip —King Philip, as he is always termed in American history — the leader in the last of the Indian wars of New England. It seems certain that there was no conspiracy; the origin of the war was accidental. An Indian informer was killed by his tribe; the murderers were arrested, tried, and convicted by a jury, of which, it must be observed, one half were Indians, and hanged. In revenge, the young Indian braves attacked an English settlement and killed eight or nine Englishmen (1675). King Philip is said to have wept when he heard that a white man's blood had been shed. He had but 700 warriors, and was surrounded by the English; he knew that victory was impossible. Within a week the Indians were driven from their quarters; within a month Philip was a fugitive among the Indians of the interior. But it was only now that the real danger of the war for the colonists began. Philip moved from place to place among the Indian tribes, urging them to war against the English. From Maine to Connecticut they rose, almost to a tribe; the Mohegans forming the one signal exception. The Narragansetts, who had promised neutrality, were dragged into the fray. For a whole year terror reigned. Twelve or thirteen towns were destroyed, and 600 houses burnt. The same number of colonists perished, forming, it was reckoned, one-twentieth of the whole number of able-bodied men. But the continuousness of civilised warfare soon broke the energy of the Indians. The Narragansetts were destroyed. The New Hampshire tribes gave in. Philip, chased from place to place with the remnant of his braves, broken-hearted through the capture of his wife and child, turned his face once more to the hunting-grounds of his fathers. Here at last he was surprised in a swamp by a body of partisans, and shot by an Indian among them. His body was brutally treated, his head carried round the colony in triumph, his son sold as a slave in Bermuda. So perished the last of the blood of Massasoit, the first Indian ally of the Pilgrims (1676).

King Philip's war lasted but a year. The struggle of Massachusetts against the oppressions of the Restoration may be said to have lasted twenty-eight years. In the course of it her charter was declared forfeited (1684). The Assembly of Rhode Island was dissolved; the surrender of the Connecticut charter, which was hidden

away in a 'charter oak' till the Revolution of 1688, was
demanded; and three years of despotic rule,
during which almost every vestige of popular
government in New England was swept away,
were endured under Sir Edmund Andros, in
whose hands was concentrated the government
of all the northern colonies as far south as
the frontier of Maryland. But on the news of the Revolution of 1688 a single wave of insurrection swept away from every colony the whole fabric of his despotism, and William and Mary were proclaimed everywhere with enthusiastic rejoicings.

<small>Struggle of Massachusetts against the Restoration Government. The Revolution of 1688.</small>

Two years after the Revolution—war having broken out between England and France in 1689—the government of Massachusetts established after the fall of Andros (1690), summoned together at New York a congress of delegates from all the colonies as far as Maryland. The result of their deliberations was nothing less than a resolution to attempt the conquest of the then French province of Canada, by a land attack on Montreal, while a fleet from Massachusetts should assail Quebec. Considering that the French population of the North American colonies, by the census of 1688, was only 11,249, or, say, a twentieth of that of the English colonies, the design might seem an easy one. The maritime province of Acadia (now Nova Scotia) was indeed soon annexed. But the French, as has been mentioned, were on friendly terms with the Indian tribes, except the Iroquois; and a war with France was nearly the same thing as a general Indian war. Although the Iroquois took Montreal, the colonists were everywhere repelled, and their frontiers desolated by the inroads of the Indians, whether led or not by the French. The English were driven from Hudson's Bay by the Canadian d'Iberville (p. 19), and Acadia was recovered.

<small>Warfare with the French till 1748.</small>

The result of the war was favourable to France. The Peace of Ryswick (1697) caused little more than a suspension of hostilities, and the war that broke out again in 1701 was marked by the conquest of Acadia, and by an attempt to conquer Canada, but was otherwise nearly as disastrous to the English colonists of the north as the former one. It was, however, terminated by a very favourable peace, that of Utrecht (1713), the terms of which have been already mentioned. From this period till the middle of the century there was only border warfare with the Indians, during which the French missions in Massachusetts, among their allies, the Abenakis of Maine, whose territory had been comprised in the French cessions at the peace, were ruthlessly destroyed; cessions of territory being obtained, by fair or foul means, from the Indians. These gave local occasion to a war known in colonial history as 'King George's War,' corresponding to the war termed that of the Austrian succession in Europe, in which a force consisting of New Englanders only took Louisburg, the stronghold of the then French colony of Cape Breton, and the strongest fortress in North America. It was, however, restored to France (to the great disgust of the colonists) at the peace of 1748.

We have now come to the period when there begins to be, for the English settlements of North America, a general colonial history. But before entering upon it, as must be done in order to make our acquaintance with some of the future leaders, military or civil, in the War of Independence, a few words must be said of the third element in the colonial population.

III. THE BLACK MAN.

It has been already said that the first negro slaves were brought by Dutchmen for sale into Virginia in 1620.

The New England public generally was at first opposed
to the practice, and there is even a record of
a slave, who had been sold by a member of the
Boston church, being ordered to be sent back to Africa
(1645). Yet negro slaves were to be found in New
England as early as 1638. Massachusetts and Connecticut recognised the lawfulness of slavery; Massachusetts,
however, only when voluntary, or in the case of captives
taken in war. Rhode Island, more generous, made illegal the perpetual service of 'black mankind,' requiring
them to be set free after two years, the period of white
men's indentures—a condition which, however, would only
tend to the working slaves to death in the allotted time.
But although there was no importation of negroes on any
considerable scale into New England, the ships by which
the slave trade was mainly carried on were those from Massachusetts and Rhode Island, which carried rum to Africa,
and brought back slaves to the West Indies and the southern colonies. In Maryland slavery had been established
at once; in South Carolina, as before observed, it came
into birth with the colony itself. The failure of the attempt
to exclude it from Georgia has been told already.

The guilt of the institution cannot, however, be fairly
charged on the colonists. Queen Elizabeth had been a
partner in the second voyage of Sir John
Hawkins, the first English slave captain.
James I. chartered a slave trading company
(1618), Charles I. a second (1631); Charles II. a third
(1663), of which the Duke of York was president, and
again a fourth, in which he himself, as well as the Duke,
was a subscriber. Nor did the expulsion of the Stuarts
cause any change of feeling in this respect. England's
sharpest stroke of business at the peace of Utrecht (1713)
was the obtaining for herself the shameful monopoly of
the 'Asiento,'—*i.e.* the slave trade with the Spanish West

Growth of slavery.

Royal slave traders, the Asiento.

Indies—undertaking 'to bring into the West Indies of America belonging to his Catholic Majesty, in the space of thirty years, 144,000 negroes,' at the rate of 4,800 a year, at a fixed rate of duty, with the right to import any further number at a lower rate. As nearly the whole shores of the Gulf of Mexico were still Spanish, England thus contributed to build up slavery in most of the future Southern States of the Union. Whether for foreign or for English colonies, it is reckoned that from 1700 to 1750, English ships carried away from Africa probably a million and a half of negroes, of whom one-eighth never lived to see the opposite shore.

In the same spirit England dealt with her colonies. When Virginia imposed a tax on the import of negroes, the law had to give way before the interest of the African Company. The same course was followed many years later towards South Carolina, when an act of the provincial assembly laying a heavy duty on imported slaves was vetoed by the crown (1761). Indeed the title to a political tract published in 1745, 'The African slave trade the great pillar and support of the British plantation trade in America,' appears fairly to express the prevalent feeling of the mother country on the subject before the War of Independence. The most remarkable relaxation of the Navigation Laws in the eighteenth century was the throwing open the slave trade by the act 'for extending and improving the trade to Africa' (1750; 23 Geo. II., c. 31), which after reciting that 'the trade to and from Africa is very advantageous to Great Britain, and necessary for the supplying the plantations and colonies thereunto belonging with a sufficient number of negroes at reasonable rates,' enacted that it should be lawful 'for all his Majesty's subjects to trade and traffick to and from any port or place in Africa, between the port of Sallee in

Support of slavery and the slave-trade by the mother country.

South Barbary and the Cape of Good Hope.' By 1763, there were about 300,000 negroes in the North American colonies.

General Colonial History, 1748-64.

When 'King George's War' ended by the restoration of Louisburg to the French, it seemed as if it had been fought out for nothing. Yet it was destined to have a place in the history of the world, through the connexion with it of a certain ex-printer's-devil, who was to become one of the leaders in the coming struggle between England and her colonies. This was Benjamin Franklin.

Connection of King George's War with Franklin.

Franklin represents, under its noblest aspect, the shrewd side of the American character, before it has developed into 'cuteness' or 'smartness.' The son of a soap and candle manufacturer in Boston (born 1706), he had been employed at ten years of age in cutting wicks and filling candle-moulds, but was already an insatiable reader. At twelve he was apprenticed to an elder brother, a printer, who in 1721 established a paper called the 'New England Courant,' and young Benjamin at fifteen both helped in printing, distributed the copies, and contributed matter of his own. But the paper got into trouble through a too free criticism of the ministers of religion. James Franklin was thrown into prison for a month, and forbidden to print the paper except under previous supervision; Benjamin escaped with an admonition. The outlook was not promising, and moreover his brother was of violent temper. At seventeen Benjamin ran away to New York; found there no employment, and after various wanderings reached Philadelphia with a dollar in his pocket. Here, however, he obtained a situation in one of the two existing printing offices, and soon prospered.

Benjamin Franklin; the author of the first military organisation in the colonies.

He was able to come to Europe, and after eighteen months' residence in London returned to Philadelphia, and set up a printing press of his own. Besides being ready to put his hand to any branch of the printing trade, he could 'make types and woodcuts, and engrave vignettes in copper.' He became printer to the Assembly; established a newspaper; the first American circulating library (1730); a celebrated almanac, called 'Poor Richard's Almanac' (1732), which he continued for twenty-five years; and the American Philosophical Society (1736). He also became clerk to the Assembly. To him again was due the first permanent military organisation in the colonies, through the establishment, during King George's War, of a militia in Pennsylvania (1747), comprising over 120 companies of 100 men each. Franklin was elected to the command of a regiment, but would only serve as a private. A few years later his discoveries in electricity, crowned by the feat of drawing lightning from the clouds by means of a key and a silken kite (1751), rendered his name famous in science throughout the world.

Like King George's War, a desultory colonial warfare known as the 'French and Indian War,' which preceded and at last merged in the war known in Europe as the Seven Years War, has become historical, as having first brought into prominence a young surveyor named George Washington. The boundary between the French and English colonies to the west of the latter had never been fixed. A company called the Ohio Company, of which Augustine Washington was a member, had obtained from the English crown a grant of 500,000 acres on the Ohio. But the valley of that river had already been taken possession of by the French, who broke up a British post on the Miami river, one of the northern

The 'French and Indian War'; George Washington.

affluents of the Ohio, carrying off its occupants to Canada, and severely punishing the Indian allies of the English. Two posts were even established in north-western Pennsylvania. George Washington born 1732, son of Augustine Washington, had attracted the notice of Lord Fairfax, an extensive landowner in Virginia, and through his influence had been appointed at nineteen adjutant-general. He was now sent by Governor Dinwiddie of Virginia (1753) to the two new French posts, to ask the reason of the French intrusion on British territory. The French commanders made no secret of their purpose; they were to take possession of the whole of the Ohio valley, and destroy every English post. Amidst many dangers, Washington found his way back, and reported the results of his mission. By his recommendation, the Ohio Company began constructing a fort on the site of what is now Pittsburg, at the junction of the Alleghany and Monongahela rivers. But it was taken by the French before the spot could be reached by a body of soldiers to whose command Washington had succeeded on the march; and the fort was completed by the French under the name of Fort Duquesne. A successful night skirmish with the French and a gallant defence in a stockade, for which Washington had thrown up with his own hands the first shovelful of earth, only resulted in his being allowed to march away with the honours of war, retaining stores and baggage. The French occupied the whole country to the Alleghanies.

The state of things was felt to be serious. Delegates from all the colonies north of the Potomac met at Albany (1754), the Iroquois being invited to the council. A plan was brought forward by Benjamin Franklin, and adopted for reference to the colonies themselves. According to this plan a congress, composed of from two to seven delegates, was to meet an-

Franklin's proposed congress.

nually at Philadelphia, with power to originate all laws, appoint civil officers, issue money, deal with the Indians, regulate trade, govern new settlements, raise soldiers, and levy taxes, subject, however, to the veto of a governor-general appointed by the crown, each colony retaining its own legislature and independence in internal affairs. Nothing came of it at that time; the seed was one which needed yet nearly a quarter of a century for its growth.

The English Government became alarmed, and sent over troops under General Braddock. Four expeditions at once were planned, the principal one, commanded by General Braddock himself, with George Washington as his aide-de-camp, against the French in the Ohio valley. Braddock derided all warnings of Indian surprises, and with his 2,000 men advanced slowly, striking terror at first both into the French and the Indians. On July 9, 1755, moving along the back of the Monongahela river, on a path about twelve feet wide, with wooded ravines ten feet deep on each side, which eventually met, he was suddenly attacked at the point of junction by a much smaller force of French and Indians, extending on both sides. The war-whoops and the shots from unseen foes struck a panic terror into the English troops, and only the Virginia Rangers, a colonial corps, offered an effectual resistance. Braddock, after seeing all his aides-de-camp disabled except Washington, after having five horses wounded under him, and receiving a musket ball through the lungs, at last by Washington's advice gave the signal for a retreat. The retreat became a rout, and stores and artillery, and the private papers of the general, were left behind. The loss amounted to 26 officers killed, 37 wounded, and 714 privates, while the enemy lost only 3 officers and 30 men killed, and as many wounded. Washington, after displaying conspicuous bravery on the battle-field, did his

General Braddock's defeat.

best to cover the retreat; but the panic spread to the garrison of Will's Creek, on which the fugitives fell back. Will's Creek was evacuated, and 100,000*l.* of stores and artillery destroyed. Braddock died the fourth day after his defeat.

Of the other three expeditions, the first resulted in the rebuilding and garrisoning of a fort at Oswego, at the south-east end of Lake Ontario; a second after a victory over the French in the erection of Fort William Henry, at the southern end of Lake George. The third, landing near the Bay of Fundy, subdued the country now known as New Brunswick, between Maine and Nova Scotia. This was followed by the barbarous measure of the expulsion of the Acadians, or French of Nova Scotia, 7,000 of whom were shipped off to the southern colonies, an event to which Mr. Longfellow's well-known poem of 'Evangeline' owes its subject.

Conquest of New Brunswick; expulsion of the Acadians.

War was only formally declared in 1756, and its first operations were again entirely favourable to the French, who under the distinguished general, Montcalm, reduced successively both Fort Oswego and Fort William Henry, the capture of the latter being followed by a massacre of the garrison by the Indian allies of the French. At the close of 1757, it is stated that the English possessions in America were to those of the French but as one to twenty.

French successes.

On the accession to power of the elder Pitt, the 'great Lord Chatham' of history, more efficient measures were taken by the English, and the tide of fortune turned decidedly in their favour. One expedition occupied Louisburg, and took possession of Cape Breton and Prince Edward's Island. An attack on the French fort of Ticonderoga on Lake George failed; but Washington, with his Virginia

The French defeated; Canada conquered; Peace of Paris.

Rangers, forming part of an army under General Forbes, drove the French out of Fort Duquesne (1758), and changed the name of the place to Pittsburg, in honour of the great minister. On his return from this expedition, he was elected (at twenty-seven) a member of the Virginian House of Burgesses. The next year was marked by the driving of the French from the country between Pittsburg and Lake Erie, from their fort of Niagara, from Ticonderoga and Lake Champlain, and still more by the magnificent achievement of the battle and taking of Quebec, in which the commanders on both sides, Wolfe and Montcalm, perished. This event was followed in 1760 by the surrender of Montreal, with the whole of Canada, and the two important posts of Mackinaw, at the junction between Lakes Michigan and Huron, and Detroit, which commands the water communication between Lakes Huron and Erie. When, three years later, peace was concluded (February 10, 1763), Spain gave up Florida to England; and France formally ceded, in North America alone, Louisiana to the Mississippi (without New Orleans), all Canada, Acadia, Cape Breton and its islands, and the fisheries with a few reservations. Never it was said, was so glorious a war, so honourable a peace.

Although extending beyond the period of which we have been speaking, there is a sequel which belongs to it, in the shape of a war with the Indians, named after their leader, an Ottawa chief, Pontiac's War.

'Pontiac's war.' Misled by his eloquence, a number of Indian tribes suddenly rose on the English, surprised nine garrisons in a day, occupied the fort of Mackinaw, and besieged Pittsburg and Detroit. But the garrison of the latter held out for months, and, as usual, the Indians could not keep together. Pontiac held on till all but his Ottawas deserted him. All the hostile tribes, two only excepted, successively treated with the English (1764). Pontiac took refuge among the Illinois, and tried to form another confederacy against the English, but was stabbed at a council by an Indian who was friendly to them. This was Virginia's last Indian war, as King Philip's war had been the last Indian war of New England.

At the close of this period the most populous of the American colonies were Massachusetts and Pennsylvania, Boston and Philadelphia containing nearly 18,000 inhabitants each, while New York had as yet only 12,000. The population was chiefly agricultural, though manufactures were already largely carried on in the North. There was a brisk coast trade, and the New Englanders had engaged in the whale fishery. Rice, indigo, and to some extent cotton, were produced in the South; tar and turpentine in North Carolina; tobacco, as well as the almost universal maize, in Virginia and Maryland.

The colonies in 1763.

CHAPTER III.

CAUSES OF DISCONTENT.—STRUGGLE BEFORE THE WAR (1763-75).

MONTCALM, it is said, predicted that if France lost America, in ten years more America would be in revolt against England. He was not far out in his prediction.

Montcalm's prediction.

It may have already appeared from the preceding sketch that the history of the English colonies in North America presents a curious blending of loyalty and disaffection. The colonists were always ready to fly to arms for the honour of the British name—and the enlargement of their own borders—

Mingled loyalty and disaffection of colonies.

against their French and Spanish neighbours; but within their own limits there was a constant straining, rising not unfrequently to rebellion, against the authority which the crown, its representatives or grantees, sought to exercise over them.

One abiding source of irritation, since the latter half of the seventeenth century, lay in the English Navigation Laws. The Navigation Act of the Commonwealth had had for its object the securing to English vessels the carrying trade of the colonies with England. The Navigation Acts of Charles II. confined to English vessels, navigated by Englishmen, all importation of merchandise into and exportation from the colonies, and even forbad any importation of European commodities into colonies except from England, whilst aliens were also forbidden to act as merchants or factors in the colonies (1660, 1662). Still more monstrous was a subsequent act, which forbad all the principal colonial staples to be exported otherwise than to England, so that a duty equivalent to the English customs duty was laid on the importation of such articles from one colony into another. *The Navigation laws.*

All the colonies soon began to suffer under this legislation. We have seen by what wild expedients Virginia sought to defend herself against its ill effects. The struggle against it in New England deserves closer notice, as having been carried on by means of legislation. On the first passing of the Navigation Act the General Court of Massachusetts published a declaration of rights, which included that of rejecting 'any parliamentary or royal imposition prejudicial to the country, and contrary to any just act of colonial legislation.' It was only after this that Charles II. was proclaimed. Ten years after the passing of the Navigation Act it was not enforced in Massachusetts. It was only in 1679 that the General

Struggle against the Navigation Laws, in New England especially.

Court, whilst declaring that 'the Acts of Navigation were an invasion of the rights and privileges of the subjects of his Majesty in the colony, they not being represented in parliament,' and that 'the laws of England do not reach America,' yet gave them effect by an act of its own. Then came the confiscation of the charters of the northern colonies, and the appointment of Sir Edmund Andros as governor of all New England.

The history of the struggle of the American, or, we might say the New England, colonies against the government of the Restoration has been scarcely studied enough. It prefigures most remarkably that larger struggle which a century later was to rend thirteen colonies away from the mother country. The principle at issue was exactly the same— the right of the mother country to interfere in the internal matters of the colonies, and with the carrying on of their trade. It is supposed that at the period of the Revolution of 1688 the colonies of North America contained together not much more than 200,000 souls. Had there been 2,000,000, the rule of governors like Berkeley and Andros would probably never have been tolerated, whatever might have been the course of politics in England. Moreover, the discontents engendered by the Restoration were not appeased by the successors of James II. Notwithstanding the enthusiasm with which William had been proclaimed, Massachusetts had to spend two years in obtaining a new charter, and lost under it the right of electing officers, who were henceforth to be appointed by the governor or the crown. In New York, as will be recollected, Leisler, the elected governor, after ruling for nearly two years in the king's name, was executed for high treason. He was looked upon as a martyr, and pieces of his clothes were saved as relics.

At the Peace of Utrecht (1713) the Navigation Laws

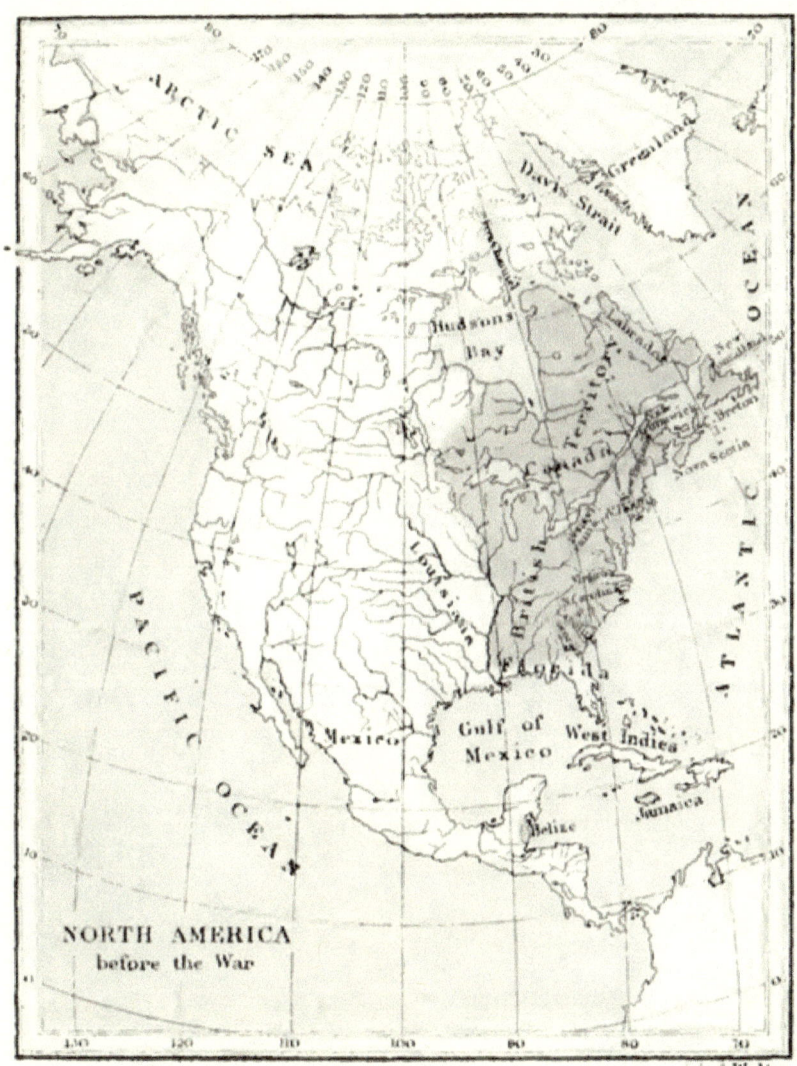

were so far relaxed that trade was permitted between Great Britain and Spain, and their respective plantations and provinces, 'where hitherto trade and commerce had been accustomed'—a clear indication of the habitual violation of the law up to that time. Sir Robert Walpole indeed made it a maxim to encourage the trade of the American colonies, passing over some of their 'irregularities' in trading with Europe. But the growth of manufactures in the colonies was discouraged on the express ground, as stated in a resolution of the House of Commons, that it 'tended to lessen their dependence on Great Britain.' The transport of hats, for instance, from one colony to another, was forbidden, because the manufacture of them was 'daily increasing in the British plantations in America' (1732). An absolute prohibition of the manufacture of iron wares was all but carried. Any relaxations of the navigation laws that were enacted, were mainly in favour of tropical products, as sugar and rice; but parliament went so far as to impose a customs duty on the import of foreign wines and sugars into any of the American colonies (1793). If bounties were given on the import of naval stores from the North American colonies, the timber trade was hampered (as was indeed that of Scotland also) by the rights of preemption of the Commissioners of the Navy, and also by the requirement of a license for cutting down white pine. To these causes of discontent were added the impressment laws, the enforcement of which during the war of 1744-8 was openly resisted. Sir Charles Knowles, the British naval commander, finding his seamen desert while lying off the Massachusetts coast, sent his boats to Boston to impress men in their stead. The people seized on the officers of the fleet who were in the town, and detained them for three days. The House of Representatives had to mediate before they were re-

Other causes of discontent.

leased, and most if not all of the impressed men were dismissed.

An ugly temper was rising on both sides. There was a disposition in England to look upon the colonists as headstrong and rebellious—as a transatlantic Jeshurun, that had waxed fat under the protection of the mother country, and kicked now at its protector. The colonists complained that the mother country crippled their trade, taxed them against their will, sought to thrust on them the worst features of its legislation. Every complaint seemed only to irritate English statesmen the more. One grievance on their part against the colonists was that the colonial Houses of Assembly claimed by their votes of supply to make the representatives of the crown their dependents; another, that the customs establishment in America was, owing to smuggling and sinecures, only a burden on the British customs. Smuggling in particular was so extensively practised that not one-tenth of the 1,500,000 lbs. of tea consumed annually in the colonies was estimated to come from England, whence alone it could be legally supplied.

Mutual com- plaints be- tween the mother country and the colonies.

The remedy devised was to levy a revenue from the colonies, and to charge upon it a civil list for the salaries of the governors and other officers of the crown, including the judges, who were to hold office henceforth at its pleasure, and for the maintenance, after the first year, of twenty regiments. Strange to say, the statesman who eventually took upon himself to attempt the administration of such a remedy, George Grenville, was one who 'doubted the propriety of taxing colonies without allowing them representatives;' but he also held that 'colonies are only settlements made in distant parts of the world for the improvement of trade,' and that 'they would be intolerable except on the conditions contained in the Act of Navi-

The attempt to raise a revenue from the colonies. George Grenville.

gation.' In other words, he was incapable of knowing a nation when he saw one, so long as it was an offshoot from another: he could not admit that slips and cuttings would ever grow into trees.

The act of 1733 by which a customs duty was laid on certain foreign imports into the American colonies had been continued from time to time. In 1763, on the ground that it was 'just and necessary' that a revenue should be raised in his Majesty's dominions in America, 'for defraying the expenses of defending, protecting, and securing the same,' a new act was passed which, whilst reducing some of the existing duties, levied new ones on a number of other articles, including wines, besides enacting many harassing regulations. The navigation laws were at the same time more strictly enforced. *The colonial Revenue Act.*

The colonists protested, but submitted. What they claimed as yet was only representation in the British parliament. James Otis of Boston, who had been advocate-general for the crown, in a pamphlet entitled 'The Rights of the British Colonies Asserted and Proved' (1764), wrote: 'When the parliament shall think fit to allow the colonists a representation in the House of Commons, the equity of taxing the colonies will be as clear as their power is at present of doing it without.' With Otis, Samuel Adams was the most prominent of the protesting colonists. 'We claim British rights,' he said at a Boston town meeting, 'not by charter only, for what is that but a parchment? but we claim them because we were born with them.' *Protests of the colonists; Otis; Samuel Adams.*

The dislike to the new customs duties was, however, far enhanced by the announcement already made (March 1764) by Grenville as Chancellor of the Exchequer, of his intention to apply the stamp duties to America. This intention was carried into effect *The Stamp Act, 1765.*

by the famous American Stamp Act in the following year 5 Geo. III., c. 12, in spite of petitions from the Assemblies of six colonies, and the representations of their agents, conspicuous amongst whom was Franklin, agent for Pennsylvania. It was signed by commission on behalf of the king—then suffering from a malady which is supposed to have been in fact the first visitation of his subsequent insanity—March 22, 1765. It contained sixty-two sections, and imposed fifty-four separate duties, ranging from a halfpenny per copy on every pamphlet or paper not exceeding half a sheet, to 10*l.* on the admission to practice of any 'counsellor, solicitor, attorney, **advocate, or proctor.'**

The measure **was** received **in America** with very various feelings. Franklin thought **that** 'the sun of liberty was set.' Otis declared **it to** be the duty of all 'humbly and silently **to** acquiesce in all the decisions **of** the supreme legislature.' **Younger** men **were** less desponding and less submissive. **In** the Virginian House of Burgesses, Patrick Henry, its youngest member, carried five resolutions asserting the rights of the colonies, and denying the authority of the British parliament to tax them. A passage in his speech has often been quoted as an instance of rhetorical adroitness. 'Cæsar,' he exclaimed, 'had his Brutus; Charles **I. had** his Cromwell; and George III.'. . .—'Treason, treason!' was the cry that rose from all sides—'and George III. may profit by their example,' was Henry's deft conclusion. Resolutions similar to those of the Virginian house were passed in New York, Massachusetts, and other colonies.

Patrick Henry's resolutions.

The Massachusetts Assembly convoked a Congress at New York for the month of October, November 1 being the date **on** which the Stamp Act was to come into force. The proposal hung fire for awhile, till, in July, South Carolina accepted the invitation **of** Massachusetts, **and** other legislatures gradually did the same. Meanwhile agitation spread amongst the people. At Boston, in August, Lord Bute, the English minister, and Oliver, the Boston stamp-master, were hung in effigy, left hanging all day, taken down at night, and carried on biers, in a great torchlight procession through the streets, to the cry of 'Liberty, Property, and No Stamps.' The stamp office, then being built, was levelled and set fire to, and the windows of Oliver's house broken, after which the figures were burnt amid the cheers of a vast multitude. Notwithstanding Oliver's public announcement that he would resign, riots broke out a few days later, in which the house of Governor Hutchinson was sacked; the rioters when arrested were rescued, and remained unpunished. The stamp-masters of New Hampshire, New Jersey, New York, voluntarily resigned their offices; those of Maryland, Pennsylvania, Rhode Island, Connecticut were forced to do so. The last, a man named Ingersoll, being threatened with death by some 500 mounted farmers and freeholders, each armed with a white club, kept them at bay for three hours, but at last gave in, as it was 'not worth dying for.' As he rode back into Hartford on his white horse, with the crowd after him, he said that he now understood the meaning of 'Death on a pale horse, and hell following him.'

A congress convened; riots at Boston and elsewhere.

There was more in all this than mere rioting. Already it had been written in a Boston paper that 'North American liberty was dead, but she had left one son, Independence, the hope of all when he should come of age.' 'Join or die' was the motto of a new paper published at New York. And on October 7, the Congress met at New York, twenty-eight delegates strong, representing nine colonies—Massachusetts, Rhode Island, Con-

Independence already spoken of; New York Congress and its proceedings.

necticut, New York, New Jersey, Pennsylvania, Delaware, Maryland, and South Carolina. They drew up a petition to the king, and a memorial to parliament in which— chiefly through the vehement opposition of Gadsden, a South Carolina delegate—all arguments drawn from royal charters were discarded. The idea of colonial representation in the British parliament was disclaimed as impracticable, and whilst 'all due subordination to the parliament of Great Britain' was acknowledged, its right to tax the colonies was denied. Six colonies, by their delegates, signed the papers, and became, to use their expression, 'a bundle of sticks which could neither be bent nor broken' Oct. 25.

On October 31 Governor Colden and all the royal governors took the oath to carry the Stamp Act into effect. On November 1 there was not a stamp-master in the colonies, nor a stamp to be seen. The day was signalised in several towns by processions carrying the Stamp Act to be burned or buried, or again by the funeral of a coffin bearing the name of Liberty, which after being lowered into the grave was raised again with the inscription 'Liberty Revived.' Handbills posted at the street corners in Boston warned those who should distribute or use stamped sheets to look to themselves. Oliver was compelled to carry out his promised resignation under a tree, now known as Liberty Tree, and to take an oath before a justice of the peace never to take measures to enforce the Stamp Act in America (Dec. 17). Open rioting was confined, however, to New York. For a time (except in Rhode Island) the courts were closed, lest for want of stamps the proceedings should be illegal, and ships feared to go to sea without stamped papers; but after awhile all went on as usual.

The Stamp Act cannot be carried into effect.

There had been a change of ministry in England between the passing of the Stamp Act and the date appointed for carrying it into execution. The Rockingham Cabinet was far weaker than its predecessor, but better disposed towards America. During the recess (January 1766) Pitt's advice was asked by the Cabinet as to the measures to be taken with regard to America. He gave it from his seat in parliament, which he had not for a long time attended. 'He could not be silent,' he said, ' on a question that might mortally wound the freedom of three millions of virtuous and brave subjects beyond the Atlantic Ocean. The Americans were the sons, not the bastards of England. They were entitled to the common right of representation, and could not be bound to pay taxes without their consent.' Later on in the debate, in reply to Grenville, who had charged the seditious spirit of the colonies to the factions in the House, Pitt uttered his famous words, soon echoed from shore to shore of the Atlantic : ' The gentleman tells us America is obstinate ; America is almost in open rebellion ; *I rejoice that America has resisted.*' Yet even he, whilst recommending the absolute repeal of the Stamp Act, added : ' At the same time, let the sovereign authority of this country over the colonies be asserted in as strong terms as can be devised, and be made to extend to every point of legislation, that we may bind their trade, confine their manufactures, and exercise every power whatsoever, except that of taking their money out of their pockets without their consent.'

The Rockingham Cabinet: Pitt rejoices that America has resisted.

His advice was followed on both points.

A year after it was passed, the Stamp Act was repealed, on the ground that its continuance ' would be attended with many inconveniences, and might be productive of consequences greatly detrimental to the commercial interests of these kingdoms.' (6 Geo. III. c. 11.) But at the

The Stamp Act repealed, 1766; the Declaratory Act.

same time the Declaratory Act was passed 'for the better securing the dependency of his Majesty's dominions in America upon **the crown** and parliament of Great Britain.' This declared that the colonies and plantations in America 'have been, are, and of right ought to be, subordinate unto and dependent upon the imperial crown and parliament of Great Britain;' and that the crown, with the advice and consent of parliament, 'had, hath, and of right ought to have, full power and authority to make laws and statutes of sufficient force and validity to bind the colonies and **people of** America, subjects of the crown of Great Britain, in all cases whatsoever;' and again, that all 'resolutions, **votes, orders, and** proceedings' in any of such colonies or plantations, **whereby the** power and authority of the parliament of Great **Britain** to make laws and statutes was denied or drawn into question, are 'utterly null and void to all intents **and purposes** whatsoever.'

In the first instance **the repeal** only of the obnoxious Stamp Act was noticed by **the** colonists, the Declaratory

Rejoicings in the colonies.

Act being overlooked. The people gave themselves up **to** joy. Instead of the funereal tolling which used to greet the arrival of vessels carrying stamps, merry peals rang from church to church. The women, who had resolved not **to** wear any clothes of English stuff, bought new ones for the king's birthday (June 4), giving the old to the poor. Boston celebrated a special holiday (May 19).

This favourable temper was not suffered to last long. The British Government had not renounced its purpose

Farther oppressive measures.

of making revenue out of the colonies, nor had the parliament disclaimed the right of taxation and of interference with **their** trade. An act of 1766 forbad absolutely, under pain of forfeiture of both goods and vessel, the importation into Jamaica or Dominica of the chief staples of the North American colonies.

If another act of the same session somewhat reduced certain import duties payable in those colonies, it was more than counterbalanced by an act of the following session, known as the Revenue Act, imposing duties on the import from Great Britain into any colony or plantation in America, of glass, tea, paper, and other articles, and directing the application of the duties 'for defraying the charges of the administration of justice, and the support of the civil government.'

But there was another source of dissatisfaction. The American colonies had hitherto, for the most part, defended themselves against aggression, and had often undertaken, of their own accord, expeditions against England's enemies. When British troops had been sent over, quarters had been found for them under provincial acts. During the Seven Years War, Lord Loudoun, as commander-in-chief, had set the example of insisting on free quarters for his officers (1756). In 1765 the first 'Quartering Act'—afterwards continued yearly—was passed, requiring the colonies to provide the king's troops with certain stores, and with barracks. Massachusetts refused to supply stores in accordance with the requirements of the act; New York did the same, passing an Act of Assembly of its own for similar purposes, but with inconsistent provisions. In retaliation, the British Government now resorted to the severe measure of suspending the New York constitution; an act being passed 'for restraining and prohibiting the Governor, Council, and House of Representatives of the province of New York, until provision shall have been made for furnishing his Majesty's troops with all the necessaries required by law, from passing or assenting to any Act of Assembly, vote, or resolution for any other purpose.'

The Quartering Act. Suspension of the New York Assembly.

Strange to say, most of the above measures were

passed under the administration of Pitt, now Earl of Chatham, to whom several colonies had been voting statues. At the express invitation of the king (July 6, 1766), he had, although enfeebled by illness, become the head of a Cabinet containing several members favourable to America (Lord Shelburne in particular), but bitterly opposed by the Rockingham Whigs. Lord Chatham's infirmities so increased upon him that towards the end of 1766 he had to leave London for Bath, nevermore to appear as a minister in the House of Lords. The brilliant but reckless Charles Townshend, taking the lead in his absence, resolved to raise a revenue from America. Chatham in vain tried to get rid of Townshend, and instead of resigning, withdrew altogether from business, leaving the leadership to the Duke of Grafton (March 11, 1767). He was even led to declare that he would not retire from the ministry except by the king's command (June 1767). Virtually the Cabinet was henceforth the king himself, more especially when, after the sudden death of Charles Townshend (Sept. 1767), his place was filled by the clear-sighted but weak-willed Lord North. Two months later, the Colonial department was taken from Lord Shelburne and given to Lord Hillsborough (December), who soon manifested the purpose of coercing the colonies. At last Lord Shelburne was dismissed (Oct. 1768). This was too much for Chatham, who resigned, notwithstanding the solicitations of the king.

The old discontents of course now broke out afresh in America. The right of parliament to legislate for the colonies had been denied for the first time in the Massachusetts House of Assembly (end of 1768). Choiseul, the French prime minister, had already sent an agent to America —Colonel de Kalb, an Alsatian, who afterwards served in the war on the American side—and, through his minister in London, was paying court to Franklin. Before the time appointed (Nov. 20) for the collection of the new taxes, after a vain attempt to obtain an early convening of the Legislature, the inhabitants of Boston met (Oct. 28, 1767), and resolved to forego the importation and use of many articles of British production and manufacture, appointing a committee to obtain signatures to an agreement for this purpose, and directing their resolutions to be forwarded throughout the colonies. The Massachusetts House of Assembly (Jan. 12, 1768) adopted a letter to be sent to their agent for communication to the British ministry, protesting, amongst other things, against all acts of the British parliament for taxing the colonies. A month later they sent a circular letter to all the colonies, requesting them to join in some suitable measure of redress. Petitions to the king, remonstrances to the parliament, began to pour in. A sloop was discharged in Boston of a cargo of wines, whilst the tide-waiter on board was kept a prisoner in the cabin. The sloop was seized by the collector; the collector's boat was dragged through the streets and burnt on the common (June 10). The captain was prosecuted, but no evidence was forthcoming, and his ship was restored to him. The Massachusetts Assembly, when requested by the governor, under the direction of the Secretary for the Colonies, to rescind the circular letter, refused to do so by 92 votes to 17. The Governor dissolved the Assembly. The merchants of Boston entered into an agreement against importation, and 'appointed an influential committee, who took measures to induce or force all to come into the agreement.' Women—'daughters of Liberty'—gave up the use of tea. Choiseul was already thinking of offering a treaty of commerce to the Americans. Just at this time, moreover, the French population of Louisiana had risen upon the Spanish authorities, and claimed to be either a French colony or a republic, a proceeding which was deemed by the French to be 'at least a good example for the English colonies.' The attempt was quelled in August of the following year, but it showed that there was revolution in the air of the American continent.

Governor Bernard having refused to issue writs for a new Assembly, a convention was called in Boston, after a precedent set in 1688. This convention, attended by delegates from nearly every settlement in the colony, refused to break up at the bidding of the governor, and the members conducted their proceedings so adroitly that Attorney-General de Grey, when consulted as to whether they had been guilty of treason, declared that he doubted whether they had been guilty of an overt act, though he was sure they had come 'within a hair's breadth of it.'

The Boston Convention.

Meanwhile the news had come that a standing army was to be kept in the colonies. On September 28, just after the Convention broke up, seven vessels of war arrived in Boston from Halifax, with seven hundred men on board, and drew up in line, broadside to the town, the gunners standing to their guns with lighted matches. They landed on October 11, but quarters were refused, and it was with the greatest difficulty that any could be found. More troops followed; by the end of the year there were four thousand regulars in Boston. To the westward, on the other hand, many posts were abandoned. It was the policy of Lord Hillsborough to 'extend an unbroken line of Indian frontier from Georgia to Canada.' Lord North in parliament declared that he would never think of repealing the Revenue Act until he saw America prostrate at his feet. The Assembly met in 1769; but finding itself surrounded by soldiers, refused to do

Troops sent to the colonies. Hillsborough's and North's policy. Feelings of Washington (1769).

business. The feelings which had by this time been aroused in the breasts of men by no means of impulsive temperament, may be judged of by a letter of Washington to George Mason, dated April 5, 1769. 'At a time when our lordly masters in Great Britain will be satisfied with nothing less than the deprivation of American freedom,' he wrote, it was clearly his opinion 'that no man should scruple or hesitate a moment to use arms in defence of so valuable a blessing,' although only as 'the last resource.' Yet for years after, as will be seen, he deprecated the idea of American independence.

Nor did New England stand alone. Virginia passed strong resolutions, which were followed by others in both Carolinas, Delaware, Maryland, New York. The non-importation agreements spread everywhere —Washington laid one before the Virginia Assembly—and home manufactures sprang up. The graduates of Harvard College, in Massachusetts, stood up to take their degrees, clad in New England black cloth. The imports from England into all the colonies fell off to a serious extent. Bitter feelings grew up between soldiers and citizens. There was rioting at New York; in the 'Boston massacre' three citizens were killed, and several wounded (March 5, 1770). The victims had a public funeral, and the troops were sent to their barracks. *Spread of non-importation agreements; the Boston massacre.*

Lord North, who had succeeded to the premiership, thought to appease the discontent of the colonists through a compromise, by which all the obnoxious duties were removed, except that on tea. To this henceforth the non-importation agreements (which indeed had only been fully observed in New York) were confined, and for nearly two years there was a comparative lull in the storm. In violation of the Massachusetts charter, which reserved *Lord North attempts a compromise: the Tea Act (1770).*

to the governor the command of its forts, Castle William at Boston was surrendered by him to the royal commander-in-chief. The popular party in North Carolina, known as 'regulators,' were forcibly put down. Fugitives from among them, however, crossed the Alleghanies, descended into the valley of the Tennessee, and there by written agreement founded a small republic of their own (1772). The settlers of Illinois did not go quite so far, but refused to submit to the crown authorities, and claimed institutions like those of Connecticut. Virginia protested against the royal instructions which forbad the governor to assent to any law by which the importation of slaves should be in any respect prohibited or obstructed.

The spark of a new conflict flew out from tiny Rhode Island, always keen for trade, whether legal or not. An act had just been passed which made it a capital offence wilfully and maliciously to burn or destroy any ship or vessel of war, or any military, naval, or victualling stores, and allowed trials for any such offence committed out of the realm to take place in any county within it. In the teeth of this act, at Providence, Rhode Island, a royal schooner, the 'Gaspee,' stationed on the coast to prevent smuggling, having been led on by a vessel which she was pursuing into shoal water, was boarded, seized, and burnt by night (June 9, 1772), and a reward of 500*l.* failed to procure any evidence against the perpetrators of the outrage.

The burning of the 'Gaspee,' 1772.

Samuel Adams now propounded a plan, which he had been maturing for a whole year, for creating committees of correspondence, to be appointed by town meetings. Boston set the example, which was rapidly followed by the Massachusetts towns, then by Virginia, by South Carolina, and by all New England. Scarcely any tea was consumed but Dutch; the Revenue Act proved a

The committees of correspondence; destruction of tea at Boston (1772-3).

dead failure. In vain, to encourage consumption, did parliament grant a drawback on the export of tea to the American colonies (as also to Ireland), first of three-fifths of the English export duties, then of the whole; in vain were shiploads of tea consigned to the colonies, instead of waiting for the orders which did not come. The 'Sons of Liberty' organisations, which had now been in existence for some years, determined that it should not be landed, or if landed, not sold. At Philadelphia and New York the ships were sent back without breaking bulk; at Charleston the tea was landed, but left to rot in damp cellars. At Boston, where Governor Hutchinson's sons were the consignees, the governor gave orders that the ships should not sail till the duties were paid. For weeks the people kept watch on the docks to prevent the landing of the tea. At a great meeting of 7,000 people (December 16, 1773), to which men poured in from twenty miles round, fervid speeches were made by Samuel Adams, Josiah Quincy, and others. Towards evening, at a war-whoop from the gallery, the meeting broke up, and some fifty sham Indians proceeded to the wharf where three tea-ships were moored, boarded them, and threw the contents of 342 chests of tea into the water; the whole proceedings being carried on in perfect order, in the presence of a vast multitude. The Boston newspapers were pressing meanwhile for a Congress of American States to frame a Bill of Rights, or to form an American commonwealth. A month later (January 25, 1774), a Scotch preventive officer was tarred and feathered, and paraded under the Boston gallows.

The news of this proceeding was received with indignation by the English Parliament, and there was a talk of arresting Franklin, now the agent of four colonies. A petition which he had presented from the Massachusetts House of Assembly to the Privy Council for the removal of the governor

Indignation of Parliament; the Boston Port Act.

was dismissed, as 'groundless, vexatious, and scandalous,' and he was himself deprived of his office of deputy postmaster for the colonies. An act known as the Boston Port Act was passed, to forbid temporarily ' the landing and discharging, lading or shipping of goods, wares, and merchandise, at the town and within the harbour of Boston,' which were placed in a state of quasi-blockade.

This act was but one of a group of five statutes of the same session (14 George III.) directed against the colonies, which were now virtually in a state of rebellion. The second aimed at securing the impartial administration of justice in the cases of persons questioned for any acts done by them in the execution of the law, or for the suppression of riots and tumults, in the province of Massachusetts Bay. It gave protection to magistrates and others against local process for acts done in the execution of their duty, allowing the taking of bail and the changing to any other colony, or to Great Britain, of the place of trial of magistrates, revenue officers, or soldiers indicted for capital offences in Massachusetts. A third act, 'for the better regulating the government of the province of Massachusetts Bay in New England,' revoked in part the Massachusetts charter. It transferred from the assembly to the governor the appointment of his council; vested in him the sole right of appointment and removal of sheriffs, and of all judges of the inferior courts, and other legal officers, as well as of the chief justice after the first vacancy; vested in the sheriffs so appointed the right of returning the juries; and forbade meetings without the governor's consent, except for the election of representatives and petty officers. A fourth legalised the quartering of troops in the North American colonies. The fifth, professing to make 'more effectual provision for the government of the province of Quebec in North America,' extended the limits of

Other repressive measures.

the province to the Ohio and the Mississippi, so as to include five of the present States of the Union: Ohio, Michigan, Indiana, Illinois, and Wisconsin. Although some of these bills were vigorously opposed in parliament by Burke, Barré, and others, all were carried by large majorities. Yet the issue seemed to be clearly seen. In the debate on an address to the crown which had preceded the five measures, Wedderburn (afterwards Lord Loughborough) had declared the leading question to be 'the dependence or independence of America.' Outside of parliament, two men of very different opinions were bold enough to advocate American independence: Tucker, Dean of Gloucester, a well-known free-trader, and John Cartwright, afterwards an equally well-known radical. But public opinion ran the other way, and as a concession to it, the reporting of debates in parliament was allowed for the first time. The singular fact, that England thus owes one of the greatest safeguards of her freedom to the attempt to coerce America, has often been noted.

Lord North had declared that if his measures were firmly sustained, 'peace and quietude' would 'soon be restored.' The result was far otherwise. On the first news of the Boston Port Bill the Virginian House of Burgesses entered a protest against it on their journals, and set apart June 1 as a day of fasting, 'to implore the divine interposition for averting the heavy calamity which threatened destruction to their civil rights and the evils of civil war, and to give them one heart and one mind firmly to oppose, by all just and proper means, every injury to American rights.' The governor dissolved the House. The members met elsewhere, and resolved that an attack on one colony was an attack on all, and that it was expedient to call together a general Congress. Massachusetts took a similar course, and it was decided that

Protests of Virginia and Massachusetts; a Congress called.

a Congress should meet at Philadelphia, in September. In the interval county meetings were held—the most remarkable of which was that of Fairfax County, presided over by Washington. This assembly adopted twenty-four resolutions, which had been drawn up by George Mason, setting forth the points at issue between England and her colonies.

The 'Continental Congress,' as it was termed, met accordingly at Carpenters' Hall, Philadelphia (Sept. 5, 1774), and it is somewhat remarkable that in the Quaker city it opened with the celebration of the Church of England service. Fifty-three delegates attended, Georgia alone not being represented. The vote was to be by colonies, whatever might be the number of delegates. 'All America,' Patrick Henry declared, 'is thrown into one mass. . . . I am not a Virginian, but an American.' Among the delegates were, besides himself, Samuel Adams and George Washington. A declaration of the rights of America was drawn up. It claimed the power of legislation through provincial assemblies; consenting indeed to the regulation of trade by act of parliament, but denying the right of internal or external taxation for raising a revenue in America. It claimed further the right of trial by jury on the spot, and of holding public meetings to consider grievances or petition the king. It declared the maintenance of a standing army in any colony in time of peace without the consent of the legislature, and the exercise of the legislative power by a nominated council, to be alike illegal; and it cited as instances of the violation of colonial rights the Sugar Act, the Stamp Act, the Quartering Act, the Tea Act, the Act for suspending the New York legislature, the Acts for trial in Great Britain of offences committed in America, the Boston Port Act,

The Continental Congress at Philadelphia (Sept. 1774).

the Massachusetts Government Act, and the Quebec Act. Resolutions were adopted for a non-consumption and non-importation agreement, for an address to the people of Great Britain, a memorial to the inhabitants of America, and a loyal address to the king, besides one approving the resistance of Massachusetts to the acts of parliament, and declaring that if these were enforced, all America ought to support her. In addition to the above addresses, one was drawn up to the people of Canada, inviting them to join the colonial league. After sitting for fifty-one days, the Congress broke up, to meet again on May 10, 1775.

It might have been thought that the calling together of a Congress to protest against and sanction resistance to the government of the mother country was itself an act of independence. Although this was generally felt to be the case in Europe, the Americans themselves did not yet understand what they were doing. *Washington still disclaims the idea of colonial independence.* While the Congress was sitting (Oct. 9, 1774) Washington wrote to an old comrade, who looked upon the proceedings of Massachusetts as aiming at independence: 'I think I can announce it as a fact that it is not the wish or interest of that government, or any other upon this continent, separately or collectively, to set up for independence. . . . . I am well satisfied,' he repeats, 'that no such thing is desired by any thinking man in all North America.' Yet at the same time he declared that none of the colonies would 'ever submit to the loss of those valuable rights and privileges which are essential to the happiness of every free state, and without which life, liberty, and property are rendered totally insecure,' and predicted that if the ministry were determined to push matters to extremity, 'more blood would be spilt than ever had been in the annals of North America.'

Massachusetts was indeed at this time taking a bold lead. The Assembly had been convoked to meet on October 5. Under the charter it should have elected the council. Of the members of the latter, who were henceforth to sit under writs from the crown, a third refused their appointments, and the greater part of those who accepted them were forced by public indignation to resign, while the new judges appointed by the crown were not allowed to sit. General Gage, the governor, now countermanded by proclamation the writs for the Assembly. The elections were held nevertheless, and the members met; but the governor not making his appearance to open the session, they resolved themselves into a provincial congress, to consider the affairs of the colony. Although General Gage, besides being governor of Massachusetts, was also commander-in-chief for all North America, with four regiments of regulars under his orders, measures were taken for organising a militia of 12,000 men, one quarter of whom were to be enlisted as 'minute-men,' bound to assemble in arms at a minute's warning. General officers were named, large stores collected, and two committees appointed—one of safety, to determine when the services of the militia were required, to call them out, and direct the army; the other of supplies. Delegates were sent to New Hampshire, Rhode Island, and Connecticut, requesting aid to make up 20,000 men, and a correspondence was opened with Canada. Corps were accordingly formed in Virginia, Rhode Island, and Carolina. General Gage wrote to Lord Dartmouth (November 2) that the 'edicts of the provincial congress' were 'implicitly obeyed,' that Massachusetts was 'without courts of justice or legislature,' the whole country 'in a ferment, many parts of it actually in arms, and ready to unite.' No 'decency' was 'observed in any place but New York,' which indeed had

The Massachusetts provincial congress; raising of troops.

alone disapproved of the resolutions of the Continental Congress.

Parliament met on November 30. The king's speech complained bitterly of the spirit of resistance and disobedience to law in the American colonies, and announced his firm resolution to withstand any attempt to weaken or impair the supreme authority of the British legislature. The House of Lords declared its 'abhorrence and detestation of the daring spirit of resistance and disobedience to the law' which so strongly prevailed in Massachusetts, and humbly thanked the king for taking measures to enforce the laws. The House of Commons followed suit. In vain did Chatham, coming forward after a long retirement, urge conciliation, and the withdrawal of the troops from Boston. 'I contend,' said 'the old man eloquent,' 'not for indulgence, but justice to America. . . . Resistance to your acts was as necessary as just; and your vain declaration of the omnipotence of parliament, and your imperious doctrines of the necessity of submission, will be found equally impotent to convince or to enslave your fellow subjects in America, who feel that tyranny, whether ambitioned by an individual part of the legislature, or by the bodies who compose it, is equally intolerable to all British subjects. . . . Woe be to him who sheds the first, the inexpiable drop of blood, in an impious war with a people contending in the great cause of public liberty! . . . The Bostonians have been condemned unheard. The indiscriminating hand of vengeance has lumped together innocent and guilty; with all the formalities of hostility has blocked up the town, and reduced to beggary and famine 30,000 inhabitants. . . . I have read Thucydides, and have studied and admired the master-states of the world, and I must declare and avow that for solidity of reasoning, force of sagacity, and wisdom of conclusion,

Large majorities in parliament against concession; Chatham's warnings.

under such a complication of difficult circumstances, no nation or body of men can stand in preference to the general Congress at Philadelphia. All attempts to impose servitude upon such men—to establish despotism over a mighty continental nation—must be vain, must be futile. We shall be forced ultimately to retract; let us retract while we can, not when we must.' But he preached to deaf ears. His motion to address the king for a removal of the troops from Boston was negatived, as was also a conciliation bill which he brought forward. In the Commons, urgent petitions from the merchants of London and others for inquiry into the commercial policy pursued towards America were, notwithstanding Burke's efforts, shelved by reference to a committee. To Horace Walpole conduct such as that of the ministry seemed to be ' that of pert children; we have thrown a pebble at a mastiff, and are surprised it was not frightened.'

The policy of the ministry was indeed pitiful. Lord North, affecting conciliation, proposed and carried by a large majority, in spite of Barré and Burke, a resolution that parliament should forbear to tax any colony that might of its own accord provide for the expenses of its defence and civil government, hoping, in fact, to divide the colonies, since 'if one consents, a link of the great chain is broken.' On the other hand, the attempt to quell Boston alone by crippling her trade having failed, the same system of quasi-blockade was extended first to New England generally, then to New Jersey, Pennsylvania, Maryland, Virginia, and South Carolina, by a similar but somewhat less extensive Act. New York, Delaware, North Carolina, and Georgia, although as yet left out of the pale of the restrictions, remained so only for a few months longer. It is almost needless to say that counter-proposals by Burke and Hartley

Lord North's new measures; the prohibition of trade extended.

allowing the colonies to tax themselves, or even for only suspending for three years the act for the better regulation of the government of Massachusetts Bay, were rejected. Of the reception of the restraint of trade bills in parliament, Burke wrote bitterly :—'We talk of starving hundreds of thousands of people with far greater ease and mirth than the regulations of a turnpike.'

In America events were rapidly ripening. Massachusetts continued to lay in stores and prepare for war, providing even linen rags for the wounded of the coming conflict, and issuing provincial bills of credit for 50,000*l*. As early as February 27, 1775, the first blood might have been shed. There was a depôt of military stores at Salem. General Gage sent Colonel Leslie with 140 men to take possession of them, but they had been removed before his arrival. Going then to the place to which they had been taken, he found a drawbridge which he had to cross drawn up, and when he attempted to cross the river, his boats were split up by the axes of the peasantry who awaited him on the other side. By way of compromise he was at last allowed to cross, but left the stores uncaptured. Massachusetts prepares for war; a collision barely averted.

In Virginia the convention met again (March 26, 1775). Patrick Henry introduced resolutions for putting the colony in a state of defence. A committee was named for the purpose, which included George Washington. A letter of his of the 25th of this month, addressed to his brother, shows him to us already in command of the Independent Company of Richmond, and ready to accept that of another, 'if occasion require it to be drawn out, as it is my full intention to devote my life and fortune in the cause we are engaged in, if needful.' Virginia prepares for war; Washington ready to devote his life to the cause.

The train was laid; there needed but a spark to kindle it. Before, however, narrating the circumstances which constituted the actual outbreak of the war, let us cast a glance at the state of the world in this fateful year 1775.

The train ready for the spark.

CHAPTER IV.

1775.

SINCE the Peace of Paris in 1763, which virtually blotted France out from the list of the greater colonial powers, these were reduced to four; England, Spain, Portugal, and Holland. England and Spain divided the North American continent between them—since the Indians and their chiefs were only recognised as creatures to be protected if friendly, and put out of the way or out of existence if troublesome. Spain and Portugal in like manner divided South America, with the exception of Dutch Guiana, comprising both English and Dutch Guiana of the present day, and French Guiana, then a mere foothold for France on the continent. The flags of several European nations floated on the West Indian islands, and in most cases from those where still they wave; but that of France was far more prominent than it is now, and in particular she held the largest and richest part of St. Domingo, the second largest island of the whole group, whilst she retained as now an islet or two on the Newfoundland waters, and the right of fishing off one of its coasts. In Africa the preponderant colonial power was Portugal, whose dominion was still a reality on the eastern as well as on the western coast; Spain also had several ports on the Barbary coast. Holland had the Cape of Good Hope, and the Guinea and Gold Coast

The colonial powers.

were studded with as many different flags as the West Indian islands themselves—slave-catching and slave-driving being then deemed to be the two most profitable businesses in the world. In the eastern hemisphere the only real colonial empire was that of Holland in the eastern islands; and if she had not yet completed the subjugation of Java, she had on the other hand a flourishing colony in Ceylon, and various settlements on the mainland of India. Spain had then, as now, her Philippines; Portugal had her Goa and her Macao, and was still rather more than a name in India; the English East India Company was already at Bombay, at Madras, at Calcutta, had acquired rights of territorial sovereignty, had possessed itself of the viceroyalty of India's three richest provinces, Bengal, Behar, and Orissa, and was virtually sovereign of them in the name of the Mogul emperor. France, lastly, though retaining some territory in India, was reduced to struggle rather for influence than for power, but through her possession of Bourbon and the Isle of France (now Mauritius) she still held a strong position as a naval power in the East. Hence, though she could no longer be said to have a colonial empire, she could still, through her navy and her yet numerous possessions abroad, hold her own with the great colonial powers themselves.

Let us now give a glance at Europe. Great Britain and Ireland were still two kingdoms under one king, who was also king of Hanover. France, within limits not much differing from her present ones (except that Savoy and Nice had not been annexed, nor Alsace and Lorraine torn away) was still a congeries of provinces, and had recently (1768) acquired Corsica. Germany retained her clumsy federal empire of the middle ages, but in her midst Prussia had sprung from an electorate of Brandenburg into a kingdom, and under

Europe.

Frederick the Great had defied at once the two greatest
Continental powers, Austria and France, riveted on herself the attention of Europe, and given a foretaste of that
energy which in our own days has placed her at the head
of a new German empire. Poland had still the name of a
kingdom, but the first partition of her territory between
Russia, Prussia, and Austria had taken place, and 3,925
square miles of country had been stripped from her
by these kind neighbours (1772). Unable to bear their
country's degradation, many Poles were emigrating, and
the names of more than one will appear in the history of
the war of American independence. Russia, which had
for the first time entered into the sphere of western
politics during the Seven Years War, was making herself
felt as a great power under Catherine II. Turkey had
vainly endeavoured to support Poland; but the Russians
had invaded Moldavia, Wallachia, and the Crimea, had
sent a fleet into the Mediterranean, roused the Morea
into insurrection, and burnt the Turkish fleet in the Archipelago. The Peace of Kainardgi, concluded through
Austrian mediation (1774), had restored in great measure
the *status quo*, except that Russia retained Azow and a
few Black Sea ports, with the right of free navigation in
Turkish waters.

The territories of the three great states of Eastern
Europe, Russia, Prussia, and Austria, had thus been
greatly enlarged, whilst their fellowship in a common
spoliation created amongst them a bond of union, which,
though snapped asunder more than once, has always
welded itself together again by a kind of magnetic force,
and binds them to this day. In Austria, whose flag waved
over the Spanish Netherlands, the clever Joseph had
reigned since 1765, with his mother, Maria Theresa.
Joseph was a philosopher-king like his fellow spoliators,
Catherine II. and Frederick II., but he could not be

brought to favour the revolted colonists, frankly averring, philosopher though he might be, that 'his trade was to be a king.' In Sweden, which had yet lost but a fragment of Finland, and retained a part of Pomerania, a half-mad despot, Gustavus III., imagined himself destined to renew the fame of a Gustavus Adolphus or a Charles XII., but was never to realise his dream. Denmark, with Norway united to her, under Christian VII. had scandalised the world by the imprisonment and divorce of a queen, herself an English princess, and the beheading of two noblemen accused of intriguing with her (1772), and had tied a knot which the sword alone has cut through in our days, in the arrangement for connecting Holstein and Sleswig with the Danish monarchy (1767). Italy, parcelled out into states of all sorts, two or three republics included, had not even the nominal unity of Germany, and was literally—though the insolent phrase had not yet been uttered—a mere 'geographical expression;' but Sardinia, the Italian counterpart of Prussia, was already a kingdom; and Bourbons reigned over the two Sicilies, as they did over France and Spain. Spain, under Charles III. (formerly Charles I. of Naples), generally followed the lead of France, for whom, thanks to her yet vast colonial empire and not inconsiderable fleet, she was by no means a despicable ally. She was at this moment engaged in an unprofitable war with the Barbaresque powers. England, besides Gibraltar, held Minorca, but Malta still belonged to its knights. Portugal, under Joseph I., was what it is. The Swiss confederacy and Geneva were separate republics. The Netherlands were also a clumsy republican confederation under a stadtholder.

Clearly, in any struggle which might break out between England and her American colonies, the powers most directly interested would be France and Spain, the only near neighbours to those colonies; and more re-

motely, Holland, through her extensive trade. No other
power would be likely to take more than an
indirect interest in the contest; or indeed, with
the exception of Russia, Sweden, Denmark,
and Portugal, could, through the possession of
a navy, take any part in it; and since France
dragged Spain in her wake, the disputants could practically look to the former alone as a valuable friend or foe
in the struggle.

<small>France and Spain the only powers directly interested in the American struggle.</small>

In France a young king of spotless character, Louis
XVI., had lately succeeded his grandfather, the heartless
debauchee, Louis XV. Though humbled in the
course of the Seven Years War in Europe by
Prussia, and by England beyond seas; stripped
of her colonies, her finances in hopeless confusion, her people steeped in misery to the
neck; France was yet the intellectual centre of Europe.
French was not only the universal language of diplomacy,
but that of nearly every court in Europe. Frederick the
Great wrote in it, and on the eve of one of his great battles
had composed an epistle in French verse to Voltaire.
French had been the habitual language of our own
George II. George III. was the first of our Hanoverian
kings to whom English was a native tongue. Gibbon
had begun by writing in French. Voltaire corresponded
in French with almost every sovereign in Europe, and
with nearly the whole world besides. The best Italian
comic dramatist of the age, Goldoni, had resided in
Paris since 1761, and written in French all his later
comedies. Although the golden age of German literature
had begun, it was scarcely known as yet outside of Germany. France, on the other hand, was a literary world
in herself, and the two greatest names in the literature
of the century were beyond all question those of Voltaire and Rousseau, the latter indeed not French but

<small>France the intellectual centre of Europe. Voltaire. Rousseau.</small>

French-Swiss. If there was a recognised pope at Rome, there was an unrecognised one at Ferney, near Geneva, whose edicts were in fact far more authoritative with the world at large. Yet the 'patriarch of Ferney,' as Voltaire was often termed in the language of the day, now eighty-one years of age, was near the end of his reign. The influence of Rousseau went far deeper than his. The one might rule in princely style over two leagues of territory, enriched not only by the sale of his works, but by speculations of all sorts: the other, a prey to morbid and misanthropic delusions, might be eking out a pension of 58*l*. a year by copying music. But the one addressed himself solely to the intellects of men, the other to their feelings. The one supplied the age with denials, the other with new beliefs. Voltaire's writings might inspire a passionate hatred towards what existed; those of Rousseau excited a passionate desire for a better future, and a belief that it could be realised.

One noteworthy feature of the age in France for many years now had been the sense of a coming revolution. 'After us the end of the world; after us the deluge,' Louis XV. used to say. 'We are approaching the age of revolution,' wrote Rousseau in 1760; 'I hold it impossible that the great monarchies of Europe can have long to last.' 'All that I see,' wrote Voltaire in 1762, 'is casting the seeds of a revolution which must come without fail.' M. de Tocqueville, in his admirable work, 'L'Ancien Régime et la Révolution,' has convincingly shown that this revolution was actually proceeding long before it was recognised as existing; that France had been already revolutionised in her administration before she was so politically. But in the political sphere blows had been already struck in 1775, though as yet from afar, which served to familiarise the public mind with the idea of change, and Malesherbes had gone so

Sense of a coming revolution.

far as to propose to Louis XVI. the calling together of the 'États-Généraux,' national assemblies which had been disused since 1614.

For the moment indeed all was hope. The court was purged from its scandals. Among the ministers whom the young king had called to his counsels were two of the purest characters of France, Turgot and Malesherbes. Of the former it has been said that he proposed all the improvements which the Revolution effected. But when evil is long-rooted, the very uprooting of it may create convulsions. The corn trade in France was clogged with all manner of restrictions. There had been under Louis XV. a hideous secret society, in which the king was chief shareholder, for keeping up the price of corn and speculating upon the hunger of the people. It seems to have lasted till 1774. Turgot, in the latter end of that year (September 13, 1774) declared the trade in corn and flour absolutely free in the interior. Grain riots, excited, there can be little doubt, by the corn monopolists themselves, ensued. The hungry people surged up to Paris, to Versailles, to petition the king for cheap bread. Some of the petitioners were arrested, and two of them hanged on a new gallows forty feet high. As they climbed to the scaffold, they called out to the people that they were dying for the people's cause (May 18, 1775),—an ill omen, surely, for the reign of a well-meaning king and the rule of a benevolent minister. In another year Turgot will lose office. The old parliaments meanwhile have been restored, to be finally swept away before fifteen years have passed by.

The new reign in France a hopeful one: Turgot and Malesherbes. The corn riots of 1775.

The instinctive perception of an approaching overthrow of existing institutions goes far to explain the interest excited on the Continent by the American Revolution; while the desire of that overthrow called forth the sympathy or enthusiasm with which it was greeted by many. But it would be a mistake to think that that interest and sympathy dated only from the Revolution itself. Turgot, in an oration delivered before the French clergy twenty-five years before it broke out (1750), had used the following words: 'Vast regions of America! Equality keeps them from both luxury and want, and preserves to them purity and simplicity with freedom. Europe herself will find there the perfection of her political societies, and the surest support of her well-being.'

French sympathy with America preceded the American Revolution.

There were moreover reasons why that sympathy should take a specially passionate form in France. England was not only the triumphant political rival of France; she was the envy of her philosophers and her patriots. Montesquieu had pointed to the British constitution as substantially the most perfect embodiment of political wisdom. His assertion that it was depictured already in the pages of the 'Germania' of Tacitus, that it had been 'found in the woods' (a hyperbole whereat Voltaire has not unnaturally his laugh), just fell in with Rousseau's declamations about the need of a return to nature and the primitive goodness of man. But Voltaire himself had as it were discovered England for France, had proclaimed the barbarian genius of Shakespeare, the greatness and bad taste of Milton, had patted Tillotson on the back, and exalted Locke and Newton to the skies. Anglomania had become the fashion of the day. But by a just retribution for the extermination of all free faith in France under Louis XIV. and Louis XV., it was only the negative side of the English mind that could influence the French. England being Protestant, whatever of faith might come from her was contraband; only her infidelity

Special grounds for such sympathy: admiration for England.

passed through the custom-house. Hence, not only the wonderful rise of Methodism, but all that rich undergrowth of genuine Christianity, springing up in the most diverse forms beneath a crust of formalism and scepticism, which is so marked and peculiar a feature of the eighteenth century in England, never touched contemporary France.

This then was the temper by which France was animated. Overshadowed nationally by England, France was compelled to look up with longing to her political liberty, her untrammelled science, her freedom of speech and thought. What if to such a France there should come to be revealed another England, still freer than the one already known in her political institutions, still bolder in speech, with men of science of her own, and withal belonging to a new world, living as it seemed to Europe on the very fringe of the wilderness, and nearer to that nature which Rousseau cried up, and, to crown all, breaking out into a life-and-death conflict with the England of the old world? Is it not clear that when such a country was engaged in such a struggle, France would give full play to all the contrary feelings which England roused in her, and that all her resentment and hatred would go towards the older England, all her admiration and love towards the new? Here then is the true secret of the passionate enthusiasm which the war of American independence raised up in France, and which afterwards influenced so greatly her own Revolution. No mere political jealousy of England could have given birth to it; it was on the contrary the setting free of feelings and aspirations which political jealousy kept under check. But political jealousy co-operated with these more generous feelings, by blinding the eyes of French ministers to the dangers involved to the monarchy in such feelings themselves.

Recent events in Eastern Europe, finally, tended to

[margin: America for France an ideal England.]

make France restless. I have already indicated the direct connexion of the fate of Poland, through the emigration of some of her sons, with the war of independence in America. Its indirect influence through France was far greater still. There was a traditional friendship between France and Poland. Choiseul, till 1771 the French Minister of Foreign Affairs (whose desire to interfere in favour of the American colonies has already been mentioned), had been ready to go to war for the sake of Poland, and had indeed sent thither 1,500 men under a commander whose name will figure both for honour and disgrace in the still distant revolutionary wars of his country, Dumouriez. But Louis XV. had steadily opposed war, and the partition of Poland, though applauded by some of the philosophers, had been felt as a disgrace to France by all the more generous-minded of the young nobility. There was an uncomfortable feeling that France was playing an inferior part in European policy, and therefore also an impatience for some daring effort to restore her tarnished honour, which in a cause capable of enlisting largely the public sympathy might ere long prove irresistible.

Influence of the partition of Poland.

Let us now consider England herself. *England.*

Culloden (1746) had blown to the winds all reasonable hopes of the Jacobite party. The 'Old Pretender' was dead (1776.) The 'Young Pretender,' the once brilliant Charles Edward, now a drunken debauchee, had been long since expelled from France. His younger brother (Cardinal York) was a Romish priest, and could beget no more claimants to the English throne. Since 1767 the English Roman Catholics had begun to pray for the Hanoverian royal family. The purchase of the Isle of Man from the Duke of Athol had brought the last outlying portion of the

The Jacobite party extinct.

British Isles under the sovereignty of the crown. The King of England was no longer a German prince. He had proclaimed in his first speech to parliament that, born and educated in the country, he gloried in the name of Briton. But although upright, painstaking, and methodical, he was ill-educated, prejudiced, and violently self-willed. Perhaps the most noteworthy element in the politics of the country was the development of his influence. From a young man of twenty-five, ruled by Lord Bute, George III. has grown into a man of thirty-seven, with high ideas of his own prerogative, checked only by his hatred of the Whig aristocracy. Minutely acquainted both with the details of administration and the springs of party organisation, he combines with his stubbornness a cunning probably nearly akin to that madness which eventually obscured his reasoning powers. In a few years he will be seen chaining Lord North to office like a prisoner.

George III.

The long struggle of the crown and parliament against John Wilkes had established the illegality of general warrants, and after three expulsions had left the famous demagogue still member for Middlesex and Lord Mayor of London (1774). 'Junius' had run his meteor-like course, declaiming with virulent rhetoric against the king and every one of his ministers by turns, except Grenville, for whom no terms of eulogy seemed too warm beneath his pen. The sun of Lord Chatham's genius was setting; that of Burke on the other hand was in its meridian splendour, and he was now the most prominent member of the Opposition, whilst the star of Charles James Fox was rising into view.

Wilkes, Junius, Chatham, Burke, Fox.

In the literary world a kind of primacy answering somewhat to that of Voltaire on the Continent had fallen to a very different man, the Tory, Johnson. Hume, after filling for two years the office of Under Secretary of State

(1766-8), had withdrawn from public life, and was this year attacked by the malady which the next would carry him off. A far greater historian, Gibbon, had entered parliament last year, and in another year would bring out the first volume of his masterpiece, the 'Decline and Fall of the Roman Empire.' Adam Smith had published his 'Wealth of Nations' in 1766. Macpherson's Ossianic fabrications or adaptations, so tasteless to the present age, were at the height of their popularity. Cowper, with reason already impaired, was taking part in the composition of the Olney Hymns, to be next year published. Boswell was taking note of Johnson's proceedings, as Horace Walpole of the proceedings of England's literary and courtly classes. Sheridan was achieving this year his first stage triumph in the 'Rivals.' In the world of art Sir Joshua Reynolds was supreme; but a not unworthy rival in portraiture, and the first great chief among English landscape-painters, Gainsborough, had come up from Bath to London last year. The Royal Academy had been founded in 1768.

Literature and art: Johnson, Hume, Gibbon, Cowper, Macpherson, Walpole, Sheridan; Reynolds, Gainsborough.

In regions mostly beyond the ken alike of Johnson, the surly literary autocrat of Bolt Court, or Walpole, the aristocratic letter-writer of Strawberry Hill, those poets of the labour-world, the inventors, whose genius was needed to enable their country to bear the burthen of a debt more than doubled by the last war, and soon to be again nearly doubled by the coming struggle, had already begun their wondrous triumphs. Jedediah Strutt had improved the stocking-frame; Hargreaves' carding-engine had been followed by his spinning-jenny; the first patent of Arkwright the barber for spinning by rollers had been taken out, and its validity established at law. The import of cotton, from 3,870,392 lbs. in 1764, had risen

Industry: the inventors—Strutt, Hargreaves, Arkwright, Watt, Wedgwood, Flaxman.

to an average of 4,760,000 lbs. in 1771–5. Calico-printing had been introduced into Lancashire (1768), and the printing on stuffs wholly made of cotton had been allowed by an act of the previous year. Yet more, that mechanical agent had been mastered which alone would develope on their full scale the results of all previous inventions. Watt, who in 1763–4 was already examining and improving Newcomen's clumsy old steam-engine, had in 1765 completed his own; and ten years later had practically secured for himself by act of parliament 'the sole use and property of certain steam-engines, commonly called fire-engines,' for twenty-five years. He had become in the previous year a partner with Boulton, and the famous Soho Works, near Birmingham, were probably very nearly what they were when Boswell a year later saw there about 700 men at work, and noted down Boulton's characteristic words : 'I sell here, sir, what all the world desires to have, power.' Our pottery and porcelain manufactures were in their full splendour. Derby ware was dearer than silver. Wedgwood, with his works at Etruria and his warehouse in St. James's Square, was at the height of his renown, and was employing, as a modeller, Flaxman, a rising young sculptor, destined ere long to be famous.

What was really, under an old name, the new science of chemistry, would powerfully contribute to the development of all new industries, and Priestley, the Unitarian minister, had just made (1774–5), his capital discovery of oxygen gas, though without understanding what he had done. On the other hand, improved means of communication were giving a new impetus to trade, and the race of our great engineers had been called into being. Under the munificent patronage of the Duke of Bridgewater, Brindley had been able to construct and open the greater part of

Chemistry and Priestley engineering Brindley, Smeaton.

the Bridgewater Canal. Smeaton, whose Eddystone lighthouse has braved the winds and waves since 1759, was at the height of his reputation. Many of our great canals had been projected, several of them had been cut, and though the country was still infested by highwaymen, every session had its crop of road bills.

The wonderful growth of population, between 1760 to 1770, had given an impetus to agriculture to which the increasing number of Enclosure Acts in each session bears witness, and our first popular writer on agriculture, Arthur Young, had already published several of his works. Junius in 1768 had declared that England would be 'undone' if the American colonies were suffered to open their trade to the world. Yet, by the various means above indicated, a silent revolution was going on, which would ere long expand English trade to dimensions never yet attained, and in no direction more remarkably than in that of England's emancipated colonies. *Growth of population; improved agriculture; Arthur Young.*

Meanwhile, two boys of six years old were growing up to be, the one the conqueror and scourge of Europe, the other the ultimate victor of that conqueror himself—Napoleon Bonaparte in Corsica, Arthur Wesley (afterwards spelt Wellesley), in the north of Ireland. *Two boys of six, Napoleon Bonaparte and Arthur Wellesley.*

CHAPTER V.

THE WAR: FIRST PERIOD; TILL THE FRENCH ALLIANCE (1775-8).

THE history of the war of American independence divides itself naturally into two periods. In the one (1775-8) the struggle is only between the mother country and her revolted colonies, and hostilities are confined to the continent of America, with some little fighting on the high seas. In the other (1778-83) France and Spain descend into the fray, Holland is dragged into it, allies are found by France in the far East, and warfare extends to all parts of the world. In the one period the story is simple, interesting, and in many instances heroic; in the latter it is complex to the last degree, and with a few brilliant exceptions, tamer ever as it goes on.

The war: divided into two periods by the French alliance.

General Gage was aware that a depôt of arms and ammunition had been established at Concord, eighteen miles from Boston. To destroy it, as also to secure the persons of Hancock and Samuel Adams, whom he supposed to be in the neighbourhood, and the latter of whom he had vainly endeavoured to buy over, he sent 800 men under Lieut.-Colonel Smith, at eleven o'clock at night, April 18, 1775. But the colonists were on the alert, and before long Colonel Smith heard the bells ring the alarm in advance of him, and sent back for reinforcements, throwing out also a detachment in advance. At Lexington, ten miles from Boston, the advanced guard thus thrown out met a body of 'minute-men,' who refused to disperse, and returned a few shots when fired upon. Concord was reached at 7 A.M., but only part of the arms and ammunition was found and destroyed, and a further skirmish with minute-men took place. The object of the expedition being as far as possible attained, the troops now fell back, until they met, eleven miles from Boston, a reinforcement of 1,000 men. This long skirmish is what is called the battle of Lexington, or Concord, and is considered to have been the beginning of the war. The results of it were on the whole unfavourable to the British, whose sole exploits were the destruction of sixty barrels of powder and some balls, the spiking of three pieces of

The first shot; battle of Lexington, April 18-19, 1775.

artillery, and the burning of a tree of liberty. They had 65 killed, 180 wounded, and lost 28 men taken prisoners; whilst on the opposite side there were 59 killed, 39 wounded, and 5 missing. Above all, the prestige of the British regulars was dispelled. Militiamen, mere armed peasants, had stood up to them, and in a manner pursued them. Franklin wrote to Burke from Philadelphia (May 15), speaking of General Gage: 'His troops made a most vigorous retreat, twenty miles in three hours—scarce to be paralleled in history—and the feeble Americans, who pelted them all the way, could scarce keep up with them.'

The whole country was now astir. The Provincial Congress of Massachusetts resolved that no obedience was in future due to General Gage, but that 'he ought to be considered and guarded against as an unnatural and inveterate foe to the country.' Before long 20,000 colonists surrounded Boston, and threatened to starve out the British army. Far away in the south, on receiving, a month later, the news of the battle of Lexington, a North Carolina town judged the time come for independence, and declared itself freed from all allegiance to the king; but this was going a little too fast for the people generally.

The whole country astir; Boston invested.

The first blow on the offensive was struck by Connecticut. There was a feud of some standing between New York and the settlers in the northern part of her territory, inhabiting what is now the State of Vermont, in which one Ethan Allen led the 'Green Mountain Boys' (as the Vermonters are called). To Ethan Allen was now given the command of a force, 270 strong, which was to surprise the fort of Ticonderoga, on Lake Champlain. There were not boats enough to carry them all over, but with his officers and eighty-three men Allen pushed on, surprised (May 10), the sleeping garrison, and claimed of the

Surprise of Ticonderoga, May 10.

commandant his surrender 'in the name of the Great Jehovah and the Continental Congress.' No resistance was possible, and without the loss of a man the colonists obtained a fort, 122 **cannon**, several vessels, and a considerable quantity of stores and powder. Two days later another post, **Crown** Point, was taken without resistance.

The Continental Congress met for its second session at Philadelphia on the day (May 10), when **Ethan Allen** was invoking its authority at **Ticonderoga**. Besides Washington, Thomas Jefferson and **John Adams**, two future presidents of the United States, were among the members. Urged by Massachusetts and other colonies, the Congress prepared for war, voted 15,000 men as a Continental army (to include 13,000 men of the New England regiments encamped before Boston), and issued bills for 2,000,000 dollars.

Second Continental Congress; a Continental army voted.

Whilst they were deliberating, a fleet stood into Boston (May 25), with 2,000 men on board, commanded by Generals Hall, Clinton, and Burgoyne. General Gage, on June 12, proclaimed martial law, offering, however, pardon to all who should come in, Samuel Adams and John Hancock (formerly president of the Massachusetts Provincial Congress, and now of the Continental Congress) only excepted. The proclamation had little success, and was in effect answered by Congress, through the unanimous vote, by which it appointed George Washington, of Virginia, commander-in-chief.

General Gage proclaims martial law. Washington commander-in-chief.

Washington was now forty-three years old (born 1732) 6 f. 3 in. in height, still fond of athletic sports and feats of agility, a passionate fox-hunter and duck-shooter. His handsome and open good-natured countenance, if we may judge from his portrait taken three years before, had not yet been stiffened by the trials of

Washington.

command into the severity that marks his later busts or portraits, especially about the lines of the mouth. He was unquestionably the best known among colonial officers. After his services in Braddock's campaign he had been spoken of from the pulpit by an eminent preacher of the time, as 'that heroic youth, Colonel Washington, whom I cannot but hope Providence has hitherto preserved in so signal a manner for some important service to his country.' He had served his apprenticeship of command during five years of warfare (1753-8) at the head of the Virginian troops. He had sat for fifteen years in the Virginia House of Burgesses (1759-1774), always returned by large majorities. Punctual in his attendance, studying every question, he seldom spoke, but then he spoke clearly and firmly. Naturally quick-tempered, he had by the effort of a strong will schooled himself to a studious moderation both in language and conduct. Elected a delegate to the first Continental Congress, he so soon made his weight felt, that Patrick Henry, whilst naming Rutledge of South Carolina as by far the greatest orator in Congress, declared that, 'if you speak of solid information and sound judgment, Colonel Washington is unquestionably the greatest man on that floor.' Appointed commander-in-chief, he refused all pay for his services, only reserving the right to claim reimbursement of his expenses.

Before Washington could take up his command, a new blow had been struck in the contest. The celebrated though misnamed battle of Bunker's (now oftener called Bunker) Hill, had been fought (June 17). Bunker's or Bunker Hill is an eminence 110 feet high, near the neck of the peninsula on which Charleston is situated, and which is divided from Boston by the Charles river. Learning that General Gage intended to occupy and fortify it, Colonel Prescott with 1,000 men was sent at night from Cambridge, the

Battle of Bunker's Hill, June 17, 1775.

head-quarters of the colonists, to anticipate the British. But they mistook, strange to say, for Bunker Hill another eminence called Breed's Hill, to the south of it, standing nearer to Charlestown and Boston, and intrenched themselves there before the morning. The eminence commanded the British camp, and, if armed with batteries, would have compelled the evacuation of Boston. When the intrenchments were discovered, 3,000 regulars were sent to attack them, under Generals Howe and Pigot. Instead of landing at the isthmus of Charleston so as to take the Americans in the rear, the troops, covered by the fire not only of the British batteries but of the fleet, marched straight up the hill. Two assaults on the intrenchments failed, but General Clinton having joined the assailants with 400 men, a third was made. The Americans had exhausted their ammunition, and Colonel Prescott ordered a retreat, which was effected in good order, and though only one piece of artillery out of six could be carried off, they encamped at Prospect Hill, a mile from the battle-ground. As was natural, the loss of the assailants was the greater—226 killed and 828 wounded and missing, as against 115 killed and 337 wounded and prisoners on the American side. The battle had taken place in sight of Boston, whose roofs and steeples were crowded with spectators. These, besides the battle itself, had witnessed a sight which sank deep into the hearts of the American people, the burning of Charleston by the British soldiers, provoked, it is said, by their having been fired on from its houses.

On the day of the battle the Congress elected four major-generals, and a few days later eight brigadiers. *Washington in command. His difficulties.* Agents with presents were sent to the Indians to obtain their neutrality. Washington (June 21) set out to take up his command, meeting on the way an express who brought tidings of the battle of Bunker's Hill. The day after reaching the army he issued a general order, reminding his forces that 'they are now the troops of the United Provinces of North America;' expressing the hope 'that all distinctions of colonies will be laid aside, so that one and the same spirit may animate the whole, and the only contest be, who shall render on this great and trying occasion the most essential service to the great and common cause in which we are all engaged.' His first task was to establish discipline. Although he found fewer men than he expected (16,000, of whom only 14,000 were fit for duty, instead of from 18,000 to 20,000), the forces under his command were far larger than those with which in after times he would have to keep British armies in check. But his lines formed a semicircle of eight or nine miles, within which lay between 11,000 and 12,000 of the enemy, who commanded the water entirely. The officers were inefficient, the men insubordinate. The commander-in-chief showed himself strict even to severity. Frequent courts martial, and daily hard work upon fortifications, were the chief means by which he gradually welded into an army a crowd of men enlisted for short periods under different conditions, which as freeholders or freeholders' sons they claimed the right to construe for themselves. The lines were drawn so close round Boston that the British and American sentries could almost have spoken together. Frequent raids and skirmishes gradually inured the provincials to war. Yet the situation was almost desperate. There was less than a ton of powder for the whole army, making about nine rounds per man, and Washington had to write to Rhode Island, New York, New Jersey, Pennsylvania, for every pound of powder and lead that could be spared. 'No quantity,' he declared, 'however small, is beneath notice.' By September the first troops enlisted by the authority of Congress, twelve companies of riflemen, had joined the camp. The army seemed about to melt away. The term of service of the contingents of Connecticut, and of Rhode Island, would expire on December 1, that of the Massachusetts men on the 31st. The paper of the Congress was being daily depreciated in value, and even of this depreciated paper the paymaster had not a dollar in hand. The country was expecting to hear of the occupation of Boston, and it would have been madness to attack it. At length, on Washington's urgent representations of the seriousness of the crisis, a committee was appointed by Congress, with Franklin at their head, to confer with Washington and the New England colonies. A scheme was now devised for raising a new army of nearly 23,000 men (Oct. 1775).

In the south the royal authority had been practically shaken off. The governor of Virginia, Lord Dunmore, having seized on the powder in Williamsburg magazine, was compelled to pay for it, and the amount paid was transmitted to Congress. Soon after he took refuge on board of a British vessel, to which he summoned the legislature; they refused to come, called a convention, and formed a government. The governors of both the Carolinas followed a similar course, escaping on board ship. Thus, whilst the British navy commanded the sea and threatened the coast, the Revolution was triumphant on shore. Walpole, writing to his friend William Mason, a little before this time (Aug. 7), thus describes the situation with somewhat exaggerated satire : 'Mrs. Britannia orders her senate to proclaim America a continent of cowards, and vote it should be starved unless it will drink tea with her. She sends her only army to be besieged in one of their towns, and half her fleet to besiege the *terra firma*; but orders her army to do nothing, in hopes that the American senate at Philadelphia will be so frightened at

Proceedings in the south: the governors on board ship.

the British army being besieged in Boston that it will sue for peace. At last she gives her army leave to sally out; but being twice defeated she determines to carry on the war so vigorously till she has not a man left, that all England will be satisfied with the total loss of America.'

Franklin on leaving England (April 1775), in paying a last visit to Burke, had warned him that separation was inevitable. Burke, however, did not yet agree with him; and there was indeed still room for conciliation. Richard Penn, late governor of Pennsylvania, was in England as the bearer of what is known as the Second Petition of Congress, or the 'Olive Branch,' adopted after Bunker's Hill (July 1775). In this document the colonists offered to submit to every enactment of parliament up to 1763, including the Navigation Acts and the Acts for regulating trade, on condition of being freed from the new system of government. Vergennes, the French minister, deemed it impossible that such terms should be refused. The French ambassador, De Guines, persisted in thinking the contrary, and he was right.

Last attempts at conciliation by Congress: Richard Penn and the 'Olive Branch.'

Penn could not obtain an audience. When he applied for an answer to the petition, he was informed that 'no answer could be given.' But an answer was given, and a bitter one, exactly ten days after Penn's arrival in England. A royal proclamation was issued (August 23), for suppressing rebellion and sedition. Gage was recalled, his command being divided between Sir Guy Carleton (afterwards Lord Dorchester), in the north, and Howe. A body of Hanoverians were enlisted. German princes were ready to sell their subjects. Applications were made to Holland and to Russia for the loan of troops, but were refused.

Proclamation against rebellion; application to German princes for troops.

The English people generally hardly understood the

gravity of the crisis. There were those who, like the
Duke of Richmond, looked on America as lost
already, but could comfort themselves with
thinking 'that in our present state we are not
fit to govern ourselves, and much less distant
provinces; and if ours emancipate, it will at least be some
good to humanity that so many millions of brave men
should be free and happy. (Duke of Richmond to Burke,
June 16.) Merchants, sharing the same conviction that
America was lost, were already looking to the Government for an indemnity. (Burke to Rockingham, Aug. 23.)
Others at Bristol saw nothing in what was taking place
but a third non-importation agreement. The two former
ones, they said, 'had broken up, much to the advantage
of the merchants, and particularly the second.' They had
then had 'a demand with 20 per cent. advance on everything, which paid them amply for the delay.' They had
'even sold at that advanced price goods of such a quality
as at other times they could not sell at any price at all.
(Burke to Rockingham, Sept. 14.) Why should they be
alarmed? The popular idol, Wilkes, was a friend to the
American cause. But a great part of the nation was
plunged in a 'shocking indifference and neutrality.'
(Burke to Duke of Richmond, Sept. 26.) The king was
full of confidence; nothing could equal his 'ease, composure, and even gaiety.' (Burke to Rockingham, Aug. 4.)
The proclamation had been hissed on the Stock Exchange, but, to Lord North's surprise, loyal addresses
began to come in from the country.

Parliament met Oct. 26. The king's speech was
violent, charging the Americans with levying a
rebellious war for the purpose of establishing
an independent empire. The announcement
of the employment of Hanoverians to garrison Gibraltar and Minorca afforded a strong
ground of attack to the Opposition. Barré, Charles Fox,

and General Conway, led the attack. Fox declared that neither Lord Chatham, the King of Prussia, nor Alexander the Great had gained so much in a campaign as had been lost by the ministers. In the Lords, Lord Shelburne strongly condemned the ministerial policy, and the Duke of Grafton, still Privy Seal, took the opportunity of announcing his disapproval of it, which he soon followed up by resignation. The American department was transferred to Lord George Germain, formerly known as Lord George Sackville, who, though he had distinguished himself at Dettingen and Fontenoy, had misconducted himself at Minden, and had been cashiered and struck off the list of the privy council. Loyal addresses poured in more and more. Everything seemed to encourage the king and his ministers in their present policy of what Lord Strafford would have called 'Thorough.'

One of the earliest acts of the new session enabled the crown to call out and embody the militia, 'upon occasion of the present rebellion in America.' It was followed by the Prohibition of Trade Act, termed by Burke, in his passionate language, the 'most wicked and sacrilegious of all measures,' 'to prohibit all trade and intercourse with the colonies of New Hampshire, Massachusetts Bay, Rhode Island, Connecticut, New York, New Jersey, Pennsylvania, the three lower counties on Delaware, Maryland, Virginia, North Carolina, South Carolina, and Georgia;' *i.e.* with the whole of the thirteen colonies. When the bill was brought in (Nov. 10), Lord Mansfield spoke of it as 'passing the Rubicon,' but crudely justified the measure on the ground that 'if you do not kill them they will kill you.' The votes of the session included payments, not only for Hanoverian troops, but for '4,300 Brunswickers,' a 'regiment of foot of Hanau,' a 'regiment of Waldeck,' the 'artillery of the Landgrave of

The General Prohibition of Trade Act; votes for German troops.

Hesse-Cassel,' the 'artillery of Hanau.' On the other hand a step was taken in the direction of conciliation. In the Prohibition of **Trade Act itself** a provision was inserted authorising any persons named by the Crown, to grant pardons, **or to declare** any **colony or** province, county, **port, district, or place, to** be 'at the peace of his Majesty.' **The intention of this provision, which was** shortly afterwards **carried out, was** to appoint **royal** commissioners **who should have power to put a stop to the war.**

In America the king's proclamation against rebellion **was received (Nov. 1) with** divided feelings. **In authorising** New Hampshire **and South** Carolina to frame new **constitutions, Congress virt**ually asserted independence. **Pennsylvania, on the** other hand, **instructed her** delegates **to** dissent from and **utterly reject any proposition**s which might **cause or lead to a** separation from the **mother-country, or a change in** the form of government. **New** Jersey followed the example **of** Pennsylvania, and **her influence paralysed** Delaware **and** Maryland. But **rules were adopted by Congress for** the government of **the** American **navy.** Authority was given for enlisting **two** battalions **of** marines, **for** seizing ships carrying for **the** British army or navy, and for appointing tribunals **for their confisca**tion.

<small>America receives with divided feelings the proclamation against rebellion.</small>

The most important warlike undertaking **on the** American **side** during the autumn was the **i**nvasion of **Canada, a measure of which the Congress had in June expressly disclaimed the** intention. Of all the enterprises of the war, this was the **most** gallant and the most fruitless. The command was **given** to Brigadier-General Montgomery, an English officer who had joined the American standard, **and a** gentleman of chivalrous **bravery.** He had served in the Seven Years War, had been **a** comrade of Colonel

<small>The invasion of Canada by Montgomery.</small>

Barré, one of the Opposition leaders in the House of Commons, and had also been with Wolfe at the taking of Quebec. Everything at first favoured the invaders. The French, and even the Indians, showed themselves friendly, and many of the former joined the Americans. Although an unauthorised attempt by Ethan Allen to repeat upon Montreal his surprise of Ticonderoga failed, that city, after the reduction of Fort St. John, was occupied without resistance (Nov. 12). Here Montgomery's difficulties began—difficulties such as every other American commander after him would have to grapple with. The bulk of his soldiers had enlisted only for a few months; their time was up, and they insisted upon returning home.

Meanwhile, from the border of Maine, a man of very different stamp from Montgomery, but of reckless courage, Benedict Arnold, formerly a horse-dealer, was pushing towards Quebec. He had been detached by Washington from his army (Sept. 11), with about 1,100 men. The difficulties of the march were extreme. The second in command deserted with three companies; the invaders had to eat not only their last ox, but their last dog; then to feed on roots and moose-skin moccasins, and were two days altogether without food. By the time Arnold reached the walls of Quebec, he had but 900 barefoot and ragged men,—too few to attempt anything. When Montgomery joined him in December, he could only bring 300 more, so that the combined American forces made up less than 1,000 men, besides 200 Canadian volunteers. With this small force an insanely heroic attempt was made, on the last day of the year, to storm 'the strongest fortified city in America, defended by more than 200 cannon of heavy metal, and a garrison of twice the number of the besiegers.' It failed of course: Montgomery was killed, and more than a third of the

Arnold; the failure before Quebec (Dec. 31, 1775).

American force were taken prisoners. But Arnold remained encamped outside the walls with the fragments of the army, declaring that he would not leave the place till he entered it in triumph, but asking for 10,000 men, whom he was little likely to get, to achieve his triumph.

The new year did not open more auspiciously for the American cause than the old year had closed. There had been some hostilities in the south, in South Carolina and Virginia. Dunmore, the governor of Virginia, of whom Washington wrote (Dec. 26), that if he were not 'crushed before spring,' he would prove 'the most formidable enemy of America,' issued a proclamation declaring martial law, and offering pardon to 'all indented servants, negroes, or others, appertaining to rebels,' if they would join him. Driven out of Norfolk on New Year's day, he cannonaded and burnt it, as Gage had cannonaded and burnt Falmouth six weeks before. Measures like these stirred far and wide among the Americans feelings of hatred towards the mother-country, and longings for revenge. On the same New Year's day (1776) on which Norfolk was burnt, the American flag was first unfurled, having no stars as yet, but with thirteen stripes of alternate red and white, the crosses of St. George and St. Andrew being still retained on a blue ground in the corner. The Congress had in the previous month voted the building of thirteen ships of war.

Lord Dunmore in Virginia: Norfolk burnt (Jan. 1, 1771): the American flag.

Washington was still before Boston, struggling always against the difficulties of short enlistments, insufficient ammunition, and want of money; credited with an army of 20,000 men, and actually in command of less than half that number. The Connecticut men were especially unruly, and many would not even wait the expiration of enlistment to return home. The same desire of 'retiring into a chimney corner' as Wash-

Washington's difficulties continue.

ington graphically expressed it, 'seized the troops of New Hampshire, Rhode Island, and Massachusetts, so soon as their time expired.' In vain did Congress authorise him to attack Boston, even at the risk of destroying the town; he had not more powder than was absolutely necessary to defend the lines if attacked (Dec. 4, 1775), and he durst not say so. 'Search the volumes of history through,' he wrote to a friend, 'and I much question whether a case similar to ours can be found; namely, to maintain a post against the flower of the British troops for six months together, without powder, and then to have one army disbanded and another to be raised within the same distance of a reinforced enemy. It is too much to attempt.' If he should be able to rise superior to his difficulties, he wrote to the same correspondent 'I shall most religiously believe that the hand of Providence is in it to blind the eyes of our enemies.' About three weeks later he had nearly 2,000 men in camp without firelocks (Feb. 9). Still he had come by this time in his slow way to a conviction which would be worth many victories to America, that independence must be declared.

His patient toil was at last rewarded. On March 4 he succeeded in one night in occupying and intrenching Dorchester heights, which commanded the city and harbour of Boston. A violent storm prevented an early assault by the British, whilst the lines of the Americans were pushed forwards; and on the 17th General Howe with the British troops evacuated Boston, which was at once taken possession of, the main body of the Americans entering on the 20th. The British fleet remained ten days longer in the harbour or in the roads, but attempted nothing further. New England was from henceforth substantially free. *Boston evacuated, March 1776.*

Congress, which some months before had authorised

Washington to employ armed vessels (the crews of which seem to have been even greater trouble to him than his own soldiers), now took the bold step of authorising privateers to cruise, but against the ships of Great Britain only, and not of Ireland (March 23). A still more important resolution—the result probably in great measure of Governor Dunmore's offer of freedom to the slaves—was one against the import of slaves 'into any of the thirteen united colonies.' Last of all, on April 6, the trade of the colonies was thrown open to all the world 'not subject to the King of Great Britain,' a step which must be considered to have been the virtual death-blow to the old colonial system throughout the world, as well as, what Mr. Bancroft calls it, 'a virtual declaration of independence.' The commercial interests of the world at large were henceforth engaged in the struggle on behalf of the revolted colonies.

Measures of Congress: resolution against the slave trade. Free trade.

Already a 'committee of secret correspondence' had appointed Silas Deane, an ex-schoolmaster, 'commercial commissioner and agent,' to solicit from France clothing and arms for 25,000 men, 100 field-pieces, and ammunition. But long before his arrival, the question of aiding the Americans was being discussed in the French cabinet. On the very day when the colonial trade was thrown open (April 6), the far-sighted and benevolent Turgot signed a memorandum in which, whilst insisting that nothing could arrest the course of events which sooner or later would 'certainly bring about the absolute independence of the English colonies, and, as an inevitable consequence, effect a total revolution in the relations of Europe and America,' he yet deprecated any measures of aid tending to involve France, still less Spain, in the war. But the spirit of intrigue was strong among French diplomatists, and

America secretly aided by France and Spain.

there was money to be gathered by fingering contracts. Vergennes, the French Minister of Foreign Affairs, was strongly in favour of aiding the Americans. Turgot was overruled. In May, Louis XVI. announced to the King of Spain that he was about to advance a million of French livres to the Americans. The King of Spain, 'assigning a false reason at his own treasury for demanding the money,' sent a million more. The chief go-between in the matter had been a wondrously clever jack-of-all-trades, the watch-maker, musician, playwright, financier, Beaumarchais, the creator of that personage of Figaro, whose name is now naturalised in every European language.

From this time to that of the Declaration of Independence (July 4, 1776), the dissolution of the old fabric of colonial government proceeds apace. South Carolina had established a constitution for itself as early as March 26. In North Carolina the Chief Justice, in his opening charge to the grand jury, declared to them 'that George III., King of Great Britain, has abdicated the government, that he has no authority over us, and we owe no obedience to him.' The General Assembly of Rhode Island (May 4) discharged the inhabitants of the colony from allegiance to the king. The Virginia House of Burgesses, on the ground that the ancient constitution of the colony had been subverted by the king and parliament, dissolved itself (May 6). A convention of delegates which assembled the same day instructed the representatives of Virginia in congress to propose that the United Colonies be declared 'free and independent States, absolved from all allegiance or dependence upon the crown or parliament of Great Britain' (May 15); and issued (June 12), a celebrated declaration of rights, which became substantially the foundation of the still more celebrated

Dissolution of the old colonial governments; Declaration of Independence proposed.

Declaration of Independence. Meanwhile the Congress had adopted a resolution proposed by John Adams, for allowing the colonies to frame their own governments, with a preamble that it was 'absolutely irreconcilable with reason and good conscience' for the people of the colonies to bear allegiance to 'any government under the crown of Great Britain,' and that it was necessary that the exercise of every kind of government under the crown should be totally suppressed. On June 7 Richard Henry Lee, on the part of Virginia, proposed, and John Adams seconded, a resolution declaring the independence of the United Colonies, the expediency of forming foreign alliances, and of framing a plan of confederation. The two latter portions of the proposal were at once assented to, and committees appointed for carrying them into effect; the consideration of the first was postponed for three weeks, but a committee was also appointed for drawing up a declaration to the effect proposed.

Whilst the committees are sitting, let us cast a glance at military events. Perhaps that which most affected British attack on Fort Moultrie; American disasters in Canada; the retreat. men's minds was the attempt of a British fleet and troops upon Charleston, and the cannonade, though by the fleet alone (June 28), of a fort on Sullivan's Island, since known as Fort Moultrie, in honour of the gallant and successful resistance of its commander. One of the frigates which had run aground had to be deserted and set on fire, and the total British loss in killed and wounded was 205, as against 37 on the American side. This success, small as it was, served to make up for the disastrous results of the expedition to Canada, where, as before mentioned, Arnold, after Montgomery's death, had been left below Quebec with a few hundred men. Of the 10,000 men asked for by Arnold, only 1,500 had reached Montreal by the middle of March. The general in chief command,

Wooster, was aged and inefficient; he had as usual neither money nor supplies; the peasantry were irritated by requisitions; the population, at first favourably disposed towards the invaders, soon became hostile almost to a man, and a party of Canadians attempted, though unsuccessfully, to raise the blockade of Quebec. In vain by the orders of Congress did Washington send more than 3,000 men as reinforcements from the continental army. Smallpox broke out, a retreat was ordered, which a sally turned into a rout, and although the Congress still made further efforts to send more men, the remnants of the army, which in little more than two months had lost by desertion and death more than 5,000 men, had to fall back within the American frontier in a most pitiable condition, so that an eyewitness declared that he did not look into a tent or a hut in which he did not find 'either a dead or a dying man' (early days of July 1776).

Not long after the evacuation of Boston, Washington had removed his head-quarters to New York (April 13), which it was supposed would be the object of the next attempt on the part of the English, as the State contained many Loyalists or Tories, and the late Governor Tryon (who like several of his fellows had taken refuge on board ship), was able, active, and influential. Washington began by inducing the New York Committee of Safety to prohibit all intercourse with the king's ships, and then proceeded to fortify the town and the Hudson river. But the condition of Washington's army itself, notwithstanding his late success, was most precarious. On April 28 the whole number of rank and file, present and fit for duty, was only 8,101. On June 12 it was only 6,749, all under temporary engagements. Many men were without arms; 'one regiment had only 97 firelocks and 7 bayonets;' the artillery consisted of only one regiment and one company. Conspi-

Washington at New York; miserable state of the army.

racy even existed, in which some of Washington's own guard were involved, and one of them was hanged after conviction by court martial in the presence of 20,000 persons. This was the first military execution of the war (June 28). Towards the end of June Congress authorised enlistments for three years or for the war.

On June 29 Washington informed the Congress that General Howe, who with Lord Howe had received a joint commission under the conciliatory provisions of the Prohibition of Trade Act, had arrived at Sandy Hook with forty-five ships or more, the rest of the fleet being expected in a day or two. Thirty thousand men were supposed to be on board. Joseph Reed, Washington's adjutant-general, deemed the odds hopeless, and declared that had he known the real position of affairs, no consideration would have tempted him to take part in them. A few months before (March 15), the same officer had written to Washington that he was 'infinitely more afraid' of the British commissioners 'than of their generals and armies.'

<small>Arrival of a British fleet, and of royal commissioners.</small>

It was under these circumstances, when most of the separate colonies had by this time passed resolutions in its favour, that the Congress adopted the famous Declaration of Independence, penned by Thomas Jefferson of Virginia. It declared as self-evident truths that all men are created equal; that they are endowed by their Creator with certain inalienable rights, among which are 'life, liberty, and the pursuit of happiness; that to secure these rights governments are instituted among men, deriving their just powers from the consent of the governed; that whenever any form of government becomes destructive of these ends, it is the right of the people to alter or to abolish it, and to institute a new government.' It enumerated a long string of acts with which the King of Great

<small>The Declaration of Independence, July 4, 1776.</small>

Britain was charged, 'all having in direct object the establishment of an absolute tyranny over these States;' as for instance, 'He has abdicated government here by declaring us out of his protection, and waging war against us; he has plundered our seas, ravaged our coasts, burnt our towns, and destroyed the lives of our people; he is at this time transporting large armies of foreign mercenaries to complete the works of death, desolation, and tyranny already begun, with circumstances of cruelty and perfidy scarcely paralleled in the most barbarous ages, and totally unworthy the head of a civilised nation; he has constrained our fellow citizens, taken captive on the high seas, to bear arms against their country, to become the executioners of their friends and brethren, or to fall themselves by their hands; he has created domestic insurrections amongst us, and has endeavoured to bring on the inhabitants of our frontiers the merciless Indian savages, whose known rule of warfare is an undistinguished destruction of all ages, sexes, and conditions.' It recounted the petitions for redress which had been presented, the appeals to the 'native justice and magnanimity' of 'our British brethren,' who had been 'deaf to the voice of justice and consanguinity,' and concluded as follows:—

'We, therefore, the representatives of the United States of America, in General Congress assembled, appealing to the Supreme Judge of the world for the rectitude of our intentions, do, in the name and by the authority of the good people of these colonies, solemnly publish and declare that the United Colonies are, and of right ought to be, free and independent States; that they are absolved from all allegiance to the British crown, and that all political connection between them and the State of Great Britain is and ought to be totally dissolved; and that, as free and independent States, they have full power to levy war, conclude peace, contract alliances, establish commerce, and do all other acts and things which independent States may of right do. And for the support of this declaration, with a firm reliance on the protection of Divine Providence, we mutually pledge to each other our lives, our fortunes, and our sacred honour.'

Only one important paragraph had been struck out of Jefferson's draft—one charging upon the king the guilt of the slave trade, which it characterised as a 'cruel war against human nature itself;' and speaking of the recent offers of freedom to the negroes as the 'paying off former crimes committed against the liberties of one people with crimes which he urges them to commit against the lives of another.'

<small>A paragraph relating to slavery and the slave trade struck out.</small>

Reading it at the present day, we can see how the passionate and declamatory rhetoric of the Declaration of Independence has left its stain to this hour on most of the political writing and oratory of America, and may wish that the birth of a great nation had not been screamed into the world after this fashion. Nothing would have been easier than, in the like rhetorical language, to draw up a list of the various acts of lawlessness and outrage committed by the colonists. Some of the charges will not bear examination. For instance, the aid of the Indians had been willingly accepted by the colonists in the Canadian expedition since September 1775; the general question of their employment had been considered by Washington in conference with a committee of Congress and delegates of the New England governments in October of the same year, and the main objection which Washington and other officers urged against it, as shown by a letter of his to General Schuyler, January 27, 1776, and the answer from the latter, was that of expense. He had nevertheless (April 19) advised Congress 'to engage them on our side,'

<small>Declamatory character of the Declaration; its unfairness.</small>

as 'they must, and no doubt soon will, take an active part either for or against us;' and Congress itself had, on June 3—not a month before the Declaration of Independence was actually accepted—passed a resolution to raise 2,000 Indians for the Canada service, which shortly afterwards was extended by another (referred to in a letter of Washington's of June 20) authorising General Washington to employ such Indians as he should take into the service, in any place where he might think that they would be most useful, and to offer them bounties—not indeed for scalps, but for every officer and soldier of the king's troops whom they might capture in the Indian country, or on the frontiers of the colonies. When all this had been done, it needed the forgetfulness and the blind hypocrisy of passion to denounce the king to the world for having 'endeavoured to bring on the inhabitants of our frontiers the merciless Indian savages;' yet the American people have never had the self-respect to erase this charge from a document generally printed in the forefront of their constitution and laws, and with which every schoolboy is sedulously made familiar. Perhaps indeed it would have been otherwise, had not the charge been one which circumstances appeared to confirm. For in fact, owing to causes already indicated, the Americans never could make friends of the Indians in the contest, and consequently the 'merciless savages' continue in history to figure on the side of the British. Who could wonder at it? At the date of the Declaration of Independence, the Indian child had only just reached man's estate, who in the year of his birth might have escaped being a victim to the bounty of 20*l.* held out for the scalp of every Indian woman and child by Massachusetts in 1755, whilst one of 40*l.* had been offered for that of his father, raised in 1756 to 300*l.* It did not require the retentive memory of the redskin to make him look with suspicion on solicitations to friendship from men who might have been parties to such schemes of extermination to his race.

But Jefferson's violent pamphlet should in fact be looked upon less as a declaration of independence than as a declaration of war—less as an assertion of right than as a cry of defiance, uttered in an hour of grave peril, in the face of a formidable foe. The spirit in which it was adopted is well indicated in some words of Joseph Reed's: 'I have no notion of being hanged for half treason. When a subject draws his sword against his prince, he must cut his way through.' Viewed in the light of attendant circumstances, the declaration itself, and the practical unanimity with which it was adopted (by twelve States out of thirteen, New York alone abstaining) became heroic.

<small>The Declaration in fact one of war.</small>

But it would be entirely dwarfing the importance of the declaration to consider it with reference to America alone. Through the general principles which it put forth, it appealed to all peoples that should deem themselves oppressed, and became as it were the charter of revolution throughout the world. The French declaration of the Rights of Man flows directly from it. It virtually cost Louis XVI. his head, as well as half a continent to George III.

<small>Its influence on foreign countries.</small>

Throughout the revolted colonies the Declaration of Independence was received with unbounded enthusiasm. Its adoption was rung out to Philadelphia from the great bell of Independence Hall, which bore for motto 'Liberty throughout the land to all the inhabitants thereof,' and the royal arms were brought from the State House and burned publicly. In Virginia an act was passed to substitute the Commonwealth for the king in the liturgy. At New York the leaden statue of George III. was pulled down and cast into bullets.

<small>Its enthusiastic reception in America.</small>

On the evening of the day when he received the declaration, Washington had the troops paraded, and each division listened bareheaded whilst it was being read (July 9).

Nevertheless, few saw the truth that the independence of the States must be a dream unless based upon their union. A draft of confederation was brought into Congress by John Dickinson of Pennsylvania on July 12. So feeble was the sort of union proposed, that all power of taxation was to be withheld from the 'United States assembled,' except for postage. Yet Rutledge of South Carolina, in language characteristic of his State, treated the plan as 'destroying all provincial distinctions, and making everything of the most minute kind bend to what they call the good of the whole,' and thus in fact saying 'that these colonies must be subject to the government of the eastern provinces,' the force of whose arms he held 'exceedingly cheap,' while he dreaded 'their low cunning, and those levelling principles which men without character and without fortune in general possess.' The whole secession war of our days is prefigured in these words. As it was, Congress only deliberated on the plan, and then postponed it. Meanwhile, the Declaration of Independence was signed (Aug. 2) by every member of Congress. *The need of union still scarcely felt. Postponement of the plan of confederation.*

Dark days were at hand. On July 8 General Howe landed 9,000 men on Staten Island. On the 12th, part of Lord Howe's fleet stood in, and two men of war with their tenders sailed up the Hudson, passed the batteries of New York uninjured, took soundings, and returned. Before proceeding to hostilities Lord Howe sent ashore a proclamation promising pardon to all who should come in. Washington forwarded it to Congress, which caused it to be published. Attempts were even made to *The royal commissioners and Washington; New York threatened.*

communicate with Washington, by letters directed to 'George Washington, Esq.,' or 'George Washington, &c., &c.;' but he refused to receive any that did not recognise him as commander of the American army. Before hostilities began, some weeks more elapsed, during which the English received further reinforcements, making up their forces to about 24,000 men, besides the fleet, whilst Washington strengthened the fortifications of New York. Many of the king's troops were Hessians and other foreigners; and—perhaps as a set-off to Lord Howe's proclamation of pardon—resolutions of Congress were circulated offering citizenship and bounties in land to all foreigners who should leave the British service (Aug. 14, 27).

The city of New York, divided on the west from the coast of New Jersey by the Hudson river, a channel of which, further south, called the Narrows, separates Staten Island from Long Island, is itself divided on the east from the latter by East River, a ferry over which connects it with the village, now suburb, of Brooklyn. Here General Putnam had his camp, and in front of it were 9,000 Americans under General Sullivan and General Stirling commonly called Lord Stirling, though his claim to the title had been rejected by the House of Lords). Washington remained in New York with a garrison already too small for its defence. On August 22 the British under Sir H. Clinton crossed from Staten Island, 10,000 strong, to the south of Long Island, which was undefended, and in three divisions advanced through the island. An important road, which led to the rear of the American position, called the Jamaica road, had been left open. In the engagements which ensued (August 27) the Americans found themselves surrounded; both their generals were taken prisoners, with 1,076 men (including some militia taken after the action), and their total loss was 1,650,

Battle of Long Island, August 27, 1776.

against 379 on the British side, of whom 94 were killed and missing. Washington crossed from New York during the battle, but could only save the remnant of the army. General Howe did not attack the fort on Brooklyn Heights till the next day, and a heavy fog interrupted hostilities. On the night of Aug. 29-30 Washington succeeded in embarking the whole army for New York, but the heavy artillery had to be left behind. The loss of the battle of Long Island is ascribed partly to the illness of General Greene, who had superintended the works and knew the ground thoroughly, whilst his hastily appointed successor, General Putnam, knew neither. In fact it appears that during the engagement no one officer was actually in command.

Worse than the defeat of Long Island were its effects. 'Our situation,' wrote Washington to Congress (Sept. 2), 'is truly distressing. The check our detachment sustained on the 27th ultimo has dispirited too great a proportion of our troops, and filled their minds with apprehension and despair. The militia are dismayed, intractable, and impatient to return. Great numbers of them have gone off; in some instances almost by whole regiments, by half-ones, and by companies at a time. . . . . Their want of discipline, and refusal of almost every kind of restraint and government, have produced a like conduct but too common to the whole, and an entire disregard of that order and subordination necessary to the well-doing of an army. . . . . I am obliged to confess my want of confidence in the generality of the troops.' He was convinced, he went on to say, that no dependence could be put in a militia, and 'that our liberties must of necessity be greatly hazarded if not entirely lost, if their defence is left to any but a permanent standing army, I mean one to exist during the war.' On September 8 the Connecticut militia had

Discouragement of the troops; Washington's position desperate.

become reduced in a few days from 6,000 men to less than 2,000. At least one-fourth of the army were sick. Pay was two months in arrear, and the military chest was empty.

Admiral Howe, after the battle, had anchored with the fleet in New York harbour, within cannon shot of the city. On September 11 a fruitless conference with a view to peace took place on Staten Island, between Lord Howe, Franklin, Rutledge, and John Adams. But hostilities were not suspended. On September 13 some of Lord Howe's ships sailed up East River, and began cannonading. Two days later a large body of troops was disembarked, and the Americans were so demoralised that eight regiments left their lines without firing a shot on the approach of seventy men of the British. Washington tried in vain to check their flight, threatening them with sword and pistol, and in endeavouring to set them an example he rode so near to the enemy that he had to be forced away by an aide-de-camp. Fearing to be again taken in the rear, Washington, supported by the great majority of a council of war, now ordered the evacuation of the city. Greene, probably the ablest commander after Washington, had been foremost in urging evacuation, and—to use his own words—the Americans made a 'miserable, disorderly retreat,' losing a considerable part of their baggage, and leaving behind most of their heavy cannon and part of their stores and provisions (Sept. 15). Washington encamped with the main body of his forces on Haarlem Heights, on the neck of land forming the northern end of New York (or Manhattan) Island, which he proceeded to fortify; a fort called Fort Washington, in particular, was constructed on a rocky height overlooking the Hudson. Meanwhile General (now Sir William) Howe, sending a detachment to occupy New York (in which a fire broke out five days later, and de-

Fruitless peace conference. New York evacuated (Sept. 15).

stroyed about a tenth part of the city), encamped in front of the American lines. A successful skirmish between advanced parties of both armies somewhat inspirited the American troops.

At the urgent entreaty of Washington, who declared success impossible unless the military system was changed (Sept. 24), Congress now ordered a new army of eighty-eight battalions to be raised, which was to serve throughout the war, bounties both of money and land being offered to soldiers and officers. *Congress raises a new army to serve during the war.* Yet the plan thus entered upon seemed likely to defeat itself. The States in turn offered additional bounties, particular towns higher bounties still, and in this competition for soldiers men began to hang back for the sake of obtaining better terms, whilst the different conditions of enlistment produced jealousies and bickerings. The different States quarrelled about the appointments, without regard to the qualifications of officers, and nominated, to use Washington's words, such as were 'not fit to be shoeblacks, from the local attachments of this or that member of Assembly.'

Sir William Howe was not sleeping on his laurels. He sent up the Hudson two ships, which cut off Washington's communications by water, and moved up himself to the north-east of Washington's camp, in order to take him in the rear. The Haarlem Heights lines now became untenable, and leaving—against his own judgment—a strong garrison at Fort Washington, Washington withdrew northwards to White Plains, and again, after an engagement (October 28), in which the Americans had to fall back, to the heights of North Castle. *General Howe's advance; Fort Washington taken (Nov. 16).* Howe now fell back, and Washington profited by the occasion to cross the Hudson with part of his army, at the only place left free by the British ships, and took up his position at Fort Lee, opposite Fort Washington, in order to cover Philadelphia. But from this spot again he had to witness disaster. Fort Washington was attacked (November 16) from four points at once by a large force, the ammunition failed, and after a few hours' defence the fort surrendered, with 2,818 men, besides artillery, arms, and ammunition; the British had, however, lost nearly 1,000 men in killed and wounded in the action. Washington, it is said, cried like a child at seeing the slaughter of his men, whom he could not relieve.

Three days later, 6,000 British troops under Lord Cornwallis crossed the Hudson above Fort Lee, which Washington had to evacuate in haste, leaving a large booty behind. All the troops he had with him were only about 3,000 men, without tents, baggage, or entrenching tools, many of them without shoes. With these he had to retreat across New Jersey, the inhabitants of which, as he afterwards wrote, 'either from fear or disaffection, almost to a man, refused to turn out' to his aid. He was pursued so closely by Lord Cornwallis that the advance guard of the latter entered Newark before the American rear-guard had left it. Having crossed the Delaware into Pennsylvania he sent one of his generals to represent in person to the Congress the weakness of the army and its need of early succour. Fortunately perhaps for the American cause, Lord Cornwallis did not attempt to cross the river. Sir Guy Carleton, meanwhile, had from Canada occupied Crown Point (October), and Sir H. Clinton, with a detachment of 6,000 men from New York, had recovered Rhode Island (Dec. 6). The result of the campaign of 1776 was to leave nearly 2,000 more American prisoners in British hands, than British in American (4,854 against 2,860); and among the captured Americans were 304 officers, whilst there were not more than 50

Washington's retreat through New Jersey; Rhode Island recovered by the British: results of the campaign.

among the British, a pretty clear proof that the American rank and file were not to be depended on.

In England the Declaration of Independence had been generally received with indignation. Parliament met on October 31. There was much abuse of America, and though Wilkes, Barré, and Fox spoke energetically on an amendment to the address by Lord John Cavendish, their minority was only 87 to 128, whilst in the Lords an amendment of Lord Rockingham's obtained only 26 votes, and from this time he and his party pointedly kept aloof from public business. The warnings of Fox and Barré as to an impending war with France were treated with scorn by the ministers. But the king himself was anxious as to this danger. He had ground for being so. On December 21 Franklin reached Paris, where his fame as a man of science had long preceded him. In his plain brown coat and powderless grey hair he took the streets and the drawing-rooms alike by storm. Before the year closed he had already obtained permission to bring American prizes into both French and Spanish ports, and initiated negotiations for a treaty. An attempt to fire Portsmouth dockyard by a man named James Aitken, nicknamed John the Painter, created considerable alarm just before this period (Dec. 6). It was said that there was a plot to destroy all the English dockyards, and that Silas Deane, American commissioner in Paris, was privy to it. The incendiary was hanged a few months later.

Indignation caused in England by the Declaration of Independence; Franklin in Paris; John the Painter.

It was in America that the American cause looked worst. To the bulk of mankind, success always implies genius, and disaster incapacity. Loud was the outcry against Washington after his late reverses. Some of the officers nearest to his person lost their trust in him. Having to open in their absence all official letters to his generals, he opened one day a letter (dated Nov. 24, 1776)

Outcry in America against Washington. Reed and Lee; Lee's capture.

addressed to his own secretary and confidential friend, Colonel Joseph Reed. The writer was General Lee, who had been left east of the Hudson—in his own opinion, and in that of many, the rightful claimant to the command in chief. The letter contained the following passage: 'I lament with you that fatal indecision of mind which in war is a much greater disqualification than stupidity or even want of personal courage. Accident may put a decisive blunderer in the right, but eternal defeat and miscarriage must attend the man of the best parts if cursed with indecision. To confess the truth, I really think our chief will do better with me than without me.' Washington inclosed the letter to Reed, magnanimously excusing himself for having seen it, as 'having no idea of its being a private letter, much less suspecting the tendency of the correspondence,' and did not even seek to remove Reed from his secretaryship; the latter, however, soon retired from the army. Yet a singular retribution was at hand. Lee, after disobeying for a long time Washington's orders and disregarding his entreaties to cross the Hudson into New Jersey, and even seeking to draw away 2,000 men from another division of the army, in the hope of making a dash on New York, was captured at night by a British scouting party. General Sullivan (the prisoner of Long Island, who had some time since been exchanged) succeeded to his command, and promptly joined Washington, who by this means, and through the receipt of other reinforcements, had soon 5,000 men under him.

The situation was none the less most serious. The British had Rhode Island and nearly all New Jersey; Pennsylvania was threatened, and Congress withdrew to Baltimore. So little public spirit was there in Pennsylvania that the militia not only refused to obey the summons of the Council of Safety and that of their commanding officers, but exulted at the approach of the British and the late misfortunes of the Americans. Washington had to urge the prudence of disarming them. To his brother he went so far as to write, ' If every nerve is not strained to recruit the new army with all possible expedition, I think the game is pretty nearly up' (December 18). Still, he was so persuaded of the justice of the cause that he could not entertain an idea that it would ' finally sink.'

To its credit be it said, Congress lost neither heart nor yet trust in the commander of its choice, but invested Washington with a temporary military dictatorship, resolving that, until otherwise ordered, General Washington should ' be possessed of all power to order and direct all things relative to the department and to the operations of war' (December 12). The measures taken for obtaining more permanent forces were already beginning to tell; but Washington at once began to raise more troops, including a corps of engineers, and promised increased pay to soldiers re-engaging.

And now this 'indecisive' commander showed what stuff he was made of. The British were ready to cross into Pennsylvania, and indeed were only waiting till the Delaware was frozen over. On Christmas night, 1776, though the number of his forces was less than he 'had any conception of' (the adjutant-general's return of December 22 only gave 4,707 rank and file present and fit for duty), Washington himself, with 2,400 men and twenty pieces of artillery, crossed the river, swollen with floating ice, into New Jersey, surprised Trenton, where there were 1,500 Hessians with a body of English cavalry, took a thousand prisoners, a thousand stand of arms, and six field-pieces, and re-crossed the Delaware with prisoners and booty, leaving the Hessian commander mortally wounded, with six of his officers and between thirty and forty of his men killed,

The surprise of Trenton, December 25, 1776.

whilst the Americans had only lost four men, of whom two were frozen to death.

The British having fallen back to Princeton, Washington again crossed the Delaware, and established himself at Trenton. But Lord Cornwallis, at the moment of embarking for England had been ordered back by Sir W. Howe to New Jersey, and soon came up with overwhelming forces. Washington now tried to surprise Princeton, and would have entirely succeeded but for his meeting a British brigade marching to Trenton. In the engagement which followed, known as the battle of Princeton, January 13, 1777, the American advanced troops at first gave way, but were rallied by Washington, and the result was a loss of 400 on the British side, and about one quarter that number on the American. Cornwallis was substantially outmanœuvred. Washington went into winter quarters at Morristown, raised by authority of Congress sixteen more battalions of regular troops, and so harassed the British that at last they retained two posts only in New Jersey. Even from these they withdrew after a few months (July), General Howe having vainly endeavoured to tempt Washington to a general engagement.

The battle of Princeton, January 1777; New Jersey nearly recovered.

Yet in spite of all measures for increasing the army, Washington's forces were always slipping through his hands. We find him writing on January 26: 'The enemy must be ignorant of our numbers, or they have not horses to move their artillery, or they would not suffer us to remain undisturbed.' On February 20: 'At this time we are only about 4,000 strong.' On March 14 the whole force fit for duty in New Jersey was under 3,000, all except 981 militia engaged only till the last of the month. Smallpox raged terribly. Vaccination had not yet been thought of, and inoculation—a practice now penal—was the only available

Washington's winter difficulties; smallpox disastrous.

remedy. The number under inoculation, with their attendants, was about 1,000. Apprehension of the smallpox greatly retarded enlistments (April 13). Pay was as usual in arrear, and the desertions were 'amazing' (April 27). Indeed Washington wrote, as late as June 1, that the numbers of his troops diminished more by desertions than they increased by enlistments. It was under such difficulties that Washington gradually pressed back the British troops towards New York.

It is right to say, on the other hand, that the ravages exercised by the British troops in New Jersey, where 'Tories' and 'Whigs' were plundered alike, roused a feeling against them which all the appeals of Washington and of Congress had failed to call forth. By July 4 we find Washington writing that the spirit with which the militia of New Jersey and Pennsylvania had turned out lately on the alarm of a movement of General Howe's, had 'far exceeded' his 'most sanguine expectations.' *The ravages of the British alienate the people.*

Strange to say, one of the difficulties of Washington and of the Congress at this period arose from the sympathies which the American cause was beginning to create in Europe, or perhaps, to speak more correctly, the attraction which the war offered to unquiet spirits while peace prevailed in the Old World. The American commissioners in Paris were lavish in promises of commissions, and for a time Congress was generous in fulfilling those promises. We find Washington (May 17), asking almost angrily of his friend Richard Henry Lee of Virginia, what Congress expects him to do 'with the many foreigners they have at different times promoted to the rank of field officers, and by the last resolve, two to that of colonels.' Eventually it came to this, that a French officer named Ducoudray came out with the promise, not only of a major-general- *Foreign volunteers: they become a difficulty.*

ship, but of the command of the whole artillery. So disgusted were the American officers at this, that three generals—Greene, Sullivan, and Knox—wrote to Congress threatening to resign if he were appointed. They were reprimanded; but the promise made by Commissioner Deane was not ratified.

Many of the new-comers were no doubt adventurers, but not all. A young French officer of eighteen, the Marquis de la Fayette, afterwards the General Lafayette of two French revolutions, being on military duty at Metz, was present at a dinner (1776), given by his commandant to the Duke of Gloucester, brother to George III., then passing through the city. The Duke had just received despatches from England relating to American matters, and referring to the Declaration of Independence. La Fayette listened, asked questions of the royal guest, took fire for the American cause, and resolved from that hour to devote himself to it. He went to Paris, sought out Silas Deane the American commissioner, who promised him a major-generalship, with a passage on board a ship which was to be sent out with arms and supplies for the Americans. But when the news came of Washington's flight from New Jersey, the credit of the insurgents fell so low that no ship could be had, and Americans even dissuaded the young Frenchman from going out. Instead of being daunted by such tidings, he bought and equipped a ship for himself, and undertook to carry despatches for Washington. His own Government as well as the English one sought to intercept him—the story of his escape is a romance in itself—but he got away through Spain in safety, and eventually landed near Georgetown in South Carolina. Among twelve officers, his companions, was the veteran De Kalb, whom Choiseul had sent ten or twelve years before as secret agent to America. On his arrival

The Marquis de la Fayette: Kosciusko.

at Philadelphia, La Fayette's application for employment was at first coolly received; but when he wrote that his conditions were that he should serve without pay as a volunteer, the marked difference of such terms from those demanded by others procured attention to him. A captain of dragoons, although not yet twenty, La Fayette received (July 31) a major-general's commission, and soon became intimate with Washington, towards whom he conceived an enthusiastic attachment. Another foreign officer who did good service to the American cause from this period was the young Polish engineer Kosciusko. In the same month of July the national flag—'the stars and stripes'—was adopted by Congress; and we may also mention the bold capture in Rhode Island of the English general Prescott, by an American party; a kind of set-off to that of Lee by the English.

In England, George III. and his ministers were carrying all before them, although an adversary, whom they had not had to reckon with for some time now, again confronted them. On May 30, 1777, Lord Chatham, who for two years had not been present at the House of Lords, appeared in his place, a gouty figure swathed in flannels.

<small>Lord Chatham's reappearance: expedition from Canada decided on.</small>

He urged peace with America, before France and Spain became parties to the war. 'You cannot,' he exclaimed, 'conquer the Americans. I might as well talk of driving them before me with this crutch.' His motion was rejected by 99 votes to 28. Yet it was difficult to obtain troops. Only 3,252 men were sent in the course of the year to America from Great Britain and Ireland, and 726 to Canada; nor could more than 3,596 be obtained from Germany. Much reliance was however placed upon the American loyalists, and upon the Indians. To give the largest scope to the services of the latter, an expedition from Canada was planned, the command of which was given to General Burgoyne, a famous wit and man of fashion, author of a successful comic opera and comedy.

With 3,724 British soldiers, 3,016 Germans, 250 provincials, 473 artillerists, besides Indian auxiliaries, Burgoyne, having left Crown Point on July 1, moved up Lake Champlain, intending to effect a junction with the southern army under Howe. The expedition was at first successful. Ticonderoga was evacuated without striking a blow, through the erection of batteries on a height deemed inaccessible, which commanded the fort (July 6). The British came up with the rear-guard of the retreating corps, and defeated it with a loss of about 400 in killed and prisoners, took Skenesborough and the stores collected there, compelled the evacuation of Fort Edward on the Hudson (July 30, invested Fort Schuyler on the Mohawk, and defeated with great loss a body of militia which were marching to relieve it. But now the tide turned.

Burgoyne's advance at first successful.

The Americans had large supplies at Bennington, in New Hampshire: Burgoyne sent a party to surprise the place, under Colonel Baum. The latter finding strong intrenchments, halted, and sent word to his commander-in-chief. Before reinforcements could reach him, he was attacked in his own intrenchments and defeated by General Stark, who was marching with a militia force to join General Schuyler, the American commander. The reinforcements, which joined too late, were in turn defeated, and the result of the two engagements (Aug. 16),—known as the battle of Bennington—was a loss to the British of 207 killed, about 600 prisoners, 4 cannon, and 1,000 stand of arms, the Americans losing only 200 in killed and wounded. Colonel St. Leger, who was investing Fort Schuyler with New York loyalists (or 'Tories') and Indians, fled in a panic to Canada, leaving tents, artillery, and much baggage behind.

Battle of Bennington, August 16, 1777.

Three days after the battle of Bennington, General Schuyler had been superseded in favour of General Gates, an Englishman born, who had served in the French and Indian wars, and had been wounded at Braddock's defeat. Great pains were taken to strengthen him, and reinforcements were sent to him from Washington's army, which, as the event even now proved, was ill able to spare them.

Washington meanwhile, with enfeebled and now vastly inferior forces, was holding Howe in check, whilst eluding any general engagement. At last Howe put to sea with about 18,000 men, leaving Clinton with a strong force at New York, and after keeping the Americans for about three weeks in doubt as to his destination, entered Chesapeake Bay the day after a council of war had unanimously decided that he must have sailed for Charlestown, and landed on the Elk river, about fifty miles from Philadelphia. Washington marched to meet him with about 14,000 men, of whom only about 8,000 were fit for service. The battle took place on Brandywine Creek (Sept. 11, 1777), and the Americans were defeated, with a loss of 300 killed, 600 wounded, and nearly 400 prisoners, besides 7 or 8 pieces of cannon, as against 90 killed, and 500 wounded or missing, on the British side. La Fayette was wounded. Another foreign volunteer, the Polish Count Pulaski, also distinguished himself in the action, and was made a brigadier-general. *Battle of Brandywine, Sept. 11, 1777.*

Having received reinforcements, Washington again offered battle a few days later, but a violent storm stopped the contest and injured his ammunition. He was obliged to retreat. A skilful movement of the British, which threatened his supplies, through a part of the country from which he could not derive, as he wrote to Congress, the least intelligence, the inhabitants, 'being to a man, dis- *Philadelphia occupied by the British, Sept. 26; battle of Germantown, Oct. 4.*

affected,' compelled him to leave open the road to Philadelphia. General **Wayne, who was left to** check the advance with **1,500 men, was surprised and** defeated, and on the **26th the British entered** Philadelphia, **from** whence Congress had adjourned to the town of Lancaster. Eight days **later, a surprise of a British division at** Germantown **seemed likely to prove a great success (Oct.** 4), but a thick fog arose, **the American** ammunition **failed,** the **British rallied, and the assailants fled in panic with a** loss **of 1,000 men. Four days later Sir** Henry **Clinton, from New York, carried by storm Forts Montgomery** and Clinton **on the Hudson river, two American frigates being** also **destroyed. An attack on the Delaware forts** indeed failed **in the first instance (Oct. 22), but even here** matters looked **so** threatening **that, by Washington's advice, some** frigates **which were being built on the Delaware** river were **sunk. A** few weeks **later the forts, after a stubborn defence, were evacuated (Nov. 15-20). Washington** withdrew to **White Marsh, fourteen miles from** Philadelphia, and **from thence, after an attempted surprise** by Howe, into **winter quarters at Valley Forge, on** the other side of the **Schuylkill, about twenty-two miles from** the city.

Of course the outcry was greater **than** ever against **a**
Renewed   commander **so** seldom successful, **so** often
outcry   defeated. **Just now the clamour** was inten-
against
Washington. **sified by** the brilliant **successes of** Gates **in** the north.

Despite **the defeat at** Bennington and the failure before Fort **Schuyler, Burgoyne** had still pressed on. **On**
The battles **September 14 he crossed** the Hudson **and en-**
of Stillwater, **camped at** Saratoga, **thence** marched slowly
Sept. 19,
Oct. 7. along the **Hudson till he met** the Americans **encamped at Stillwater or** Bemus's (alias Behmus's) **heights (Sept. 19), within lines planned by Kosciusko. The** battle continued till nightfall, when **the Americans**

withdrew to their camp; but the British loss was the greater, 500 to over 319. Burgoyne's Indian allies and many of the loyalist volunteers now deserted him. What remained of his army was on half-rations; his horses were without forage. Meanwhile Gates was daily receiving reinforcements. On October 7 Burgoyne again engaged the Americans. The fight was so fierce that one gun was taken and retaken five times. Benedict Arnold, who had already been the hero of the previous battle, but who had been deprived of his command by the jealousy of Gates, resumed it under fire in spite of the latter's orders, and only left the field when wounded in the leg. General Frazer, the most brilliant of the English officers, was killed; and though again night only separated the combatants, the British loss was far greater than the American,—700 as against about 150.

Burgoyne fell back to Saratoga, and was about to withdraw to Fort Edward, when he learnt that it was in the enemy's hands. He was surrounded, his men were starving, and only 3,500 of them were fit to fight, whilst the enemy were not less than 14,000. *Burgoyne's surrender at Saratoga, Oct. 16.* A council of war was deliberating on capitulation, when an eighteen-pound ball swept across the table. On October 16, 5,791 British troops, with arms and baggage, 42 guns and ammunition, surrendered, receiving indeed the honours of war, and being allowed (though the stipulation remained long unfulfilled) to embark for England, on condition of not serving again against the Americans until exchanged. The conduct of the American soldiers on the surrender was excellent; as the famished remnant of veterans came out, 'all was mute astonishment and pity.' Sir Henry Clinton's movement up the river Hudson came too late to help Burgoyne; nor after the storming of the American forts on the western bank had it any further result than the capture of stores and destruction of property, Forts Montgomery and Clinton being evacuated (Oct. 26).

Gates did not even apprise Washington of Burgoyne's surrender, but made his report direct to Congress, which voted him thanks and a gold medal, and when Washington urgently pressed him now to send back troops, Gates refused to part with them. Yet, as Washington shows in his letters, he had to fight two battles with forces inferior to those of his antagonists, in order, if possible, to save Philadelphia, in a State abounding in 'the disaffected and lukewarm,' whilst 'the States of New York and New England, resolving to crush Burgoyne,' had 'continued pouring in their troops' till his surrender. It was indeed only from a distance that Washington's work was appreciated. Vergennes, at an interview with the American commissioners (Dec. 12, 1777), declared that nothing had struck him so much as General Washington's attacking and giving battle to General Howe, with 'an army raised within a year.'

Gates and Washington.

In England the news of the capture of Philadelphia caused 'in the minds of all sorts of people,' Burke wrote, a 'wild tumult of joy.' As the seat of Congress, Philadelphia might well look to the European observer like a capital, whereas it was in fact but one among several great American cities. On the other hand, when the gain of the campaign came to be dispassionately weighed, it appeared that the whole result of British success was only the 'acquisition of good winter quarters for the British army' in the Quaker city. When parliament met on November 20, more than one warning voice was raised. Pownall declared that the Americans would never return to subjection, and that until men were convinced 'that the United States are an independent sovereign people,' and 'prepared to treat with them as

Rejoicings in England over the evacuation of Philadelphia; Chatham's inconsistency.

such,' no schemes of conciliation could be of much use. Chatham, who moved an amendment in the Lords, was more hopeful; but he again declared conquest impossible. 'You may swell,' he said, 'every expense and every effort still more extravagantly, pile and accumulate every assistance you can buy or borrow; traffic and barter with every little pitiful German prince that sells and sends his subjects to the shambles of a foreign prince, but your efforts are for ever vain and impotent.' He denounced with furious invective the employment of Indians, 'hellhounds of savage war' (Dec. 2). But the inconsistency of his policy was palpable. 'Lord Chatham,' wrote Horace Walpole to the Countess of Ossory, 'is an Irishman; he would recall the troops and deny the independence of the Americans' (Dec. 5). The Duke of Richmond, on the other hand, representing the Rockingham Whigs, declared that he would 'sooner give up every claim to America than continue an unjust and cruel civil war.' But the quiescent attitude of the party left the ministry undisturbed, justifying Walpole's bitter sarcasm of a few months previous: 'The cruellest thing that has been said of the Americans by the Court is, that they were encouraged by the Opposition. You might as soon light a fire with a wet dish-clout.' (Walpole to Mason, Oct. 5.)

But even whilst returning from the debate of December 2, the news reached Lord North of the surrender of Saratoga. The minister could neither eat nor sleep, and was anxious to give up all, or to retire. The king was in an agony of grief. The Opposition plucked up heart of grace. Fox, Barré, Burke vehemently attacked the ministry, urging agreement with the Americans anyhow, a recognition of independence, or even alliance. The Duke of Richmond followed the same line in the Lords (11th). Parliament adjourned to January 20, 1778.

Gloomy impressions produced by the Saratoga surrender; France ready to treat with America.

During the recess, it is said that the king sent over to Paris an old deaf Moravian, named James Hutton, well known to Franklin, to sound the latter as to the possibility of making terms. The reply was 'too late.' Nor could it be otherwise. On December 12, at an interview already referred to, Vergennes announced to the American commissioners that a treaty would be entered into with them, but that Spain must be consulted. On the 17th they were informed that American independence would be not only acknowledged but supported by France. Yet it was only on the 28th that Lord Stormont, the British ambassador at Paris, could warn his chiefs that Spain and France were plotting.

There was a sense in England of an impending crisis, and the king's thoughts began to turn to Chatham, though he was still determined not to give him control as well as place. When parliament met again on January 20, Lord Rockingham and the Duke of Richmond again urged the recognition of American independence, though Lord Chatham, and even Lord Shelburne, could not yet entertain the idea. Lord North was always anxious to retire, and only remained in office under pressure of his sovereign. The king himself by this time (January 1778), contemplated the possibility that a time might come when it would be 'wise to abandon all America but Canada, Nova Scotia, and the Floridas;' but while he disclaimed 'any absurd ideas of unconditional submission' (Jan. 31), he put the continuance of the war on the plea that the country had a 'right to have the struggle continued till convinced that it is vain.'

Sense of an impending crisis; the king has forebodings.

In America, in spite of discord and weakness, Congress was feeling its way towards the establishment of American nationality. On Nov. 15, 1777, the scheme of confederation, which had been under consideration since July 1776, was, with various amendments, adopted, and remitted to the several States for acceptation. Weak as it eventually proved — reserving to each State 'its sovereignty, freedom, and independence, and every power, jurisdiction, and right not expressly delegated to the United States in Congress assembled'—it declared a perpetual union, and withheld from the several States the power of treating with foreign countries, or with each other, and other functions of sovereignty. It was not however acceded to by any State till 1778, nor by all, as we shall see, till 1781. *The scheme of Confederation adopted by Congress, Nov. 15, 1777.*

But Congress itself was little more than the shadow of a name. The number of members present at its sittings rarely rose to 17, fell sometimes to 9. It tried in January 1778 to borrow, but no one would lend. It could only issue more and more paper money. It could not even recover its debts, and had in February to beg the States to enact laws for enabling it to do so. *Impotency of Congress.*

All this impotency told of course with twofold force upon the army. There had been dark days already for the commander-in-chief, but those of the winter at Valley Forge were the darkest. The neighbourhood was chiefly Tory; the English paid in cash for their supplies; Washington had nothing but the depreciated paper-money of Congress, and in this paper-money a general's pay scarcely kept him in clothes. Three days before Christmas the last ration had been served out. Washington declared in writing to the President of Congress, that unless 'some great and capital change' suddenly took place, the army must inevitably either 'starve, dissolve, or disperse in order to obtain subsistence in the best manner they can. For want of shoes or clothing 2,898 men were unfit for duty. He was compelled to send out foraging parties, *Washington's miserable winter at Valley Forge.*

whilst warning Congress that such measures ruined discipline. By February the neighbourhood was exhausted, the horses were dying for want of forage, and the commissaries could see no means of supply beyond March 11. For six days running the soldiers were without meat; and there was hardly a whole pair of shoes in the camp. Putrid fevers and other deadly diseases were rife. Desertions were 'astonishingly great.' In little more than six months, between 200 and 300 officers threw up their commissions. Had Sir W. Howe attacked the army, he must have annihilated it. The Pennsylvania legislature censured the commander-in-chief. A cabal was formed against him, the moving spirit in which was an Irishman named Conway. Congress appointed his opponents on a new board of war, and made Conway inspector of the army. Propositions were made for putting Gates or Lee (lately exchanged for General Prescott) in his place. An effort was made to detach La Fayette from him by giving the former the command of an expedition to Canada, planned without consulting the commander-in-chief, with Conway for second in command. But La Fayette saw through the design: the attempt was felt to be impracticable, and was given up. Washington was maintained, and on his representations measures were taken for better organising the army and the war.

Meanwhile the British were wasting the fruits of their late successes in inaction. Philadelphia proved 'the Inaction of Capua of the British army.' As Franklin the English phrased it, instead of Howe's taking Philadelphia, Philadelphia took Howe. The officers were spending their time in amateur theatricals and amusements of all sorts, gambling for high stakes, and disgusting the staid Quaker population not only with their levity but their debaucheries.

But the news which reached America in May 1778 startled the English out of their gaieties, and woke the Americans out of their torpor. On February 6 not only a treaty of amity and commerce, but of eventual defensive alliance, was concluded at Paris between France and the United States. The absolute and unlimited independence of the United States was put forth as the essential object, each party agreeing not to lay down their arms till this independence should be ensured by treaty. By a separate secret convention, power was reserved to the King of Spain to accede to the treaties. *The treaty between France and America, February 6, 1778.*

To call such a treaty a defensive one was a transparent subterfuge. Since England was at war to prevent the independence of her American colonies, to make that independence the essential object of a treaty, and to guarantee it, was equivalent to a declaration of war upon her. From henceforth virtually the area of the conflict becomes that of the globe itself. *The theatre of the war enlarged.*

CHAPTER VI.

THE WAR. SECOND PERIOD: FROM THE ALLIANCE WITH FRANCE TILL THE END OF THE WAR (1778-83).

THE treaty between the King of France and the United States was not immediately published in the former country. Voltaire, in a letter of March 15, speaks of its publication as a recent event. His view was that 'without a declaration of war there would be blows struck.' France indeed was but ill prepared for war. Her finances had lately been entrusted to the Genevese banker Necker. His credit was *France and the treaty.*

good, and he found money, where his predecessors had failed to do so. The device of a State lottery, amongst others, was tried in France, as it was also tried in England; but already, at the time when Voltaire wrote, the tickets were at 8 per cent. discount, and there were 5,000 which had found no purchasers. Vast sums had however been spent on the fleets, and France hoped once more, with the eventual help of Spain, to dispute with England the supremacy of the seas.

In England the existence of the treaty was soon known to the ministry. It is said that the king's first idea on hearing of it was to withdraw at once all land and sea forces from America, and concentrate all the efforts of England against France alone. This was not done; but now, when it was too late, concessions were offered which, if granted before, would no doubt have averted the war. On February 17— which Horace Walpole describes as 'a day of confusion and humiliation that will be remembered as long as the name of England exists'—Lord North brought forward a plan of conciliation, in which the independence of the United States was acknowledged, to use his words, not 'verbally' but yet 'virtually.' He was asked if he did not know that the treaty between the Americans and France was signed. 'He would not answer till Sir George Saville hallooed out, "An answer, an answer, an answer!" His lordship then rose, could not deny the fact, but said he did not know it officially.' There was no opposition to speak of, either now or during the progress of the measures through Parliament, and by the month of April three acts were passed (known as 'Lord North's Conciliatory Bills,' 18 Geo. III., cc. 11, 12, 13), one of which repealed the act for regulating the government of Massachusetts, on the ground of its having been 'found to create great uneasinesses in the

Lord North's conciliatory bills.

minds of the inhabitants of the said province,' and having 'occasioned jealousies and apprehensions of danger to their liberties and rights in several others of the colonies and plantations in North America.' A second, besides repealing the Tea Act, renounced the right of taxation by the king and parliament for any of the colonies in North America or the West Indies, except as regarded duties for the regulation of commerce, and even these duties were to be applied for the use of the respective colonies in the same manner as duties collected by authority of their general courts or assemblies. A third empowered the crown to appoint two commissioners, with power (until June 1, 1779) to treat 'with any body or bodies politic or corporate, or with any assembly or assemblies of men, or with any person or persons whatsoever,' for the redress of grievances, &c., to order a cessation of hostilities by sea or land, suspend any act of parliament passed since Feb. 10, 1763, grant pardons, &c. Any term implying rebellion was carefully avoided in these acts, in which the strongest expression, besides that of 'hostilities,' was that of 'disorders among his Majesty's faithful subjects,'—which 'faithful subjects had, in the Declaration of Independence, now nearly two years old, pronounced his Majesty's character to be 'marked by every act that may define a tyrant,' and himself thereby 'unfit to be the ruler of a free people.' Conciliation in this form could be held only as a demonstration of weakness.

In the meanwhile, on March 17, the ministry had laid before parliament a notification from France of her treaty with America, which was ironically declared not to be an exclusive one. Lord Stormont was at once recalled, and the cry swelled for Lord Chatham as premier. How unfit he was for the office, the course of another short month would prove.

The king will not have Lord Chatham as premier.

But his name seemed to be a tower of strength against France, and was no doubt so felt in France itself. The king obstinately refused to give him more than high office.

'No consideration in life,' he wrote on that very March 17 when France was known to have virtually thrown down the gauntlet to England, 'shall make me stoop to opposition. . . . Whilst any ten men in the kingdom will stand by me, I will not give myself into bondage. . . . It is impossible that the nation should not stand by me; if they will not, they shall have another king.' With relentless hatred towards Chatham he could look forward to the day 'when decrepitude or death puts an end to him as a trumpet of sedition.' So Lord North, vainly beseeching to be released, remained in the pillory of his office.

A few weeks later occurred (April 7) the last scene in Lord Chatham's political life. The Duke of Richmond had brought forward a motion for the withdrawal of the fleets and armies from America, and for the use of none but amicable means towards her. And now Lord Chatham, who had repeatedly declared that America could not be conquered, rose up to express his indignation at an idea which had gone forth of giving up America. 'As long,' he said, 'as I can crawl down to this house, and have strength to raise myself on my crutches, or lift my hand, I will vote against giving up the dependency of America on the sovereignty of Great Britain.' He had spoken, Walpole tells us, 'with every symptom of debility, repeated his own phrases, could not recollect his own ideas.' The Duke of Richmond, in very measured terms, replied to him. Lord Chatham rose again, staggered, and fell in an apoplectic fit. The House adjourned. He lingered till May 11. Parliament voted him a public funeral and a monument, with a perpetual pension of 4,000*l.* a year to his heirs, and a large sum of money for payment of his debts. The funeral took place

Death of Chatham, May 11, 1778.

on June 7 ; but Walpole observed that the funeral of Garrick the actor had been ten times more largely attended.

Meanwhile the sending of reinforcements to America was stopped, and an act was passed for strengthening the militia and to encourage volunteers. The prospect of a war with France called forth the warlike energies of the country, and by July 7 Walpole could write to Sir H. Mann : 'The country is covered with camps. General Conway, who has been to one of them, speaks with astonishment of the fineness of the men, of the regiments, of their discipline and manœuvres.' Various concessions, both fiscal and ecclesiastical, were made to Ireland. It was not, however, till the end of July that France formally declared war, and as late as September communications remained open between France and England. *Preparations for war with France.*

On May 3, 1778, news reached Congress, and was forwarded by it to Washington, of the treaty with France. By an order of the day (May 6), stating that 'it has pleased the Almighty Ruler of the universe to defend the cause of the United American States, and finally to raise us up a powerful friend among the princes of the earth, to establish our liberty and independency upon a lasting foundation,' Washington set apart the following day as one of solemn rejoicing, which was celebrated with thanksgiving by the brigade chaplains, military evolutions, *feux de joie*, and huzzas of 'Long live the King of France!' 'Long live the friendly European Powers and The American States.' Congress at first took steps for reinforcing the army ; replaced the inspector-general Conway, who had resigned in a huff, by an experienced Prussian lieutenant-general, Baron Steuben, late aide-de-camp of Frederick the Great ; and pledged to the officers the payment of half-pay after the close of the war. *Rejoicings over the treaty in America.*

Yet the promotion of foreign officers created such discontent, and often led to results otherwise so unsatisfactory, that a few months later we find Washington writing, 'I most devoutly wish that we had not a single foreigner among us except the Marquis de la Fayette' (July 24).

The haste with which Lord North's Conciliatory Bills had been passed had been so far successful that drafts of them, together with Lord North's speech introducing them, had reached New York several weeks before the French treaty. So entirely unexpected were such concessions, that for several days neither Washington nor Laurens, then President of Congress, could believe them genuine. When Washington became convinced of their genuineness, it is obvious that he felt considerable doubts as to the effect they would produce. There were symptoms to authorise an opinion that the people of America were 'pretty generally weary' of the war; and it appeared to him doubtful whether many 'might not incline to an accommodation rather than persevere in a contest for independence.' Hence 'to enter into a negotiation too hastily or to reject it altogether' might 'be attended with consequences equally fatal.' Congress however promptly decided (April 22) 'that these States cannot with propriety hold any conference or treaty with any commissioners on the part of Great Britain, unless they shall, as a preliminary thereto, either withdraw their fleets and armies, or else in positive and express terms acknowledge the independence of the said States.' The news of the French treaty could only strengthen the grounds for such a course.

When therefore the commissioners under the late act arrived in the Delaware (June 4), their undertaking was foredoomed to failure. They were three in number—the Earl of Carlisle, William Eden, afterwards Lord Auckland, and George Johnstone, a former Governor of West Florida, hence

Reception of the Conciliatory Bills.

Arrival of the royal commissioners (June 4, 1778).

commonly spoken of as Governor Johnstone. Lord Howe and Sir William Howe were also included in the commission, but the latter having resigned, his successor, Sir Henry Clinton, took his place. The conciliatory acts as passed were in the first instance forwarded to Congress (June 6). They replied that they had in April expressed their sentiments on bills not essentially different, and that when the king should be 'seriously disposed to end the unprovoked war waged against these United States,' they would 'readily attend to such terms of peace as may consist with the honour of independent nations and the sacred regard they mean to pay to treaties.'

On that very day the commissioners arrived at Philadelphia, to find it in course of evacuation. The French alliance alone, without any active measures on the part of the Americans, had determined Lord George Germain to order this step by a secret despatch, of which the commissioners seem to have been unaware. The occupation of the Quaker city by the British had terminated with the same levity which had characterised it all through. Before Sir William Howe had left (May 24) a grand tournament or 'mis chianza' had been held by the officers in his honour. But when Lord Carlisle landed, the British territory did not extend more than two miles from the city. The order for evacuation had been received with the gloomiest feelings; 3,000 loyalists were embarking to escape with the troops. The commissioners had just time to write to Congress, offering to the 'States' perfect freedom of legislation and internal government, representation in parliament, and exemption from the presence of troops, except with their own permission, and then pledging themselves to take their departure on board ship. But the answer (June 17) was the same as before, and required from the king 'an explicit acknow-

The evacuation of Philadelphia ordered.

ledgment of the independence of these States, or the withdrawing of his fleets and armies.'

In the course of that night (June 17-18) Sir Henry Clinton finally evacuated Philadelphia, crossing the Delaware with over 17,000 men. Philadelphia was before long re-occupied by the Americans, and Arnold placed in command there. Clinton advanced slowly through New Jersey, retreating on New York, weakened daily by desertions, his baggage occupying a line eight miles long.

<small>Philadelphia evacuated. Battle of Monmouth (June 28). Lee and Washington.</small>

Washington, whose forces had been slowly recruited during the spring, endeavoured to obstruct his march, and against the advice of a council of war, gave battle at Monmouth Court House (June 28). The weather was such that on the British side the Hessians refused to engage, alleging that it was too hot. Three sergeants and fifty-six men dropped down dead from the heat. Lee, who at first, as disapproving the movement, had handed over to La Fayette the conduct of the attack, afterwards claimed to retain it, but blundered and retreated, and was found by Washington, who was marching to his support with the main body, in the rear of his division. Washington gave him a severe rebuke, and sent him back to the battle, which was sharply contested, and ended by leaving the Americans masters of the field, whilst the British took up a strong position covered by woods and marshes, with only a narrow pass in front, out of which however they effected a safe retreat during the night with all their wounded who could be moved. Leaving about 250 of their dead to be buried by the Americans, besides 100 prisoners, they made good their way to New York. The American loss was about 200 in killed and wounded. The day after the battle Lee sent a challenge to Washington. He was thereupon tried by court-martial for disobedience of orders, misbehaviour before the enemy, and disrespect of the commander-in-chief, found guilty on all the charges, and sentenced to be suspended from all command for a year. He never rejoined the army, and died four years later.

On July 2 Congress met again at Philadelphia. On the 9th the articles of confederation were signed by eight States, and a circular was issued the next day to the five remaining ones, pressing them to conclude the 'glorious compact,' an invitation which was acceded to in the course of the month by two of them,—North Carolina and Georgia. Articles of Confederation signed by several States.

Meanwhile, Clinton had scarcely reached New York, when a French fleet with a strong land force under Count d'Estaing appeared off the mouth of the Delaware (July 8). An attack on New York was projected, with a view to the capture or destruction of the British fleet which lay in the bay. D'Estaing and the French investment of Newport. But the French ships could not cross the bar of the Hudson, and it was resolved to attack the British at Newport, Rhode Island, which was invested by the Americans from the land side under General Sullivan, supported by La Fayette and Greene, and by the French fleet from the sea. But the American troops were not ready for a week after D'Estaing's arrival. Then a British fleet under Lord Howe suddenly made its appearance, and Count d'Estaing sailed out to meet it; but a violent storm, still remembered in Rhode Island as 'the great storm,' separated the combatants, and so damaged the French fleet that before long D'Estaing, in spite of the efforts of La Fayette and Greene to persuade him otherwise, announced that he must return to Boston to refit, so that Sullivan (August 28) had to retreat. All the American general officers except La Fayette and Greene protested against the French admiral's departure.

Events which, although of little military importance,

sank deep into the hearts of the Americans, and proved
Indian massacres. to be of terrible moment for the fates of the
red men, were the incursions of the Indians
(Iroquois, headed or aided by loyalists, into the valley of
the Susquehannah and Cherry Valley, and the massacres
which ensued, accompanied by all the barbarities of
Indian warfare. That of Wyoming in particular has been
immortalised by the poet Campbell in his 'Gertrude of
Wyoming.' (July and November 1778.)

The peace commissioners themselves ended by adding fuel to the flame of war. A second letter of theirs,
Failure of the peace commission. asking the authority of Congress for making
treaties, had been left unanswered (July 18,.
Governor Johnstone is said then to have tried
bribery with Joseph Reed, now in Congress. Congress,
on being informed of the circumstances, refused to hold
any further communication with him. Johnstone published a vindication of himself, but withdrew from the
commission. The commissioners published a final
address or manifesto (October 3) declaring that the
conduct of the Americans would 'change the whole
nature and future conduct of the war,' and threatening
them with the 'extremes of war.' The declaration was
strongly condemned in parliament by Coke of Norfolk,
afterwards Lord Leicester, Burke, Rockingham, and the
Bishop of Peterborough, but defended by Lord George
Germain, Johnstone himself, and Lord Suffolk. That it
was not intended as an idle threat was shown by the
ravages already perpetrated by detachments from Clinton's
army as well as by those of the Indians already mentioned.

Between France and England the war was being carried
on with varying fortunes. There had been an
The war in other quarters: Keppel, Paul Jones; Hyder Ali. indecisive action within sight of Brest (July 27),
between the French and English fleets, the latter
under Admiral Keppel, who was tried for misconduct by court-martial in the early part of the follow-

ing year, but honourably acquitted. In the West Indies Dominica was taken by the French (September), St. Lucia by the English, D'Estaing being beaten off with loss (December). The western coast of England was harried by Paul Jones, a Scotchman in the American service, who even burnt the shipping in Whitehaven. But in point of prizes the balance of profit on the war lay with England. More than two millions' worth had been taken by her cruisers by October 30. A camp established by the French in Normandy came to nothing. In India, before even accurate tidings were received of the war with France, measures were taken for seizing all the French settlements. Pondicherry alone resisted for seventy days, the others surrendered without a blow. But the taking of Mahé was the occasion of a second war with Hyder Ali, the soldier of fortune who had possessed himself of the throne of Mysore, and who, with his son Tippoo, proved one of the most formidable foes ever met by the English in India. He had warned the English that he would invade the Carnatic if Mahé were attacked. He was as good as his word, and by the end of the year there was war with the Mahrattas.

Let us now return to America. Mr. Bancroft heads one of the chapters in the last volume of his History of the United States with the title, 'A people without a government, August–December 1778.' *Increasing impotency of Congress; it solicits French 'protection.'* With keen knowledge of the character of his people, Washington had written, two days after learning of the French alliance, 'I very much fear that we, taking it for granted that we have nothing more to do, because France has acknowledged our independency and formed an alliance with us, shall relapse into a state of supineness and perfect security' (May 5, 1778). Congress remained assiduously engaged in making paper money, without even being able to obtain the sole right of doing so from the several States, and issuing loan certificates at six per cent. interest, without having the power to raise taxes to pay even the latter. Some of these certificates they succeeded in getting rid of by discharging in them their debts to the several States. A more brilliant idea was that of drawing on their commissioners in Paris, and this was actually done in the very month when the news of the French treaty was received, to the extent of 31,500,000 livres, or say 1,220,000*l.*, the expectation being of course that the commissioners, who were provided with no means whatever of meeting the bills, would somehow beg the money from France. Congress turned to an English writer on finance, Dr. Price, offering him citizenship, and requesting him to regulate their finances; he declined the invitation. And now these States, so punctilious as to the acknowledgment of their independence on the part of England, humbled themselves to France so far as to instruct Franklin (end of October) to assure the king that 'they hoped protection from his power and magnanimity,' the word 'protection' being divided against, but carried by a majority of eight States to two. There was no resource, it was admitted, but in 'very considerable loans or subsidies in Europe, and whilst Franklin was pressing for a loan in France, Laurens was sent (December) to obtain one if possible from Holland. The disgraceful feature of the matter was, that as the war was confined to a few districts of the coast or frontier, the country generally was prospering, Virginia growing abundance of tobacco, and Massachusetts gathering wealth by trade.

Whilst Washington was left too weak for offensive warfare, Clinton also in New York remained not only without reinforcements, but with an empty chest, and was moreover directed to weaken himself by sending ten regiments to the West Indies, and an expedition to the south, so that, without complaining, he had to beg that nothing might be 'expected' of him. The expedition to the South was the most important military event of the year. The region was one where the Tories or loyalists were most numerous. Already two incursions into Georgia, consisting in great measure of such refugees, had taken place during the autumn from East Florida, whilst an attempt to retaliate upon St. Augustine failed. Towards the end of December a British fleet under Sir Peter Parker, bearing Colonel Campbell with 2,000 men, appeared before Savannah. General Howe, who commanded on the American side, with 900 men under him, was completely defeated (December 29), losing 100 men killed and 453 prisoners, whilst the English lost only 24 in killed and wounded. Savannah was occupied, and in the beginning of January 1779 Colonel Prevost, who commanded in East Florida, marched through Lower Georgia to Savannah, subduing the country as he went, and though there was not such a general rising of loyalists as was expected, the whole province was practically recovered. *British operations in the south. Savannah taken (December 29), and Georgia recovered.*

The next attempt was on South Carolina; but a party of loyalists from thence, on their way to rejoin the British army, were cut to pieces (February 14, 1779), only about 200 escaping to the British lines. The prisoners taken were afterwards tried for treason to South Carolina, 70 of them convicted, and 5 hung. The American army was not, however, successfully commanded by General Lincoln, who had replaced Howe. A detachment of 1,500 North Carolina militia, with a few Continentals under Colonel Aske, was signally defeated by Prevost at Briar Arch on the Savannah river, near Augusta (March 3); and only 450 men rejoined General Lincoln out of the whole *South Carolina invaded, and Charleston threatened (May 1779).*

force. Colonel Prevost now pushed forward to Charleston (May 11), into which some hundreds of men had thrown themselves, under Moultrie, the Pole Pulaski, and others. Congress had recommended the arming of the slaves; but this was so distasteful to the council of the State that they sent to propose to the English its neutrality during the war. This was of course refused, and Prevost declined to treat with the civil government, demanding the surrender of the garrison as prisoners of war. But on the news of Lincoln's approach the English commander drew off, leaving a post at Stony Ferry, afterwards transferred to Beaufort. Soon, however, the ravages and plunder of the British troops in South Carolina went far to alienate the population, whilst the intense heat compelled both parties to give up active operations in the south till the autumn; the Carolina militia went home, and Lincoln remained with only 800 men.

The winter of 1778-9, owing to better supplies and better regulations, was less trying to the main army, encamped at Middlebrook, New Jersey, than any yet experienced, although it still required Washington's 'constant presence and attention,' and 'some degree of care and address, to keep it from crumbling' (Dec. 12, 1778). But an overweening confidence had now replaced despondency. Everything was expected from the support of the French. The British were still at New York, and Washington had great trouble to hinder Congress from attempting to conquer Canada with the aid of France. It is a remarkable instance of the combination in him of statesmanship with military skill, that although the scheme had originated with his intimate friend La Fayette, he at once discountenanced it on the ground of the 'true and permanent interests' of his country, lest France should recover Canada, and 'have it in her power to give law to these States;'

Washington's army during the winter of 1778-9. Defensive campaign.

and this although he was 'thoroughly convinced of the expediency and policy of doing everything practicable' on the part of the Americans, 'even for accomplishing the annexation of Canada to the Union.' There was great delay in the necessary recruiting. A great part of the officers, Washington wrote, were, 'from absolute necessity,' quitting the service, the 'virtuous few' who remained 'sinking by sure degrees into beggary and want,' so that 'the dissolution of the army' was again 'not an improbable event, if the situation of the officers were not improved' (Jan. 20, 1779). After a month's consultation with the commander-in-chief, Congress decided that the state of the currency and supplies would oblige them to act on the defensive during the campaign of 1779, except as related to the chastising of the Indians (April 1779). A defensive campaign is not the one to attract recruits, and by May 8 the army was 'little more than the skeleton of an army,' and the New Jersey brigade could with difficulty be restrained from abandoning the service, owing to arrears of pay. Clinton, whose forces, though weakened by the expedition to the south, were rather more numerous than Washington's, harried the country with marauding parties. Terrible ravages were committed in Virginia, on the Chesapeake, where, besides captures, over 130 vessels and 500,000*l*. worth of property were destroyed (May). Sailing up the Hudson, Clinton compelled the evacuation or surrender of Stony Point and Verplanck Point, posts fortified by Washington to protect the crossing at King's Ferry, the chief channel of communication between the eastern and middle States and West Point, where the Americans had their chief magazines and stores (June 1, 1779). General Tryon, the former governor of New York, ravaged the coast of Connecticut, plundering or burning New Haven and other towns. He was, however, recalled, owing to the recovery of Stony Point by General Wayne

(July 15), who destroyed it. Another fort opposite New York was taken a month later still (August 19).

During the summer (August and September) a terrible revenge was taken on the Iroquois for the Wyoming massacres by General Sullivan, who with 5,000 men devastated their whole country between the Susquehannah and Genesee rivers—covered, we are told, with 'pleasant villages and luxuriant corn fields'—burning every village, and giving no quarter. At one village, which is termed the 'metropolis of Genesee valley,' no less than 160,000 bushels of corn were destroyed. The Indians were pursued as far as the British fort of Niagara, and Indian agriculture was destroyed throughout the district. The total American loss did not exceed forty men. The responsibility for these cruel measures lies at Washington's own door. His instructions to General Sullivan (May 31) were, 'that the country may not be merely overrun, but destroyed.'

General Sullivan devastates the Iroquois country.

On the other hand General Maclean, who commanded the British forces in Nova Scotia, in order to check American incursions into that province, established a post of 600 men in Penobscot Bay, in what is now the State of Maine, but which then belonged to Massachusetts (June 1779). To dislodge them Massachusetts sent out the largest American armament that had yet sailed; nineteen armed ships with 300 guns, besides twenty-four transports, and nearly 1,000—other accounts say 3,000—men. The affair was a signal failure, which the arrival of Sir George Collier with a 64-gun ship and five frigates turned into a disaster. Two vessels were taken, the rest burned by the Americans themselves, the troops and crews fell to blows, many perished in the woods, and the country east of the Penobscot became British territory (July–August).

The British in Penobscot Bay.

If the American Congress failed to show itself great

in pushing on the war, it was much occupied with settling the conditions of the future peace, at first with France only, afterwards with Spain, when, as we shall presently see, she joined the Franco-American alliance. Both powers, jealous of the future extension of the republic, wished to shut her out from the region north-west of the Ohio, and from the Newfoundland fisheries, while Spain wanted to exclude her from the navigation of the Mississippi. It would be tedious to dwell on the negotiations: suffice it to say that on September 27 peace commissioners were appointed—John Adams for France, Jay for Spain. Yet a period nearly as long as that which had elapsed since the beginning of the war was to pass away before peace should be concluded. *Congress appoints peace commissioners.*

There is very little to notice in Europe during the early months of 1779. No European war was ever more uneventful than was thus far the war between England and France. The violent storm which ushered in the year 1779; the eighty-four days' frost which followed the storm; the personal quarrel between Admiral Keppel and his second in command, Palliser, the successive courts-martial on both, the riots on Keppel's acquittal; occupied England till the end of February far more than the war itself. There was indeed an inquiry by the House of Commons into the proceedings in America and the conduct of the war; but the only result was to expose Howe's blunders, and on the other hand to whitewash Burgoyne. In Ireland volunteer associations were formed to replace the troops sent to America; and the demands which they made for redress of grievances began to excite apprehension. *The war in Europe uneventful.*

Horace Walpole wrote to Sir Horace Mann (Feb. 25), 'The backwardness of Spain has saved us.' But the time was approaching when she was to be drawn into the struggle. Her position and conduct deserve now to be considered. *Spain's backwardness in going to war.*

France had little to lose, in the way of territory at least, and everything to gain in a war with a power like England, already in conflict with America. It was otherwise with Spain. A sure instinct told her that she had everything to lose by American independence; and that her vast American empire must sooner or later follow the fate of that of England. When, in January 1778, Montmorin the French ambassador read to the Spanish minister Florida Blanca a despatch announcing the determination of France to support America, it is said that the Spaniard 'quivered in every limb, and could hardly utter a reply.' For months Spain continued to reproach France with engaging in the war. But the possession by England of Gibraltar and Minorca was a double thorn in the side of Spain, and a war with England might enable her to recover them. In the spring of 1778 battering trains were already being collected at Seville, and in the Bay of Cadiz a greater fleet was gathered than any which had issued from Spain since the Armada. For another twelvemonth, however, Spain negotiated on all sides, half-sincerely, half-dishonestly, pressing her mediation on England, endeavouring in treating with France to cripple the United States in the future, and exacting from both France and America impossible conditions as the price of her co-operation. At last (April 12, 1779), a convention was signed between France and Spain, by which France undertook to invade Great Britain or Ireland, this invasion being regarded by Spain as the only means of recovering Gibraltar. If Newfoundland were recovered, France was to share its fisheries with Spain alone. She was further bound to use every effort to recover for Spain Minorca, Pensacola, Mobile, the Bay of Honduras, the coast of Campeachy, and to grant neither peace, truce, nor suspension of hostilities till Gibraltar was restored. Spain was moreover to be free to require from the United

War convention between France and Spain, April 12, 1779.

States a renunciation of the whole basin of the St. Lawrence and the lakes, the navigation of the Mississippi, and all the country between that river and the Alleghanies.

Even if the vast region in question had remained unoccupied, it would have been folly for America to accept terms which would have wholly crippled her future development. But it was too late to propose them. America had been growing as well as fighting. The 'county' of Kentucky had been incorporated by the Virginia legislature as early as December 1776, George Rogers Clark being one of its first representatives. With the approval of Jefferson and others, Clark set out in June 1779 for the conquest of the country north-west of the Ohio, surprised Kaskaskia, occupied the whole Illinois region, and after some alternations of fortune, compelled the British lieutenant-governor with a handful of men to surrender at Vincennes (February 24, 1779). Further to the south, the Cherokees and other tribes south of the Ohio having invaded the western American frontier from Georgia to Pennsylvania, were crushed, their towns burnt, their fields wasted, their cattle driven away (April 1779). During the whole of the year emigration flowed over the mountains; the Cumberland River country, in what is now Tennessee, was occupied. Further south yet, Natchez had already been occupied by a detachment which had descended the Ohio and Mississippi. Thus the eastern half of the Mississippi basin was virtually in the hands of the United States at the time when Spain proposed to exclude them from it.

The north-western territory coveted by Spain, but occupied by the backwoodsmen.

The convention between France and Spain was at first kept secret, and it was not till June 16, 1779, that war was actually declared between England and Spain. Such a provocation only roused the spirit of king and people in England. The House of Commons pledged to the crown the support of the nation, Burke and Fox joining with the Tories. Fifty thousand militia were enrolled, in addition to 50,000 troops. The funds fell only one per cent. But there was a growing impatience of the war with America. Motions against it in different forms, by Lord John Cavendish in the Commons, and by the Duke of Richmond in the Lords, received increased support. The king alone was obdurate. In his strange style, he admitted now that no man could allege that 'the laying of a tax was deserving all the evils that have arisen from it. . . . without being thought more fit for Bedlam than a seat in the senate.' But every man 'not willing to sacrifice every object to a momentary and inglorious peace,' must concur with him in thinking that England could 'never submit to' American independence. He did not yet despair that, with Clinton's activity and the Indians in their rear, the provinces would soon submit. Before he would 'hear of any man's readiness to take office' he should 'expect to see it signed under his own hand, that he is resolved to keep the empire entire, and that no troops shall consequently be withdrawn from thence, nor independence ever allowed' (June 21-22). So he prepared to face at once France, Spain, and America, and would only find fault with his admirals for over-caution.

England ready for war with Spain, but impatient of that with America. The king's obstinacy.

Three weeks after the declaration of war, Spain, flying at once at her most coveted prey, commenced the siege of Gibraltar (July 8). She was pressing France to invade England. Sixty transport vessels of 16,000 tons burthen were engaged for the purpose. The Spanish fleet was tardier than the French, but a junction was at last effected off the coast of Spain, and · bitter sight for English pride —the combined fleet, consisting of nearly seventy ships

Siege of Gibraltar; the combined fleets in the Channel.

of the line, cruised up and down the Channel, the English fleet of thirty-eight sail not being strong enough to attack it (August). It showed itself off Plymouth, picked up merchantmen, and even a blundering English man-of-war which fancied that it was rallying to its own flag. But it did nothing more. The French and Spanish commanders fell out ; dysentery raged in their fleets ; they withdrew to Brest and then separated. The Spanish admiral was ready to give his parole never more to serve against England, but was willing to serve against France. Fever and dysentery ravaged also the French camps in Brittany and Normandy, and the queen, Marie Antoinette, wrote to her mother that the doing of nothing at all had cost France a great deal of money.

There was more serious work in the North Sea, where Paul Jones, in the 'Bonhomme Richard' of forty guns, with two frigates of 36 and 32 and a brig of 12 guns (one frigate and the brig being French), endeavoured to intercept the English Baltic fleet, under the convoy of the 'Serapis' of 40, commanded by Captain Pearson, and the 'Countess of Scarborough,' of 20. The fight was desperate. The 'Serapis' was set on fire, but silenced the 'Bonhomme Richard's' guns, when the frigate 'Alliance,' one of her consorts, came up, and by her cross-fire compelled the 'Serapis' to strike her flag, as did also her consort. The 'Bonhomme Richard,' which had had 300 out of 375 men killed or wounded, foundered the next day, but Paul Jones took off his prizes to Holland (September 1779). When we add that in the West Indies two islands were lost to the French, that the Spaniards invaded Florida, and eventually reduced all the English settlements on the Mississippi, that British log-cutters on the coast of Honduras were attacked, and a fort taken and retaken ; that on the coast of Africa Senegal was taken by the French, and Goree by the English, an

Paul Jones's sea fight ; vast scale of the war.

idea will be conceived of the vast scale on which hostilities were carried on. We must also remember that in India a Mahratta war was proceeding, and the most formidable league being formed which the English had yet had to encounter,—one between Hyder Ali, the Mahrattas, and the Nizam, in whose service were able French officers.

Let us now return to the Southern United States, which were now the chief focus of the war. On September 1, 1779, the French Admiral d'Estaing appeared from the West Indies off the coast of Georgia, with thirty-three vessels, surprising four English ships of war. By the 10th the French troops had landed before Savannah, but they were not enough to invest the town, and it was not till the 23rd that General Lincoln was able to join them. In the meanwhile the garrison of Beaufort had succeeded in reaching Savannah across the swamps. The French fleet dreaded the autumnal gales, and after cannonading the town for five days (October 4-9), an assault was decided on. It failed disastrously. The French and Americans lost at least 800 men—inflicting very slight loss in return. D'Estaing was wounded twice, and the gallant Pole, Pulaski, was mortally wounded (October 1-9). D'Estaing refused to renew the attack, and drew off with his fleet and troops. Lincoln withdrew to Charleston with the remnant of his army, and the South Carolina militia went home. A somewhat ludicrous success which the Americans gained in the partisan warfare which was being waged in Georgia may be considered worthy of mention. The scene of the incident was the Ogeechee river, where Captain French was posted with one hundred men and a squadron of five vessels, four of which were armed. Colonel White, of the Georgia line, with one officer and four men, by kindling fires in different places along the bank and laying out a large encampment, led Captain French to suppose that

Failure of the French and Americans before Savannah, October 9, 1779.

he was at the head of a large force, and by this means actually obtained the surrender of the entire squadron. This feat certainly rivals that of the Irishman who related that he captured three prisoners single-handed 'by surrounding them.'

In order to push on the war more vigorously in the south, Rhode Island was now evacuated (October 1779), and the troops from thence joined Sir H. Clinton's army in New York, which had itself received some reinforcements from Europe. Leaving General Kniphausen in command in New York, Clinton embarked 8,500 men (December 26), for Tybee in Georgia, as a place of rendezvous for an attack on Charleston. Bad sailing, bad weather, and privateers hindered or damaged the expedition. Nothing was ready before the end of January, nor did the British troops come in sight of Charleston before February 26. But Lincoln, drawing all disposable forces into the town—a course of conduct of which Washington 'dreaded the event'—allowed himself to be caught as in a trap. The town was untenable, the inhabitants were disaffected almost to a man. On May 12 he capitulated, surrendering 4 frigates, 400 pieces of artillery, and a large number of prisoners, the militia being allowed to return home on parole. Clinton went back to New York, leaving 5,000 men with Lord Cornwallis, who was invested with a separate command, besides 1,000 men in Georgia. By the end of June 1780 Lord Cornwallis reported that all resistance was at an end in Georgia. But the severe measures taken by the British commanders, including a proclamation which required all the inhabitants to give actual assistance to the royal cause, as well as frequent confiscations, especially of slaves, alienated the people more and more.

Rhode Island evacuated by the British; Charleston taken (May 12, 1780), and South Carolina subdued.

The winter of 1779-80, strange to say, was worse for

the main army under Washington than the previous one. The winter itself was early and unusually rigorous. The Americans were more and more disposed to throw the burthen of the war on their allies. Gérard, the French minister in America, did not fear to express to his own court his regret that Spain should have joined in the war, since 'just in proportion as accessions to the means of opposing the enemy were afforded by foreign powers, the Americans became inactive and backward in their own efforts' (September 10, 1779). The revolution seemed bankrupt. There were 200 millions of paper dollars in circulation, but forty paper dollars were worth only one in specie; a pair of boots cost 600 dollars. In the early part of January the troops, both officers and men, were for a fortnight almost perishing for want of bread and meat, the whole time with a very scanty allowance of either, and frequently destitute of both.' The men began to plunder on their own account, and a scheme by which the several States were to furnish specific quantities of certain supplies, to be repaid by Congress, utterly broke down. Washington had again to seize provisions for them. A kind of strike was threatened by a number of officers, who declared that they must resign by a given day unless they could be better provided for. Washington wrote (April 3, 1780). 'There never has been a stage of the war in which the dissatisfaction has been so general or alarming.' A committee of Congress reported that the army was unpaid for five months, that it seldom had more than six days' provisions in advance, and was on several occasions for successive days without meat; that every department of the army was without money, and had not even the shadow of credit left; and that the patience of the soldiers was on the point of being exhausted. A mutiny in the Connecticut regiments was only with difficulty suppressed. In the first week in

[margin note: Another gloomy winter for Washington. Supineness of the Americans.]

June Washington had only 3,760 men fit for duty. Not a recruit could be obtained for six months for less than 100 hard dollars. La Fayette indeed, who had returned to France to obtain further aid, came back in April, announcing the speedy arrival of a French fleet with troops, in two divisions. When in July the first division of 6,000 men under Count de Rochambeau came into Newport harbour, Rhode Island, Washington had neither men nor supplies to co-operate with them. The second division never appeared, being blockaded in Brest, and a new British fleet ere long blockaded the first in Newport. At a time when Washington was empowered by Congress to carry on his operations beyond the limits of the United States, so as to act in concert with the French and Spanish in the West Indies, he was reduced ' to the painful alternative either of dismissing a part of the militia now assembling . . . or letting them come forward to starve.' On January 1 following, one half of his present forces would dissolve, and ' the shadow of an army that would remain would have every motive, except mere patriotism, to abandon the service.' If ' either the temper or the resources of the country ' would not admit of an alteration, they might ' expect soon to be reduced to the humiliating condition of seeing the cause of America, in America, upheld by foreign arms.' If ' something satisfactory ' were not done, ' the army (already so much reduced in officers by daily resignations as not to have a sufficiency to do the common duties of it) must either cease to exist at the end of a campaign,' or would ' exhibit an example of more virtue, fortitude, self-denial, and perseverance' than had ' perhaps ever yet been paralleled in the history of human enthusiasm.' Nothing on the other hand was done on the English side beyond an incursion into New Jersey.

It was on the seas that the war was now the most
active. A great seaman had appeared on the
English side. When the war with France
broke out in 1778 Admiral Rodney was in
Paris. He wished to return to England, but his creditors
would not let him go. Those were, however, the days
when war had its chivalry. An old French marshal, De
Biron, lent him 1,000 louis to free himself. He placed
his services at the disposal of the Admiralty, but his politics were not those of the ministry; for a twelvemonth he
could get no employment. At last (October 1, 1779) he
was appointed commander-in-chief on the Leeward
Islands and Barbadoes station, but with instructions in
the first instance to relieve Gibraltar. He put to sea three
days before the New Year, one of the king's sons, afterwards King William IV., serving on board his fleet as
midshipman. On January 8 he took a Spanish merchant
fleet of 15 sail, with 7 vessels of war. On the 16th, off
Cape St. Vincent, he defeated the Spanish admiral
Langara, taking or destroying 7 out of 11 ships of the
line, then relieved successively Gibraltar and Minorca,
and sailed for the West Indies. Here his success was
for the time less brilliant. He engaged the French fleet
under Count de Guichen more than once (April and
May), but some of his officers failed to support him sufficiently, and the actions were indecisive, nor did he
succeed in preventing the junction of the French and
Spanish fleets (June). But nothing came of this junction.
Again the two admirals disagreed; again disease broke
out in the fleets; again they separated, the Spanish
ships returning to Havana, the French to France. Rodney
sailed for the coast of **North America to** co-operate with
Sir Henry Clinton.

An abortive and insane operation of the years 1779-80
on the British side deserves to be mentioned **for** the sake

The war at sea: Rodney.

of the post-captain who led it. A party of troops was sent to cross Central America by the river San Juan and the lakes Nicaragua and Leon into the Pacific, on board the 'Hinchinbroke.' The mission of Post-Captain Nelson ended at the San Juan River; but as there was no one capable of directing the expedition, he went up the river and took 12 forts, but was beaten back by the deadly climate, scarcely 300 men out of 1,800 surviving to return, and his own health being for the time wholly shattered. Meanwhile another belligerent was being dragged into the fray. Of all the neutral powers, Holland—or, to speak more correctly, the Netherlands — was the one whose trade was the most extensive, and which consequently profited most through the war, on the one hand by the opening of the American ports to trade, on the other by fetching and carrying for the belligerents. England had early sought to engage Holland in the war on her side, on the plea of old treaty engagements, which the Dutch did not admit to be applicable. The English claim of a right to search neutral vessels for the enemy's goods, and the wide interpretation she gave to the term 'naval stores' viewed as contraband of war, pressed hardly on Dutch trade. On the other hand the shelter given in Dutch ports to Paul Jones and to his prizes was made a ground of bitter complaint by the English. In spite of these complaints, he was allowed to leave the Texel with his prizes (December 27). Four days later a Dutch merchant fleet, proceeding to Brest under the convoy of five Dutch ships of war, was stopped in the Channel by an English squadron under Captain Fielding, who claimed to search the traders. This was refused, and a shallop sent for the purpose was fired upon. Hereupon the English fired into the flagship, which, after returning a broadside, struck her colours, and those of the merchantmen that

Nelson in Central America. England's quarrel with Holland.

failed to escape were taken into Portsmouth. A few months later the existing freedom of trade between England and Holland was temporarily suspended, but it was not till nearly the end of the year that war was actually declared.

The capture of the Dutch fleet, however, together with that of two Russian merchantmen by Spain, helped on a measure to which Frederick of Prussia had for some time been urging the Empress of Russia, and which, though nominally directed against all the belligerents, told especially against England, viz. the formation of the 'armed neutrality.' On March 8 Russia issued a declaration, laying down certain principles (some of which, though not all, have been in our days acceded to by England herself), viz. the free navigation of neutral ships, even from port to port on a belligerent coast; freedom of all goods on free ships, contraband of war only excepted; limitation of contraband of war to arms and ammunition; effectual blockades. To maintain these principles the empress armed her fleets, and invited Sweden, Denmark, Portugal, and the Netherlands to join with her. Before any of the four states so invited had replied to the invitation, two of the belligerents, Spain and France, had eagerly accepted the principles of the declaration (April 1780), in doing which they were followed by Prussia. Thus encouraged, Denmark and Sweden entered into treaties for mutual support with Russia. Before the end of the year the Emperor came in, the United States having also accepted the principles of the Russian declaration in October.

The armed neutrality.

In England itself some singular events had occurred. During the recess two of the ministers, Lords Weymouth and Gower, resigned, the latter, at least, on account of disagreement with his colleagues on the American question, and Lord North was always pressing for leave to follow their example. Overtures were made, but in vain, to Lords Camden and Shelburne to join the ministry. Parliament met on November 25. The state of Ireland was beginning to cause great disquiet; 60,000 volunteers were in arms. Perfect tranquillity prevailed; but non-importation agreements against England had been entered into, and an address of the Irish parliament to the crown for freedom of trade and other matters had been carried, and had been followed by a vote of supply limited to six months (November 15). The king's speech did not mention America, but congratulated the country on the failure of the French and Spanish attempt at invasion, and called attention to the state of Ireland. Lord North admitted that the policy hitherto pursued towards Ireland had been misjudged, and his speech foreshadowed further concessions, beyond some trifling ones granted in the last two sessions, both to Irish trade generally and to Roman Catholics as such. The apprehensions of the anti-Romish party seem to have been violently excited by this course of conduct. On the other hand the classes which till now had supported the ministry were getting tired of the war. On December 30, at a meeting of 600 gentlemen whose collective fortune was said to be larger than that of the whole House of Commons, a committee of sixty-one members, known as the Yorkshire Committee, was appointed by the county of York to petition parliament and form an association for financial and parliamentary reform. Corresponding committees were formed in other counties and cities, including the city of London. Side by side with these were formed other associations, in Scotland as well as in England, against further concessions to the Roman Catholics. The two movements seem not to have been clearly distinguished by outsiders, and may

Ireland; the Yorkshire Committee; the Protestant Association and Lord George Gordon.

indeed often have run into one. Thus it is difficult from Walpole's letters of January and February 1780 to discern whether, in speaking of associations and 'orders under the title of petitions,' he means those of the financial and parliamentary reformers, or of the anti-popery men. At any rate the associations of the latter were organized into one as the 'Protestant Association.' Its president was Lord George Gordon, a half-crazy M.P., who, obtaining an interview from the king towards the end of January, read to him for an hour out of a pamphlet he had written, and when it became too dark, left only on a promise that the king would finish reading it himself. In the early days of February there were already anti-popery riots in Scotland.

By February 6 petitions had come in from over twenty counties, besides several towns. On the 8th Burke presented a plan for economic reform, to include a diminution of the influence of the crown. On March 13 he defeated the ministry. On April 6 Dunning brought forward in committee a celebrated resolution, 'that it is the opinion of this committee that the influence of the crown has increased, is increasing, and ought to be diminished,' and to the surprise of everybody, carried it by a majority of 48, whilst another resolution as to the competency of the House of Commons to correct abuses in the civil list passed also. But ministers, instead of throwing up office, obtained an adjournment of the House, and by April 24, when it met again, its temper had changed. A new motion of Dunning's, against prorogation or dissolution until the demands of the petitioners were satisfied, was rejected by 254 to 203.

Burke's plan of Economic Reform ; Dunning's resolution.

The parliamentary warfare went on with diminishing excitement, when suddenly the strangest event of the century enforced a temporary truce of parties, namely, the London No-popery or Lord George Gordon riots, lasting from Friday, June 2, to Thursday, June 8, until the last two days of which time London was left virtually without resistance in the hands of the mob, which destroyed chapels and houses at their will, stormed Newgate, attacked the Bank, though without taking any lives, and were at last put down only by a large force of soldiers and militia, with terrible slaughter; 285 civilians were killed or died of their wounds, and 173 were taken, seriously wounded, to the hospitals, besides those that perished in the flames of the numerous fires or were carried home to their friends. The total loss of property was said to be 180,000*l*. The next day Lord George Gordon was committed to the Tower on a charge of treason. Similar riots were being attempted in Bath, Bristol, and Hull, but were checked everywhere by the magistrates. On the 19th parliament met, after having adjourned in consequence of the riots. Resolutions were passed refusing to repeal the act for the relief of Roman Catholics. On July 6 those of the rioters who had been arrested were brought to trial. 'They are,' wrote Walpole, 'apprentices, women, a black girl, and two or three escaped convicts. And these Catilines, without plan, plot, connection, or object, threw a million of inhabitants into consternation, burned their houses about their ears, besieged the parliament, drove it to adjourn for ten days, and have saddled the capital with 10,000 men.' Out of those that were tried sixty were found guilty; forty were sentenced to death, and twenty of them executed; the rest were transported. Lord George Gordon, however, who was tried in the early part of the following year, was acquitted. He eventually became a Jew, and died of gaol fever whilst in prison for libel.

The London No-popery riots, June 2-8, 1780.

The No-popery riots, occurring as they did in the midst

180   *The War of American Independence.*   A.D.

of a war with three enemies at once, whilst a fourth was
being provoked into hostility, and almost all the
remainder of the European powers were arming,
virtually against England, on the plea of neutrality, show how comparatively indifferent that war really
was to a large body of the English people. Yet the riots
helped to prolong it. Spain had no sooner got into
the war than she was anxious to get out of it. She had
been negotiating since November 1779. If she could
only recover Gibraltar, she was ready to cede Porto
Rico and Oran, to pay a large sum of money, and pledge
herself not to help France. But the No-popery riots
raised the angriest feelings both in the Spanish king
and people, and peace was further off again.

Spanish negotiations stopped by the riots.

In America the South continued throughout the year
1780 to be the chief, if not the only seat of active
warfare. In South Carolina, as has been
stated, resistance was at an end. But refugees
from that State in North Carolina, who had
formed themselves into a partisan band under
Colonel Sumpter, previously in command of a
continental regiment, began with some success a guerrilla
warfare. A surprise by him of a British post at Hanging Rock (August 6) may be noticed, on account of the
presence in his ranks of a boy of thirteen, who was to be
one of the most remarkable presidents of the United
States,—Andrew Jackson. Meanwhile forces were being
sent from the north, Washington detaching De Kalb with
nearly 3,000 men, Virginia sending militiamen and arms,
till at last General Gates, who was placed in the independent command of the forces, found himself at the head of
a 'grand army,' as he termed it, which outnumbered the
British. He met Lords Cornwallis and Rawdon at
Camden. The day was disastrous to the Americans.
The Virginia militia threw down their arms and made

The war in South Carolina: battle of Camden (August 16, 1780).

for the woods 'with such speed that not more than three of them were killed or wounded.' The North Carolina militia, a few excepted, did the same, so that 'nearly two-thirds of the army fled without firing a shot. Only Washington's Maryland and Delaware troops held their ground, and De Kalb's division in particular had the advantage till the last. The American loss, according to British accounts, was 2,000 in killed, wounded, and prisoners. The whole of the artillery (eight field-pieces) was taken, and almost all the baggage. The whole army was dispersed, all but one hundred continentals, who were led off through the swamps. De Kalb had been mortally wounded, and died after three days. The Americans, General Gates foremost, fled as far as Charlotte, North Carolina, and Gates himself pushed on to Hillsborough, where the North Carolina legislature was about to meet, riding more than 200 miles in three days and a half. There now remained only Sumpter, who had been detached before the battle with 800 men to cut off a British convoy, and had succeeded in his errand. He was in turn surprised by Colonel Tarleton, who, with one hundred dragoons and sixty light infantry, cut his corps to pieces, taking two or three hundred prisoners, killing or wounding 150, and recovering all the captures. Four days after the battle of Camden, Sumpter rode into Charlotte alone, bareheaded, on a horse barebacked.

But the tide was now on the turn. Lord Cornwallis's severities once more irritated the people. Partisan bands under James Williams, Marion, and ere long again Sumpter, kept up a warfare of surprises. Through Marion's influence, according to Lord Cornwallis himself, there was scarcely an inhabitant between the Pedee and the Santee, who was not in arms against the British, and

<small>Cornwallis's march into North Carolina checked. American partisans. Greene in command.</small>

almost the whole country seemed on the eve of a revolt.
Lord Cornwallis nevertheless began in September his
march into North Carolina, hoping for aid from the
loyalists there. Detaching Major Ferguson to the high-
land country, he pressed on to Charlotte, and from thence
towards Salisbury. But on his way the tidings reached
him of a serious reverse which had befallen Major Ferguson. With a force of 1,125 men, of whom 125 only
were regulars, he had been attacked at King's Mountain,
by one of Virginians and North Carolinians, defeated,
himself killed, and the whole force obliged to surrender,
648 being made prisoners, besides 456 killed and
wounded (October 7). Cornwallis now fell back into
South Carolina, harassed on his way by the militia
and by the peasantry, whilst Marion and Sumpter were
intercepting supplies and surprising posts. At Blackstock Sumpter won from Tarleton a return match. Re-
lying on previous successes, before his light infantry
could come up, he dashed with 250 horsemen up a hill-
side at Sumpter's superior force. This time the Americans held their own. The English 63rd lost its commanding officer and two lieutenants, with one third of its
privates, and Tarleton had to retreat, leaving his wounded
behind. But Sumpter himself was severely wounded
(November 20). Of far more consequence than any partisan success to the American cause was the appointment
of Greene in place of Gates to the command of the forces
south of the Delaware, but this time 'subject to the
control of the commander-in-chief' (October 30). Washington had originally recommended him for the post
when Gates was appointed, and there seems reason to
think that he was Washington's favourite officer. None
certainly ever showed more of his great commander's
spirit.

In the north but little was doing. Incursions had

been made into New York from Canada, two American forts had been taken, much grain destroyed, and British parties had pushed on almost to Saratoga. Some correspondence was also going on, much to Washington's anxiety, between the leaders in Vermont, which Congress still refused to acknowledge as separate from New York, and the British authorities. Otherwise Washington and Clinton continued watching each other, each too weak, or deeming himself so, for successful offensive warfare. But a new danger now threatened the American cause. *Little doing in the north.*

There was no braver soldier in the American ranks than Benedict Arnold, the hero of the Canadian campaign, the real victor at Stillwater. Placed in command at Philadelphia after the evacuation of the city by the British, he irritated the people by an overbearing manner and various arbitrary proceedings, gave way to extravagance, sank into debt, involved himself still further through disastrous speculations, and resorted, it is said, to fraud and peculation. Charges were brought against him by the Executive Council of Pennsylvania, and laid before Congress. A committee, appointed to report on the case, acquitted him except as to two charges, but four were eventually sent on to the commander-in-chief, and on these Arnold was tried by court-martial (Dec. 4, 1779–Jan. 26, 1780). On two he was acquitted, but he was found guilty of having illegally granted a passport to a vessel, and of having used some public waggons for private purposes. By order of the court he was publicly reprimanded by Washington. Whilst his trial was proceeding, his accounts during his Canada command were also passing through committee in Congress. These were found confused and irregular, and large deductions were reported. Deeming himself ill-used, he appealed in vain against the *Arnold's treason, Sept. 1780.*

decision. Mortification and chagrin turned him into a traitor. He began writing anonymously to Sir Henry Clinton. Eighteen months later, having obtained the command at West Point, the most important post of any on the American side, he offered to Sir Henry to hand over to the British both West Point and other posts in the highlands. Whilst Washington had gone to Hartford to meet the French commander, Major André, adjutant-general of the British army, was sent up the Hudson in the 'Vulture' sloop of war to confer with Arnold. Terms were settled; Arnold was to receive 10,000*l.* and a brigadier-generalship. Plans of West Point, and a statement of its condition, were given to André, who hid them in his stockings. But meanwhile the 'Vulture' had been compelled to change her position. André could no longer be carried on board, and had to return to New York on foot, with a pass from Arnold under the name of John Anderson. Almost within sight of the British lines he was stopped by three militiamen, whom he tried in vain to bribe, was searched, and on the discovery of the compromising papers taken to the nearest American post. On learning his capture, Arnold hastily escaped in his barge to the 'Vulture' (September 25, 1780). André, as soon as he knew that Arnold was safe, declared his real name and rank. Tried by court-martial as a spy, he defended himself, declaring that he could be no spy, as he had entered the lines under a flag of truce on the invitation of an American general—a specious but scarcely tenable plea. He was found guilty, and could not even obtain the privilege of being shot instead of hanged. Though the justice of his sentence can hardly be denied, his execution (October 2, 1780) was useless, and is one of the few blots on Washington's fair fame. He lies now in Westminster Abbey. Arnold, though he never fulfilled his share of the contract, received his reward, and at the head of a legion of loyalists and deserters did, as we shall see, some damage to his former country; but he never distinguished himself again, and remained for all future time 'the traitor Arnold.' For the gallant young victim of his treason, André, universal sympathy has ever been felt on both sides of the Atlantic.

Not much was done in the war during the year 1780 elsewhere than in America, except in India, where Hyder Ali inflicted a severe defeat on Colonel Baillie, and might have taken Madras had he pursued his enemy. British trade was seriously damaged through the capture not only of the Quebec fleet by the Americans, but of the East and West India fleets by the Spaniards, who took them into Cadiz with 2,865 prisoners. The capture of a dozen French merchantmen from St. Domingo was a poor set-off to such losses. *The war in India and at sea, 1780.*

Parliament had been dissolved on September 1, and the new parliament had met on October 31. The new members were as many as 113 in number, and among them were the younger Pitt, Sheridan, and Wilberforce. The ministers were at first triumphant. The great event of the autumn was the declaration of war against Holland (December 20), which followed the accession of the latter to the armed neutrality. 'This good town,' wrote Horace Walpole from London, to Mason, January 4, 1781, 'is quite happy, for it has gotten a new plaything, a Dutch war, and the folks who are to gain by privateering have persuaded those who are to pay the piper to dance for joy.' Burke's plan of economical reform was again brought forward and again rejected. *The new Parliament; war with Holland declared, Dec. 20, 1780.*

An attack upon Jersey by the French in the early part of the year was easily beaten off. Spain was pressing on the siege of Gibraltar. She had prevailed on the Emperor of Morocco, from whose green hills the town then, as now, was mainly victualled, to *The war in Europe, 1781.*

refuse supplies, and scurvy had begun to rage, when the place was again relieved by Admiral Darby. A furious bombardment ensued. Nearly 80,000 balls and shells were poured in; the town was almost entirely destroyed, and the inhabitants took refuge to the south of the rock; but only about 70 persons were killed and wounded. In Minorca St. Philip's castle was besieged, and held out gallantly for months under General Murray. The combined fleets of France and Spain occupied the mouth of the Channel from Scilly to Ushant. An indecisive action took place off the Doggerbank between an English and a Dutch fleet (August 5).

Before the actual declaration of war, orders had been sent to Rodney to seize the Dutch island of St. Eustace,

Seizure of St. Eustace Feb. 3, 1781; the war in the West Indies, Florida, and India, 1781.

a free port, and probably then as rich a mart of trade as the Danish free port of St. Thomas afterwards became. On February 3, 1781, the rupture not being yet known, he carried out his orders. The prize was a splendid one. It included 3,000,000*l.* of merchandise, 150 merchantmen, a Dutch frigate and five smaller ships of war. To these were soon added 30 more merchantmen with a 60-gun ship as their convoy, overtaken on their way to Europe by a detachment from the English fleet, and 17 more which entered the harbour after the capture, the Dutch flag still flying. The other Dutch colonies in the West Indies, Demerara, Essequibo, Berbice, were reduced in March. But Rodney had to fight an indecisive action with the French fleet on April 29; on June 2 Tobago capitulated to the French, and before the end of the year they retook St. Eustatius from the English, and also took St. Martin's. On the southern coast of North America Pensacola capitulated to the Spaniards after a most gallant defence, and Spain left the British troops free to serve against the United States (March 9,

1781). In India Sir Eyre Coote disarmed the French of Pondicherry, who had risen on the arrival of a French fleet, and in a glorious campaign drove back the vastly superior forces of Hyder Ali, though at the cost of a third of his troops, whilst further north the war with the Mahrattas was virtually brought to a close by a night surprise of the latter (March 27, 1781). The Dutch settlements in India were also attacked, and Negapatam was reduced (November 1781).

Although England now stood alone against three foreign enemies, besides her own revolted colonies, it would have been difficult to say on which side was the balance of advantage. France was anxious for peace. Necker had already at the close of the last year written secretly to Lord North proposing a truce on the basis, diplomatically termed, of *uti possidetis*, each party to keep possession of what he had. A few months later Vergennes in turn took up the idea, but not liking to propose it, handed it over to the Austrian minister Kaunitz, who attempted a mediation and proposed a peace congress at Vienna, but failed. France, with nearly 160,000,000*l*. sterling of debt, was verging on bankruptcy, yet Necker was prevailed upon to consent to a loan of 10,000,000 more of French livres to America, to be negotiated in Holland in the name of the King of France. The negotiator, Laurens, was a South Carolinian, and the first use he made of it was to pay a debt of his own State to Holland. Presently Necker was dismissed from office. It was after all in America that the fate of the war must be decided.

France anxious for peace. Mediation of Austria.

Not however in the north. The winter of 1780–1 was a gloomier one than any yet for the main army under Washington. By November 20, 1780, the soldiers had been for ten months without pay. The paper money of the Congress was made more worthless still by a flood of

British forgeries. Washington deemed a foreign loan

<small>Washington's army during the winter of 1780-1. Mutinies.</small> 'indispensably necessary for the continuance of the war.' On the night of January 1, 1781, the whole of the Pennsylvanian troops, three regiments only excepted, mutinied and declared that they would march to Philadelphia to obtain redress. In endeavouring to restrain them one officer was killed, another mortally and several less severely wounded. The mutineers met with their bayonets a favourite general, Wayne, who vainly tried to stop them, and commenced their march, 1,300 strong, with six pieces of artillery. They were not, indeed, traitors, and when Sir H. Clinton sent some men to tempt them over with advantageous terms to the British side, they handed over his emissaries to General Wayne for execution. A committee of Congress met the mutineers, and compromised matters by discharging many, and giving 40 days' furloughs to others. The New Jersey brigade was the next to revolt (January 20), and Washington had to resort to force, and hang five of the ringleaders (January 27). Events like these did not promote recruiting. Washington's favourite plan of enlisting men for the war failed so completely that some of the States had to resort again to temporary enlistments (April 1); and by May, out of 37,000 men requisitioned by Congress, the whole of the northern States, from New Jersey to New Hampshire, had not 7,000 infantry in the field. Compelled to resort to impressment for obtaining supplies, Washington wrote in his Diary (May 1): 'We are daily and hourly oppressing the people, souring their tempers and alienating their affections.'

Still, the worst of the financial crisis was tided over through the exertions of Robert Morris, appointed superintendent of finance (February 1781). By means of a bank which he established, called the Bank of North

America, he succeeded on the whole from henceforth in meeting the engagements of the army, going indeed so far as to procure supplies on his own credit. A still more important event was the adoption by the last outstanding State (March 1, 1781) of the Articles of Confederation approved of by Congress since 1777. The chief cause of delay had been a question of waste lands and boundaries. It will be recollected that many of the States had been chartered with very extensive limits, extending often to the Pacific Ocean. These States claimed the benefit of their charters, and the ownership of all waste lands within the purview of those charters. The smaller States with fixed limits, on the other hand—Rhode Island, Delaware, New Jersey, Maryland—claimed that Congress should fix boundaries for all, and that the waste lands should belong to the Union at large. All, however, except Maryland had acceded to the Confederation by the end of 1779. Eventually New York (1780) consented to let Congress fix her western boundaries, and ceded her public lands to the Union. A year later Virginia, not to be outdone, ceded all her claims to what was known as the north-western territory, *i.e.* that to the N.W. of the Ohio. Thus the bone of contention was removed, and Maryland signed the articles. Yet at the very moment when the revolted colonies were thus drawing closer together the bond of union, Lord George Germain, the English secretary of state, was writing to Sir Henry Clinton (March 7), in a despatch afterwards intercepted: ' So very contemptible is the rebel force now in all parts, and so vast is our superiority everywhere, that no resistance on their part is to be apprehended that can materially obstruct the progress of the king's arms in the speedy suppression of the rebellion.'

The crisis tided over, the Articles of Confederation finally signed March 1, 1781

In the south the war was about to take a new aspect

under Gates's successor, the former Quaker blacksmith, Greene.

The state of things as Greene found it (December 1780) seemed well-nigh desperate. He had only 2,307 men, of whom one-half were militia, and only 800 were properly clothed and equipped. His army, to use his own words, was 'rather a shadow than a substance .... artillery, baggage, stores, everything had gone by the board on the fatal day of the recent defeat' (*i.e.* at Camden). The soldiers went and came as they pleased, and were only stopped from doing so when one of them was shot as a deserter. Moving on himself to the Pedee river, he sent General Morgan with 1,000 men into the north-west of South Carolina, towards the junction of the Broad and Pacolet rivers. Here at a place called the Cowpens (from one of those enclosures into which the numerous herds of cattle are driven for marking), Morgan was attacked by Tarleton with somewhat superior forces. The Americans were already outflanked on both sides, when a rear-movement of the Maryland division, which was mistaken for a breaking of the American line, drew on in turn the main body of the British under a murderous cross-fire. They were thrown into disorder, the Americans charged on all sides, and the day ended in the utter defeat of the English.

Greene in the south. Battle of the Cowpens January 17, 1781.

The fame of the victory spread far and wide. Lord Cornwallis, writing to Sir Henry Clinton the day after the battle, called it an 'unexpected and extraordinary event,' of which it was 'impossible to foresee all the consequences.' But he was bent upon an offensive campaign, in which, marching through North Carolina and Virginia, he should form a junction on the Chesapeake with the Northern British army. As the first step towards this, Arnold had already been sent by Clinton with 1,600 men

Lord Cornwallis advances again into North Carolina, Greene retreating.

to the James river (January 2), and had plundered and burnt Richmond. So leaving Lord Rawdon with a body of troops in South Carolina, Cornwallis pushed across the border into North Carolina, destroying all superfluous baggage, and proceeding mostly by forced marches. Too weak to resist the English advance, although Morgan with his victorious troops had rejoined him, Greene retreated before Cornwallis for 200 miles to the north bank of the Dan river, which he crossed the night before his pursuer reached it. Of his troops, many hundreds tracked 'the ground with their bloody feet;' they had but one blanket to four men, besides being unpaid and irregularly fed. Lord Cornwallis now proceeded by easier stages to Hillsborough, whence he issued a proclamation (February 20), inviting all loyal subjects to repair to his standard. The loyalists were indeed numerous, and as many as seven companies were formed in a day. But a body of 300 were cut to pieces by a larger force of Americans under Pickens and Lee, with 'dreadful carnage,' say the American accounts, although 'begging quarter,' say the English. The event seems to have struck terror into their party, for Lord Cornwallis wrote of his being 'among timid friends, and adjoining to inveterate rebels.'

After some marching and counter-marching, Greene at last accepted battle at Guilford Court House (March 15). His forces were, by American accounts even, twice as many as the 1,900 of Cornwallis. The Americans were very strongly posted, but in three separate positions. The first and strongest, manned by North Carolina militia, was easily taken, the militiamen taking to their heels after a first or second shot, and nearly one-half without firing at all. The second position was obstinately contested by the Virginia brigade, but a bayonet charge finally dislodged them. Round the third, commanded by Greene

Battle of Guilford Court House, March 15, 1781; Cornwallis falls back to the coast.

himself, the battle raged long with varying success. At last Greene retreated, leaving his artillery behind, but the victory was dearly won. Out of the small British force, 570 were killed or wounded, whilst the Americans lost only 419, all but 93 continentals. The battle, moreover, had been fought 200 miles from Cornwallis's communications, and his march henceforth became a retreat, in which he was in turn pursued by Greene. Falling back towards the coast, he reached Wilmington (April 7) with the relics of his army, and all North Carolina was recovered by the Americans. Cornwallis was still bent on reaching Virginia.

Hither La Fayette had been sent to oppose Arnold. His troops were as usual without pay or supplies. With characteristic generosity—serving, it will be remembered, without pay—he borrowed 2,000*l.* to equip them. With the assistance of Steuben at the head of a body of militia, he succeeded in keeping in check the already superior British force. In the last days of April, Cornwallis, without Clinton's authority, left Wilmington with 1,435 men, and marched without opposition to Petersburg in Virginia. Clinton trembled for 'the fatal consequences' which might ensue. But Lord George Germain was entirely with Cornwallis, and every despatch urged the importance of pushing the war in Virginia.

<small>La Fayette and Arnold in Virginia. Cornwallis leaves Wilmington (April).</small>

Before Cornwallis had even reached Wilmington, Greene was already taking measures for recovering South Carolina and Georgia. Three posts commanded the interior of the former, Camden and Ninety-six in South Carolina, and Augusta in Georgia. Lee and Marion were sent to operate between Camden and Charleston, Sumpter between Camden and Ninety-six, Pickens between Ninety-six and Augusta. Greene himself moved upon Camden. Near

<small>Greene recovers the greater part of South Carolina.</small>

this place he was attacked (April 18) in a well-chosen position by Lord Rawdon, with 800 or 900 men, Greene's own regulars alone outnumbering the English, whilst his total force, according to the English accounts, came up to 2,000 men. But he was defeated, losing rather more in killed and wounded than the English, who could, however, ill spare their loss of 258 men. Lord Rawdon at first pursued him, but Lee and Marion had meanwhile broken the connexion between Camden and Charleston. It became necessary to evacuate Camden, while Rawdon was obliged to retreat, marching down the north bank of the Santee. Before long the whole north-west of South Carolina had been recovered by the Americans, who took many prisoners through the surrender of the smaller posts. Then Augusta fell (June 5), whilst Ninety-six was besieged. An assault upon it, hastened by the approach of Lord Rawdon, failed, with severe loss; but it was too isolated to be thenceforth tenable, and was evacuated, whilst Lord Rawdon announced to the loyalists of the district that they could no longer be protected. He returned to Charleston ill and disgusted, and sailed before long for England. The result of the campaign had been that Greene had recovered the principal part of South Carolina, and had confined the English within the Santee, Congaree, and Edisto rivers. Thus Lord Cornwallis's rash advance into Virginia had thrown away the fruit of all previous successes in the south, and reduced the English dominion to a mere foothold or two. He himself was now convinced that the idea of the loyalists 'rising in any number and to any purpose' had 'totally failed,' and doubted whether the English force were sufficient for a war of conquest. Yet with eyes thus open did he rush upon his doom.

Whilst these things were taking place, the Opposition in the new House of Commons again endeavoured to put a stop to the war. Motions were made to this effect by James Hartley (May 30), by Fox (June 12). Fox declared that the report of Lord Cornwallis (after the battle of Guilford Court House), showed the war to be 'impracticable in its object, and ruinous in its progress.' The honours of the debate were, however, for the younger Pitt, who was declared to have equalled his father. He termed the war 'a most accursed war, wicked, barbarous, cruel, and unnatural,' and spoke of the 'impious course of enforcing unconditional submission.' The ministers won, but with diminishing majorities. The session was closed on July 18. The final catastrophe was not to be diverted by a timely peace.

Proceedings in parliament. Fox and the younger Pitt.

And yet never had America felt weaker. Her young navy had been annihilated; only two frigates remained. Congress had given up wrangling about the conditions of peace. Some of its members were in the pay of France. Boundaries, fisheries, the navigation of the Mississippi, the country west of the Ohio, all these points, hitherto deemed essential, were thrown overboard. Independence was to be the sole condition, and in the same breath such subserviency to France was acknowledged that the American commissioners were instructed not only 'to undertake nothing in their negotiations for peace or truce without the knowledge and concurrence of the ministers of the King of France,' but 'ultimately to govern themselves by their advice and opinion' (May 1781).

Weakness of America. Subserviency to France.

Cornwallis reached Petersburg on May 20. He sent Tarleton to Charlottesville, where the State legislature was sitting, and where seven of the members were taken prisoners. Meantime, he started himself in pursuit of La Fayette. With great adroitness, at the head of about equal forces, though with not nearly so many regulars, La Fayette

Cornwallis in Virginia. He withdraws to Yorktown (August 1781).

eluded and checked him; and the summer was spent in useless movements and in mere ravages, during which it is said that property to the amount of 3,000,000*l.* was destroyed. But Lord Cornwallis had received orders from Sir Henry Clinton to send back 3,000 men to New York, and to withdraw to a defensive position (June–July). He saw too late that his movement into Virginia must prove a failure, and wished to transfer the command to another general and return to Charleston. But in obedience to orders he withdrew (August 1-8) with his army to Yorktown and Gloucester—'a very advantageous place,' wrote La Fayette to Vergennes, 'for one who has the maritime superiority'—and a French fleet under De Grasse, bringing reinforcements, was then expected on the coast.

Whilst Cornwallis is fortifying himself in Yorktown, and Washington is doing his best to collect his forces for the final encounter, let us cast one more glance on the other fields of warfare in America. In South Carolina Greene was pushing what remained of the British forces more and more towards Charleston. A final engagement took place at Eutaw Springs (September 8), in which the English under Colonel Stuart, Lord Rawdon's successor, remained masters of the field through an unexpected rally, though losing not much less than 700 men against 555 on the American side. But they were too weak to hold their ground, and drew off in the night towards Charleston, after destroying 1,000 stand of arms, and leaving 70 wounded men behind. The struggle in the south was henceforth virtually closed, although Wilmington, Charleston, and Savannah remained in English hands. The English had fought like heroes, but most of their victories had been as fatal to them as defeats.

Battle of Eutaw Springs, September 8, 1781; the war at an end in the south.

Just two days before the battle of Eutaw Springs, the

war had cast up a last flicker in the extreme north.
Arnold, whom Cornwallis, on his arrival in Virginia, had sent back to New York, had been detached by Clinton against Connecticut, his native State, in order, if possible, to draw off either the French, or a portion of the main army. He plundered and burnt New London, and stormed Fort Griswold, garrisoned by some 150 militiamen under a colonel. Quarter was refused. This was Benedict Arnold's last exploit.

Arnold in Connecticut (September).

Meanwhile Washington had had time to effect a junction with the French forces. As early as May 21 he had agreed with Rochambeau that the war should be carried to the Chesapeake. In June the French from Rhode Island, including a newly arrived reinforcement of 1,500 men, left Newport for the Hudson river, whilst a timely succour in money of 2,500,000 French livres (out of a promised French loan of 6,000,000) also came in. Seeing himself thus strengthened, Washington for a time projected a combined attack on New York; Rochambeau preferred the plan of operations on the Chesapeake, which La Fayette also warmly supported, and the latter plan was finally decided on, in order to make sure of the support of the French admiral, Count de Grasse, who would not be able to remain off the coast beyond the middle of October, a time which was considered too early for the reduction of New York.

Junction of Washington and the French; operations on the Chesapeake decided on.

By August 21 the combined French and American troops were on the march. On the 23rd and 24th they crossed the Hudson without hindrance from Clinton, who was expecting to be attacked. It was September 2 before he began to suspect that New York was not their object. Meanwhile on August 31 De Grasse arrived in Chesapeake Bay with 28 ships of the line, having taken Lord Rawdon prisoner

The march to Virginia, August 1781.

while the latter was returning to Europe. A few days later he beat off the British fleet under Admiral Graves, and shortly after took two British frigates. Washington was pressing on. Having visited on the way, after more than six years' absence, his own estate at Mount Vernon, he reached Williamsburg on the 14th. The natural impetuosity of his usually self-restrained character betrays itself in a letter written the following day to General Lincoln:—'Every day we now lose is comparatively an age . . . hurry on then, my dear sir, with your troops on the wings of speed.' At the last moment a check came from the French admiral, who would have preferred to operate on New York, but Washington and La Fayette prevailed upon him to waive the plan, and join in the attack on Yorktown.

On September 28 the whole army advanced to within two miles of that place, which was completely invested, the French taking the left and the Americans the right, whilst another body under a French commander also invested Gloucester on the other side of the York river. Expecting succour, Cornwallis did not impede their operations. Trenches were opened on October 5. The batteries began their fire on the 9th and 10th; a frigate and three transports were set on fire by red-hot shot on the night of the 10th–11th. By the 11th the English could scarcely return the fire, and in the night the second parallel was begun within 100 yards of their lines. On the 14th two redoubts were taken by storm, one by the French, the other by the Americans. A desperate sally just before break of day on the 16th, at first successful, failed. On that night an attempt was made to cross the river to Gloucester Point, and cut a way through the French lines; but a violent storm prevented its success. The next day Cornwallis proposed a cessation of hostili-

Yorktown invested, September 28; Cornwallis surrenders, October 19.

ties, a capitulation was **concluded**, and on the 19th he surrendered Yorktown and Gloucester to Washington, with the troops and **100 pieces** of artillery, whilst the ships and sailors were **surrendered** to De Grasse. Clinton, after vainly trying a diversion through Arnold, **as** above mentioned, had **sailed with 7,000 men to** the relief **of Lord** Cornwallis **on the very** day of the surrender, and **only received the** news on reaching **the** Chesapeake, when he **returned to** New York.

One of Washington's aides-de-camp **bore the news to** Philadelphia. Reaching the **town** at night, he was near *Rejoicings in America.* being **taken** up **by a watchman** for **knocking** too **loud at** the President's door. **The old doorkeeper of Congress died for joy.** Washington gave a **free** pardon **to all military offenders.** There were public thanksgiving services, **votes** of thanks to the commanders and officers of the allied army; a commemorative marble column **was directed to be** erected at Yorktown itself; 2 stands **of** colours (out **of 28** captured) were presented to Washington, 2 field-pieces to Rochambeau.

The news **reached Lord** George Germain on **November 23.** He **communicated** it to Lord North, **who** *Proceedings in parliament, the ministers fiercely attacked meetings against the war.* took it **'as** he would have taken **a** bullet through **his** breast,' exclaiming, 'O God! it is all over.' Yet when, **a** few days later the king opened parliament, his speech reiterated his resolution to preserve America, and **expressed** the hope of being **able by** the valour of his fleets **and** armies to restore the blessings of peace to his dominions. The speech was fiercely attacked by Lord Shelburne in the Lords, by Fox, Burke, Pitt in the Commons. Fox declared **that** it meant, ' My rage for conquest is unquenched, my revenge unsated, nor can anything except the total subjugation of my revolted American subjects allay my animosity,' and threatened the ministers **with the** scaffold. Burke **compared the**

American war to the attempt of a man to shear a wolf because he had been accustomed to shear sheep. Lord North on the other hand declared that the late disaster in Virginia ought 'to impel, to urge, to animate' Englishmen; Lord George Germain, declared that he would never assent to reconciliation on the terms of American independence, as this country depended on America 'for its very existence.' The address was carried in both Houses by large majorities. But a fortnight later when Sir James Lowther moved a resolution that the attempt to reduce America by arms was impolitic and ought to be abandoned, Lord North avowed that it would be 'neither wise nor right to prosecute the war in America any longer on a continental plan . . . by sending fresh armies to march through the colonies, in order by those marches to subdue America to obedience.' This was a confession of failure, and Lowther's resolution was rejected by a reduced majority. Public meetings began to be held in London, Middlesex, Surrey, Westminster, asking that hostilities should be put a stop to. In this request they were joined by the West India merchants, though as yet these were ignorant of the extent to which their special trade was about to be affected.

On January 31, 1782, the French retook Demerara, and in February St. Kitt's, Nevis, and Montserrat surrendered to the Spaniards, so that of the Leeward Islands only Barbadoes and Antigua remained to the English. In the East more Dutch settlements had been reduced, and were again lost through jealousies between British commanders. The Cape of Good Hope proved too strong to be taken. A series of sea-actions fought between English fleets under Commodore Johnstone or Sir Edward Hughes and the French fleet under Suffrein, have been claimed as victories by historians of both nations. At any rate they did not prevent Suffrein from

The war almost everywhere disastrous to England. Minorca lost (Feb. 7, 1782).

being able always to refit, or from landing 3,000 men as auxiliaries to Hyder Ali, tidings of whose death (December 7, 1782) alone stopped the victorious progress of his son, henceforth Tippoo Sultan. But peace was concluded with the Mahrattas (May 17, 1782). Nearer home, Minorca had been surrendered to the French after a most gallant defence, whilst Admiral Kempenfelt returned home, after failing to intercept a superior French fleet. The mismanagement of the navy by Lord Sandwich now became a subject of loud complaint, and in the attacks upon him in parliament the majority of the ministers was seen to be waning.

The war with America had long lost all its popularity. England had been threatened with ruin to her trade if Weakness and fall of Lord North's ministry (March 20, 1782.) she lost her North American colonies, and after seven years' cessation of intercourse with them, thanks to the marvellous development of her manufacturing industry, she seemed to be none the worse. Lord George Germain, who was more especially identified in the public mind with these bugbear prophecies, had become so unpopular that Lord North himself asked him to resign; the king, however, insisting on giving him a peerage to show that no slur was put upon him. On February 22 General Conway moved an address against the further prosecution of the war, and this time the motion was defeated by a majority of one only (193 to 192). It was henceforth evident that the ministry was doomed. Five days later a similar address was carried by a majority of nineteen. The king still held out against all persuasion, Lord North always urging him to accept his resignation, and declaring in the House with truth that it was from no personal desire that he remained in office. The answer given to Conway's address being vague, the latter brought forward a second one, declaring enemies to the king and country those who would further prosecute the war on the continent of America. This time the motion was adopted without a division, and on the next day leave was given to bring in a bill for enabling the king to conclude a peace or a truce. The continuance of the ministry was impossible, and Lord North at last obtained his release from office, the king reminding him at parting, 'It is you that desert me, not I you.' On March 20, obtaining on a point of order precedence over a member who was to move a vote of want of confidence, Lord North announced his resignation, and the House adjourned. A long debate was expected; it was snowing, and Lord North's carriage was almost alone in attendance. As he went out, 'You see, gentlemen,' he said, turning to some of his opponents, 'the advantage of being in the secret.' No kindlier, pleasanter minister ever lost half an empire to his country; no minister ever did so much mischief, against his own better judgment, out of mere deference to a half-crazy sovereign.

The king, it seems, at first thought of withdrawing to Hanover, and it was with great difficulty that he was prevailed upon to accept a ministry (March 22) in which Rockingham was premier, Shelburne and Fox were secretaries of state, Conway commander-in-chief, Barré treasurer of the navy, Burke paymaster of the forces, Sheridan under-secretary of state. *The second Rockingham ministry: Shelburne treats with Franklin.* In the forming of this ministry it was made a condition in writing that there should be 'no veto to the independence of America.' Young Pitt, conscious of his power, stood aloof till he could enter the cabinet. The affairs of America were comprised in the Home Department, which Lord Shelburne took. He lost no time in sending Sir Guy Carleton as commander-in-chief to America in the place of Sir H. Clinton, with the most conciliatory instructions, and in putting himself in communication personally with **Henry** Laurens, a late president of Congress (who had been taken on the high seas, and was now a prisoner in England on parole), and with Franklin by means **of a** friendly letter through Richard Oswald, a Scotchman who had resided many years in **America,** 'a pacifical man.'

But America felt herself to be so weak, and knew England to be still so strong, that she could not yet believe in

<small>America so reduced that she cannot believe in peace.</small>

peace. Some desultory warfare was still being **carried on between** loyalists and republicans **in the C**arolinas, with much ravage and **massacre on both** sides, the result tending always against **the British** cause. **On the other** hand the American **treasury had been** drained of its last dollar by the beginning of January, and the States declared that **they could pay no taxes.** Two millions of dollars were **to have been paid by April 1**; not a cent was paid by the **23rd, and only 20,000 dollars by June 1.** There were only **10,000** soldiers in the northern army, clamouring as usual **for pay.** Under such circumstances the pacific overtures **of Sir Guy** Carleton, **who reached** New York in May, seemed too good to be true; both Washington and **the** Congress alike distrusted them, and a passport was refused for bringing despatches to Philadelphia.

Just now, indeed, occurred one of the most curious episodes of the period. The discontents of the army were **at** their height, and Washington **could**

<small>The crown offered to Washington.</small>

barely restrain **it** from violence. Robert Morris, the finance minister, unable to obtain money, was abused alike for asking it and for not giving it; 'baited,' as he wrote, 'by continual clamorous **demands;' 'paid by** invective' for 'the forfeiture of all **that is** valuable in life; tempted daily **to lay** down **a** burthen which pressed him to the earth.' **An** address **was** now presented to Washington from a number of officers and soldiers, setting forth the failure of justice from Congress, the advantages of a mixed form of government, and suggesting that their chief should take rule with the name of king. It met with a stern rebuke from Washington. But so weak was he that he wrote at the end of this month that if the British advanced he must evacuate his positions.

Negotiations meanwhile were going on on the British side, not only with America but with France, and to a trifling extent with Spain. With the second power they were hastened by a splendid victory of Rodney's in the West Indies over the French fleet under De Grasse, in which seven ships of the line and two frigates were captured, besides the French admiral and his flag-ship the 'Ville de Paris,' then the largest ship on the seas, which had taken part in the reduction of Yorktown; though, indeed, on the return passage she and four other of the prizes foundered with their crews, in a hurricane. Jamaica, which had been the object of the allied fleets, was thus saved to the English; but the Bahama Islands were surrendered to Spain, whilst in the far north La Pérouse, ere long to be better known as a scientific explorer, was destroying the settlements on the Hudson's Bay river.

Rodney's victory in the West Indies (April 12, 1782).

The death of Rockingham (July 1) did not impede the progress of negotiation, as Shelburne now took the premiership; but the ministry was weakened by the secession of Fox, Burke, and others. Pitt, on the other hand, joined the cabinet as chancellor of the exchequer, and Fox going at once into opposition, the rivalry between these two celebrated men, hitherto united in their politics, now began, which was only to end with their lives. Just about this time Georgia, where, in spite of the aid of the Creek and Choctaw Indians, the British had been gradually

The Shelburne ministry; evacuation of Savannah (July 12).

driven into Savannah, was recovered from them altogether through the evacuation of that place (July 12), the loyalists withdrawing into Florida, whilst the British regulars joined their comrades in Charleston, which was too strong to be conquered.

Although some movements on the northern frontier took place as late as February 1783, active warfare was now virtually reduced, except in the East, to the siege of Gibraltar, the prize for the sake of which Spain had against her will entered into the war, and which she was bent on recovering. This is not the place for relating that celebrated siege, with its bombardments and its sallies. We must content ourselves with mentioning the famous attack by the whole Spanish forces, ships, floating batteries, and land artillery, on September 13, 1782, and its triumphant repulse by the besieged, when the floating batteries were set on fire with red-hot balls. Shortly afterwards the place was revictualled by a fleet under Lord Howe, which next engaged the combined French and Spanish fleets in a decisive battle. Gibraltar was not yet to be recovered by Spain.

Active warfare confined to the siege of Gibraltar.

Negotiations had all this while been going on in Paris, but separately with the American commissioners, and with France. Franklin had at first treated alone, and all difficulties seemed by August to be at an end, when his colleague Jay arriving, and afterwards Adams, interposed new obstacles. In another month, however, the British negotiators laid before them an intercepted despatch from the French secretary of legation in Philadelphia, which showed underhand dealings on the part of France to the detriment of America. Jay's unwillingness to proceed was thus removed; and it was time that it should be. The loyalists of Pennsyl-

Progress of negotiations. preliminary articles of peace between England and America, Nov. 30, 1782.

vania, Maryland, Delaware, New York, were presenting addresses to Sir Guy Carleton against the negotiations, declaring their determination to resist the Congress. Washington wrote in October: 'The longsufferance of the army is almost exhausted; it is high time for a peace.' Although specifically instructed, as has been seen, to undertake nothing without the knowledge of the French ministry, and to 'govern themselves by their advice and opinion,' the American commissioners signed preliminary articles of peace behind the back of the French Government. Vergennes naturally complained. America was at that very moment begging a further loan of France. Franklin was obliged to eat humble pie; he acknowledged that he and his colleagues had been 'guilty of neglecting a point of *bienséance*,' and hoped it would be excused. The fact evidently is that he was determined to make peace at any price. France, indeed, was generous; she granted a loan of 6,000,000 livres, and paid down 600,000. But she was not just in her generosity, for to do this she was obliged to stop payment for a twelvemonth of her own bills of exchange, due in America and the East Indies. Spain, too, was so exhausted that in the course of the year she had had to borrow from Portugal at 8 per cent., whilst her paper was at a discount of 14. In fact, though standing alone against so many belligerents, England had suffered least of all.

On December 5 the session of parliament was opened, and the king announced his consent to the independence of the American colonies. 'In thus admitting their separation from the crown of Great Britain,' he said, 'I have sacrificed every consideration of my own to the wishes and opinion of the people. I make it my humble and earnest prayer to Almighty God that Great Britain may not feel the evils which might result from so great a dismemberment of

Opening of parliament, Nov. 5; the king's speech.

the empire, and that America may be free from those calamities which have formerly proved in the mother-country how essential monarchy is to the enjoyment of constitutional liberty. Religion, language, interest, affections, may, and I hope will yet prove a bond of permanent union between the two countries; to this end neither attention nor disposition shall be wanting on my part.' To the surprise of many the speech was disapproved by Fox and Burke, as well as by Lord North.

In the same month the French fleet left the coast of America, carrying with it the French troops, which had now been two years and a half in the country, and yet had never met the English except at Yorktown. Washington meanwhile was writing that the temper of the army was 'much soured,' and 'more irritable than at any period since the commencement of the war.'

<small>The French troops return to Europe.</small>

On January 20, 1783, the preliminaries of peace were signed in Paris between Great Britain, France, and Spain. The United States were acknowledged as free, sovereign, and independent, their frontier being marked by a line drawn from the north-west angle of Nova Scotia toward one of the heads of the Connecticut river, thence to Lake Ontario, and through the middle of that lake and of Lakes Erie and Huron to the Lake of the Woods, thence to the Mississippi, and along its course to Fort Mobile and the borders of Florida. The Americans obtained the right of fishing on the banks of Newfoundland and in the Gulf of the St. Lawrence; the whole course of the Mississippi was to be free to both nations. As between England and France there was substantially a general restitution of conquered territory, except that France kept Tobago; and there was some exchange of territory on the coast of Africa. Spain, unable to obtain Gibraltar, restored the

<small>Preliminaries of peace with France and Spain, January 20, 1783.</small>

Bahamas, but retained Minorca, and retained or obtained all Florida. The loyalists were recommended to the favourable consideration of Congress, which paid no heed to the recommendation.

Shortly after the conclusion of the general treaty, an armistice followed by a peace was concluded with Holland, on the same principle of mutual restitution, except that Holland lost Negapatam. The only enemy now in arms against England was Tippoo Sultan. There was fighting in India between him and his French allies on the one side, and the British on the other, after the date of the peace. When the news of this came, the French were recalled, and the sultan was invited to join in the peace. He refused to do so till he had reduced Mangalore, but having done this consented to treat on the basis of a mutual restoration of conquests (March 1784). Peace with Holland and with Tippoo Sultan.

The treaties of Paris were sharply assailed in parliament, chiefly as respects what was declared to be the desertion of the loyalists. A coalition between Fox and Lord North was now avowed, and amendments to the address were carried, then specific resolutions condemning ministers on account of the peace. Lord Shelburne resigned; and as Pitt declined to form a ministry, a coalition cabinet was formed under the Duke of Portland, comprising Fox and Lord North. Among the earliest acts of this ministry was the appointment of commissioners to inquire into the losses of the loyalists, and to allow half-pay to all who had served. From first to last over 12,000,000*l.* were paid to them. Fall of Shelburne; the coalition ministry (April 2, 1783).

The discontents in the American army were now even worse than ever. The chief grievance of the officers was that the half-pay for life, promised in 1780, had never been paid or even recognised by the requisite majority of States.

The officers offered to commute their claim for a fixed sum; but a majority of States could not be obtained even for this proposal. A meeting of officers was summoned, at which resolutions were to be offered that might have led to civil war. Washington came himself to the meeting and read an address, in which he urged patience, and pledged himself to leave nothing untried to obtain redress. The very next day news reached Philadelphia of the signature of the peace, and rather more than a month later Congress issued a proclamation for the cessation of hostilities.

Discontents of Washington's officers. Cessation of hostilities (April 17, 1783).

But it proved almost as difficult to put an end to hostilities as to continue them. The troops remained always unpaid. Washington discharged at once on furlough all who had the means of returning home, and many who were willing to go without means. But one company of Pennsylvanian recruits marched to the State House of Philadelphia, threatening the Congress with their vengeance if their claims were not satisfied, and Washington had to send a detachment to disperse them and arrest their chiefs. With the British still in New York, Congress had actually to withdraw to Princeton in order to be out of the way of its mutinous soldiers. It was owing to Washington alone that the whole army did not throw down its arms. Four months' pay out of the long arrears was all that Robert Morris could find to pay it.

Congress threatened by mutineers.

After the ratification of the treaties between Great Britain, France, Spain, and America, Congress disbanded the army, with the exception of a small force which had been enlisted for a definite time. Sir Guy Carleton had already received orders to evacuate New York. Some months elapsed, however, during which arrangements had to be

Ratification of the treaties, September 3, 1783; the slave question.

made for enabling the loyalists to emigrate, and also, sad to say, for the restoration of slaves, an article of the treaty prohibiting the British from 'carrying away any negroes or other property of the inhabitants.' It is not a little painful to find Franklin, the professed opponent of slavery, complaining to his colleague, Henry Laurens, that General Carleton 'has sent away a great number of negroes, alleging that freedom having been promised them by a proclamation, the honour of the nation was concerned.' Sir Guy Carleton, it seems, took up the position, which appears correct in point of law, that the article of the treaty could apply only to captured negroes, and not to such as had voluntarily joined the British; but it is to be feared that many an unfortunate negro did not receive from his subordinates the benefit of the distinction. It must indeed be admitted with shame that the worst feature of the war on the British side was their treatment of the negroes.

All difficulties were, however, at last surmounted; and on November 25, 1783 (observed still in New York as 'Evacuation Day'), the British troops left New York, Washington with his forces entering the city at the same time. Thus was consummated that great disruption of the British race which has placed two English-speaking peoples instead of one on the shores of the Atlantic, and has shown that, alone as yet among the races of the earth, it is equally capable of self-government under republican institutions or under a king. We may rejoice in the result, and see God's hand in it. Yet we cannot but feel that the disruption was unnecessary; that not only the same, but even a less measure of qualified independence than that which is now enjoyed by all the larger colonies of England would have preserved all the American colonies in joyful allegiance. The Canadian Dominion

Evacuation of New York, November 25, 1783.

is nearly as populous as the thirteen original States
when they revolted, and far more extensive than they
then were. The Australian group of colonies is like-
wise more extensive, whilst far more distant. New
England, Virginia, the Carolinas were as anxious to
remain united with Great Britain in 1774 as any British
colony in 1874. The very names of 'Whigs' and 'Tories,'
applied throughout the war to the contending parties in
America, show that the struggle was considered a mere
extension of party divisions in England, rather than a
war between people and people.

On December 4 Washington took leave of his officers
'with a heart full of love and gratitude,' devoutly wishing
that their latter days might be 'prosperous and
happy,' as their former ones had been 'glorious
and honourable.' Leaving them in tears, he
crossed over to New Jersey, on his way to
Philadelphia and to Annapolis, where Congress
was then sitting. At Philadelphia he gave in to the comp-
troller of finance a detailed statement in his own hand
of his expenses during the war; he had renounced from
the first, it will be recollected, all claim to pay. They
amounted to 14,479*l*. 18*s*. 9¾*d*., besides 2287*l*. interest on
a certain balance due to him December 31, 1776—a cheap
price for making a nation. He reached Annapolis on
December 19, and four days afterwards surrendered his
commission to Congress. By a strange retribution, the
President of Congress, General Mifflin, was one of those
officers who had caballed against him. Mifflin had now to
offer the thanks of the country to the chief whose tran-
scendent services he had vainly endeavoured in former
days to depreciate.

Washington's fare-well to his officers; he is thanked by Congress.

The war had cost America 135,000,000 dollars, or say
over 37,000,000*l*., besides outstanding debts
to the amount of 40,000,000 dollars, or say
9,000,000*l*. But to Great Britain it had cost 140,000,000*l*.

Cost of the war.

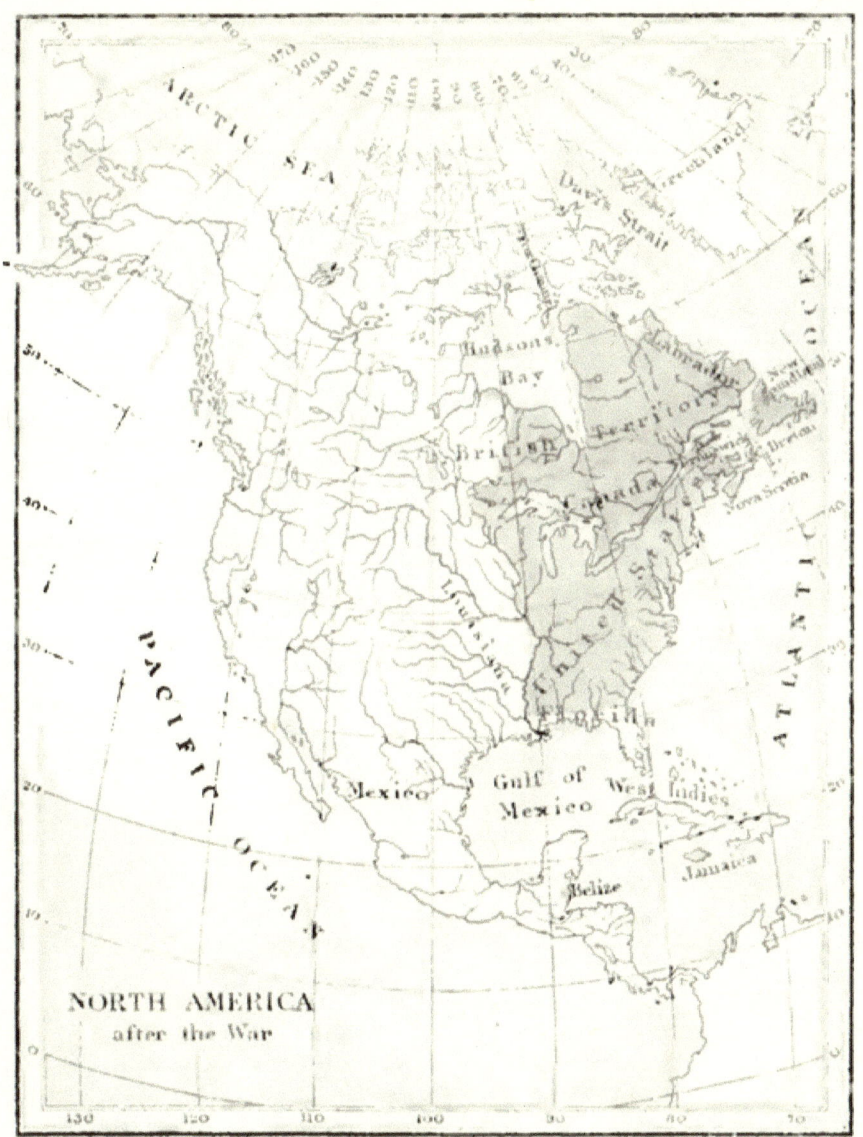

of which 115,000,000*l*. were added to the principal of her debt. The debt itself now amounted to nearly 245,000,000*l*., bearing something over 9,300,000*l*. interest.

Take it all in all, the result had been by no means discreditable to England. She had failed indeed, thank God, in a task unworthy of herself, which she should never have undertaken. But whilst engaged in the task she had held her own against three European enemies at once, and in the far East against the most formidable native foes she ever met in India, the Mysore princes; and the upshot of it all, beyond American independence, had been the loss of a small West India island, of almost uninhabited Florida, and of an island in the Mediterranean never rightly her own. Whilst she had gained a rich town in India, she had almost annihilated the fleets of France and Spain. She left America bankrupt, France and Spain on the verge of bankruptcy, whilst the skill of her great industrial inventors and the subtle fingers of her artisans were developing within her a material prosperity soon to surpass anything she had ever known. *[margin: What England had done.]*

We began by considering the position of the Red man, the White man, and the Black man at the commencement of the struggle. Let us consider it again at its close. *[margin: Results of the war for the different races.]*

The Red man had unluckily attached himself to the losing side. He has taken perhaps a few hundred scalps of pale-faces. But from the Susquehannah to the Genesee, the Iroquois country has been made desolate, and no Indian cornfields will ever again wave over it. More to the west the Illinois tribes have been subdued by Virginia. Fort Jefferson has been established (1780) on the Mississippi, near the mouth of the Ohio, a menace to all the Red men of the *[margin: (1) The Red man driven back.]*

t.e West. Further south, the country of the Cherokees and their allies has been laid waste.

Wherever the Red man has fallen back, the White man has advanced. Counties have been organised (Kentucky and Illinois) which will become States, and form more States by subdivision. The tide of emigration has flowed well over the Alleghanies, and has reached the Mississippi at more than one point of its course. Three civilised powers instead of two now divide the North American continent. The American confederation stands henceforth between England and Spain.

<small>(1) Advance of the White man.</small>

The Black man— has he gained or lost? It seemed at first as if he would gain. The mulatto Attucks was one of the victims of the Boston massacre, and was buried with honour among the 'martyrs of liberty.' At the first call to arms the negroes freely enlisted; but a meeting of the general officers decided against their enlistment in the new army of 1775. The free negroes were greatly dissatisfied. Lest they should transfer their services to the British, Washington gave leave to enlist them, and it is certain that they served throughout the war, shoulder to shoulder with white men. At the battle of Monmouth there were more than 700 black men in the field. Rhode Island formed a battalion of negroes, giving liberty to every slave enlisting, with compensation to his owner; and the battalion did good service. But Washington always considered the policy of arming slaves 'a moot point,' unless the enemy set the example; and though Congress recommended Georgia and South Carolina to raise 3,000 negroes for the war, giving full 'compensation to the proprietors of such negroes,' South Carolina refused to do so, and Georgia had been already overrun by the British when the advice was brought.

<small>(2) The Black man: what he got from the Americans.</small>

Notwithstanding the early adoption of a resolution against the importation of slaves into any of the thirteen colonies (April 6, 1776), Jefferson's fervid paragraph condemning the slave-trade, and by implication slavery, was struck out of the Declaration of Independence in deference to South Carolina and Georgia, and a member from South Carolina declared that 'if property in slaves should be questioned there must be an end to confederation.' The resolution of Congress itself against the slave-trade bound no single State, although a law to this effect was adopted by Virginia in 1778, and subsequently by all the other States; but this was so entirely a matter of State-concernment that neither was any prohibition of the trade contained in the articles of confederation, nor was any suffered to be inserted in the treaty of peace. The feeling against slavery itself was strong in the North. Vermont, in forming a constitution for herself in 1777, allowed no slavery, and was punished for doing so when she applied for admission as a State with the consent of New York, from which she had seceded in 1781; the Southern States refusing to admit her for the present, lest the balance of power should be destroyed. Massachusetts and Pennsylvania, directly or indirectly, abolished slavery in 1780, New Hampshire in 1783. They were followed the next year by Connecticut and Rhode Island, so that by 1784 slavery would be practically at an end in New England and Pennsylvania. Other States, Virginia, Delaware, New Jersey, went no further than to pass laws for allowing voluntary emancipation. In strange contrast to these, Virginia is found in 1780 offering a negro by way of bounty to any white man enlisting for the war. The great Virginians of the day, however—Jefferson, Patrick Henry, George Mason—were opposed to slavery, and large numbers of slaves were emancipated in the State.

So much and no more did the Black men get from the Americans. It seemed at first, when Lord Dunmore issued his proclamation offering freedom to all slaves who should join the British standard, as if they were to get much more from England. Accordingly, Governor Rutledge of South Carolina declared in 1780 that the negroes offered up their prayers in favour of England. But although Lord Dunmore persisted in recommending the arming and emancipation of the blacks, neither the ministry at home nor the British officers would enter into the plan. Lord George Germain authorised the confiscation and sale of slaves, even of those who voluntarily followed the troops. Indians were encouraged to catch them and bring them in; they were distributed as prizes, and shipped to the West Indies, 2,000 at one time, being valued at 250 silver dollars each. The English name became a terror to the black man, and when Greene took the command they flocked in numbers to his standard. We have seen, finally, how the terms of the peace forbade the British troops to carry away 'negroes or other property.' Whichever side he might fight for, the poor black man earned no gratitude.

The Black man badly treated by the English.

Yet in little more than three-quarters of a century, the political complications arising out of the wrongs inflicted on him were to involve the States that had just won their independence in a civil war, in comparison with which the struggle to throw off the yoke of the mother country would appear almost as child's play.

How the Black man's wrongs would avenge themselves.

CHAPTER VII.

THE PARADOXES OF THE WAR, AND ITS TRUE CHARACTER.

PARADOXICAL as it may seem, two things must equally surprise the reader on studying the history of the war of American independence,—the first, that England should ever have considered it possible to succeed in subduing her revolted colonies; the second, that she should not have succeeded in doing so. At a time when steam had not yet baffled the winds, to dream of conquering by force of arms on the other side of the Atlantic a people of English race numbering between 3,000,000 and 4,000,000, with something like 1,200 miles of seaboard, was surely an act of enormous folly. Horace Walpole had wittily said, at the very commencement of the so-called rebellion, that 'if computed by the tract of the country it occupies, we, as so diminutive in comparison, ought rather to be called in rebellion to that.' We have seen in our own days the difficulties experienced by the far more powerful and populous Northern States in quelling the secession of the Southern, when between the two there was no other frontier than at most a river, very often a mere ideal line, and when armies could be raised by a hundred thousand men at a time. England attempted a far more difficult task with forces which, till 1781, never reached 35,000 men, and never exceeded 42,075, including 'provincials,' *i.e.* American loyalists.

England's success seemingly impossible.

Yet it is impossible to doubt that, not once only, but repeatedly during the course of the struggle, England was on the verge of triumph. The American armies were perpetually melting away before the enemy, directly through the practice of short

England was often on the verge of triumph.

enlistments, indirectly through desertions. These desertions, if they might be often palliated by the straits to which the men were reduced through arrears of pay and want of supplies, arose in other cases, as after the retreat from New York, from sheer loss of heart in the cause. The main army under Washington was seldom even equal in number to that opposed to him. In the winter of 1776-77, when his troops were only about 4,000 strong, it is difficult to understand how it was that Sir W. Howe, with more than double the number, should have failed to annihilate the American army. In the winter of 1777-8 the 'dreadful situation of the army for want of provisions' made Washington 'admire' that they should not have been excited to a general mutiny and desertion. In May 1779 he hardly knew any resource for the American cause except in reinforcements from France, and did not know what might be the consequence if the enemy had it in their power to press the troops hard in the ensuing campaign. In December of that year his forces were 'mouldering away daily,' and he considered that Sir Henry Clinton, with more than twice his numbers, could 'not justify remaining inactive with a force so superior.' A year later, he was compelled for want of clothing to discharge the levies which he had always so much trouble in obtaining, and 'want of flour would have disbanded the whole army' if he had not adopted this expedient. In March 1781, again, the crisis was 'perilous,' and though he did not doubt the happy issue of the contest, he considered that the period for its accomplishment might be too far distant for a person of his years. In April he wrote: 'We cannot transport the provisions from the States in which they are assessed to the army, because we cannot pay the teamsters who will no longer work for certificates. It is equally certain that our troops are approaching fast to nakedness, and that we have nothing to clothe them with; that our hospitals are without medicines, and our sick without nutriment except such as well men eat; and that all our public works are at a stand and the artificers disbanding. . . . It may be declared in a word that we are at the end of our tether, and that now or never our deliverance must come.' Six months later, when Yorktown capitulated, the British forces still remaining in North America after the surrender of that garrison were more considerable than they had been as late as February 1779: and Sir Henry Clinton even then declared that with a reinforcement of 10,000 men he would be responsible for the conquest of America.

How shall we explain either puzzle? that England should have so nearly missed success, to fail at last; or that America should have succeeded, after having been almost constantly on the brink of failure? Puzzles to be explained.

The main hope of success on the English side lay in the idea that the spirit and acts of resistance to the authority of the mother-country were in reality only on the part of a turbulent minority; that the bulk of the people desired to be loyal. Reliance of the English on the loyalists.
It is certain indeed that the struggle was, in America itself, much more of a civil war than the Americans are now generally disposed to admit. In December 1780 there were 8,954 'provincials' among the British forces in America, and on March 7, 1781, a letter from Lord George Germain to Sir H. Clinton, intercepted by the Americans, says: 'The American levies in the king's service are more in number than the whole of the enlisted troops in the service of the Congress.' As late as September 1, 1781, there were 7,241. We hear of loyal associators' in Massachusetts, Maryland, and Pennsylvania, of 'associated loyalists' in New York, of a

fort built and maintained by 'associated refugees,' and everywhere of 'Tories,' whose arrest Washington is found suggesting to Governor Trumbull of Connecticut as early as November 12, 1775. New England may indeed be considered to have been cleared of active opposition to the American cause when more than 1,000 refugees left Boston in March 1776 with the British troops. But New York, New Jersey, and Pennsylvania remained long full of Tories. By June 28, 1776, the disaffected on Long Island had taken up arms, and after the evacuation of New York by Washington a brigade of loyalists was raised on the island, and companies were formed in two neighbouring counties to join the king's troops. During Washington's retreat through New Jersey 'the inhabitants, either from fear or disaffection, almost to a man refused to turn out.' In Pennsylvania the militia, instead of giving any assistance in repelling the British, exulted at their approach, and over the misfortunes of their countrymen. On the 20th of that month the British were 'daily gathering strength from the disaffected.' In 1777 the Tories who joined Burgoyne in his invasion from the north are said to have doubled his force. In 1778 Tories joined the Indians in the devastation of Wyoming and Cherry Valley; and although the indiscriminate ravages of the British, or of the Germans in their pay, seem to have roused the three States above-mentioned to self-defence, yet, as late as May 1780 Washington still speaks of sending a small party of cavalry to escort La Fayette 'safely through the Tory settlements' of New York. Virginia, as late as the spring of 1776, was 'alarmed at the idea of independence;' Washington admitted that his countrymen (of that State) 'from their form of government, and steady attachment heretofore to royalty,' would 'come reluctantly' to that idea, but trusted to 'time and persecution.' In 1781 the ground for transferring the seat of war to the Chesapeake was the number of loyalists in that quarter. In the Southern States the division of feeling was still greater. In the Carolinas, a loyalist regiment was raised in a few days in 1776, and again in 1779. In Georgia, in South Carolina, the bitterest partisan warfare was carried on between the Whig and Tory bands; and a body of New York Tories contributed powerfully to the fall of Savannah in 1778 by taking the American forces in the rear.

On the other hand it is unquestionable that in the extent and quality of the support which they met with, the British generals were cruelly disappointed. Up to May 1778 General Howe has declared that in 13 corps raised, with a nominal strength of 6,500 men, the whole number amounted only to 3,609, of whom only a small proportion were Americans, and that 'all the force that could be collected in Pennsylvania, after the most indefatigable exertions during eight months,' was only 974 men. *Inadequate support really afforded by the loyalists.* Of the far more numerous loyalist levies in the south, Lord Cornwallis speaks in the most disparaging terms. A whole regiment in South Carolina marched off on one occasion in a body. Speaking of the friends to the British cause in North Carolina, he wrote, 'If they are as dastardly and pusillanimous as our friends to the southward, we must leave them to their fate.' At the time of the battle of Guilford Court House (1781) the idea of such friends 'rising in any number and to any purpose had totally failed.' No 'provincial' general ever rose to eminence on the British side, although more than one was appointed, and it is clear that if the struggle was so long protracted, it was not through the valour or constancy of the loyalists.

The real causes of its protraction—though it may be hard to an American to admit the fact—lay in the incapacity of American politicians, and, it must be added, in the supineness and want of patriotism of the American people. If, indeed, importing into the struggle views of a later date, we look upon it as one between two nations, the mismanagement of the war by the Americans, on all points save one—the retention of Washington in the chief command—is seen to have been so pitiable from first to last as to be in fact almost unintelligible. We only understand the case when we see that there was no such thing as an American nation in existence, but only a number of revolted colonies, jealous of one another, and with no tie but that of a common danger. Even in the army divisions broke out. Washington, in a general order of August 1, 1776, says: 'It is with great concern that the general understands that jealousies have arisen among the troops from the different provinces, and reflections are frequently thrown out which can only tend to irritate each other and injure the noble cause in which we are engaged.' It was seldom that much help could be obtained in troops from any State, unless that State were immediately threatened by the enemy; and even then these troops would be raised by that State for its own defence, irrespectively of the general or 'continental army.' 'Those at a distance from the seat of war,' wrote Washington in April 1778, 'live in such perfect tranquillity that they conceive the dispute to be in a manner at an end; and those near it are so disaffected that they serve only as embarrassments.' In January 1779 we find him remonstrating with the Governor of Rhode Island because that State had 'ordered several battalions to be raised for the defence of the State only, and this before proper measures are taken to fill the continental regiments.' The different bounties and rates of pay allowed by the various States were a constant source of annoyance to him. After the first year, the best men were not returned to Congress, or did not return to it. Whole

States remained frequently unrepresented. In the winter of 1777-78 Congress was reduced to 21 members. But even with a full representation it could do little. 'One State will comply with a requisition of Congress,' writes Washington in 1780, 'another neglects to do it, a third executes it by halves, and all differ either in the manner, the matter, or so much in point of time, that we are always working up hill.' At first Congress was really nothing more than a voluntary committee. When the Confederation was completed — which was only, be it remembered, on March 1, 1781—it was still, as Washington wrote in 1785, 'little more than a shadow without the substance, and the Congress a nugatory body;' or, as it was described by a later writer, 'powerless for government, and a rope of sand for union.'

Like politicians, like people. There was no doubt a brilliant display of patriotic ardour at the first flying to arms of the colonists. Lexington and Bunker Hill were actions decidedly creditable to their raw troops. The expedition to Canada, foolhardy though it proved, was pursued up to a certain point with real heroism. But with it the heroic period of the war (individual instances excepted) may be said to have closed. There seems little reason to doubt that the revolution would never have been commenced if it had been expected to cost so tough a struggle. 'A false estimate of the power and perseverance of our enemies,' wrote James Duane to Washington, 'was friendly to the present revolution, and inspired that confidence of success in all ranks of people which was necessary to unite them in so arduous a cause.' As early as November 1775, Washington wrote, speaking of military arrangements, 'Such a dearth of public spirit, and such want of virtue, such stock-jobbing and fertility in all the low arts to obtain advantages of one kind or another ... I never saw before, and

Supineness and want of patriotism of the people.

pray God's mercy that I may never be witness to again.' Such 'a mercenary spirit' pervaded the whole of the troops, that he should not have been 'at all surprised at any disaster.' At the same date, besides desertions of 30 or 40 soldiers at a time, he speaks of the practice of plundering as so rife that 'no man is secure in his effects, and scarcely in his person.' People were 'frightened out of their houses under pretence of those houses being ordered to be burnt . . . with a view of seizing the goods;' and to conceal the villany more effectually some houses were actually burnt down. On February 28, 1777, 'the scandalous loss, waste, and private appropriation of public arms during the last campaign,' had been 'beyond all conception.' Officers drew 'large sums under pretence of paying their men,' and appropriated them. In one case an officer led his men to robbery, offered resistance to a brigade-major who ordered him to return the goods, and was only with difficulty cashiered. 'Can we carry on the war much longer?' Washington asks in 1778—after the treaty with France and the appearance of a French fleet off the coast. 'Certainly not, unless some measures can be devised and speedily executed to restore the credit of our currency, restrain extortion, and punish forestallers.' A few days later, 'To make and extort money in every shape that can be devised, and at the same time to decry its value, seems to have become a mere business and an epidemical disease.' On December 30, 1778, 'speculation, peculation, and an insatiable thirst for riches seem to have got the better of every other consideration, and almost of every order of men; . . . party disputes and personal quarrels are the great business of the day; whilst the momentous concerns of an empire, a great and accumulating debt, ruined finances, depreciated money, and want of credit, which in its consequences is the want of everything, are but secondary considerations.'

After a first loan had been obtained from France and spent, and a further one was granted in 1782, so utterly unpatriotic and selfish was known to be the temper of the people that the loan had to be kept secret, in order not to diminish such efforts as might be made by the Americans themselves. On July 10 of that year, with New York and Charleston still in British hands, Washington writes : 'That spirit of freedom which at the commencement of this contest would have gladly sacrificed everything to the attainment of its object, has long since subsided, and every selfish passion has taken its place.' But indeed the mere fact that from the date of the battle of Monmouth (July 28, 1778), Washington was never supplied with sufficient means, even with the assistance of French fleets and troops, to strike one blow at the English in New York—though these were but very sparingly reinforced during the period—shows an absence of public spirit, one might almost say of national shame, scarcely conceivable, and in singular contrast with the terrible earnestness exhibited on both sides some eighty years later in the Secession War.

Why, then, must we ask on the other side, did England fail at last? *Why did England fail?*

The English were prone to attribute their ill success to the incompetency of their generals. Lord North, with his quaint humour, would say, 'I do not know whether our generals will frighten the enemy, but I know they frighten me whenever I think of them.' When, in 1778, Lord Carlisle came out as commissioner, in a letter speaking of the great scale of all things in America, he says : 'We have nothing on a great scale with us but our blunders, our misconduct, our ruin, our losses, our disgraces and misfortunes.' Pitt, in a speech of 1781, aptly described the war as having been, on the part of England, 'a series *Incompetency of British generals no sufficient reason.*

of ineffective victories or severe defeats.' No doubt it is difficult to account for Gage's early blunders, for Howe's repeated failure to follow up his own success or profit by his enemy's weakness; and Cornwallis's movement, justly censured by Sir Henry Clinton, in transferring the bulk of his army from the far south to Virginia, within marching distance of Washington, opened the way to that crowning disaster at Yorktown, without which it is by no means impossible that Georgia and the Carolinas might have remained British. But no allowance for bad generalship can account for the failure of the British. Washington and Greene appear to have been the only two American generals of marked ability, though they unquestionably derived great advantage from the talents of their foreign allies, La Fayette, Pulaski, Steuben, Rochambeau,—and Washington was more than once out-manœuvred. Gates evidently owed his one signal triumph to enormous superiority of numbers on his own ground, and was as signally defeated, under circumstances infinitely less creditable to him than those of Burgoyne's surrender. Lee's vaunted abilities came to nothing.

Political incapacity was of course charged upon ministers as another cause of disaster; and no doubt their miscalculation of the severity of the struggle was almost childish. When Parliament met in the autumn of 1776—*i.e.* after the Declaration of Independence had gone forth to the world—it was held out in the king's speech that another campaign would be sufficient to end the war, whilst in spite of all the warnings of the Opposition, they persisted in blinding themselves to the force of the temptations which must inevitably bring down France, if not Spain, into the lists against them, until the treaties of these powers with America were actually concluded. The forces sent out were miserably inadequate for a war on so large

Ministerial incapacity no sufficient reason.

a scale,—'too many to make peace, too few to make war,' as Lord Chatham told the ministry. The English generals complained almost as bitterly as the American of the want of adequate reinforcements, and the best of them, Sir Henry Clinton, is found writing (1779) in a strain which might be mistaken for Washington's, of his spirits being 'worn out' by the difficulties of his position. But no mistakes in the management of the war by British statesmen can account for their ultimate failure. However great British mismanagement may have been, it was far surpassed by American. Until Robert Morris took the finances in hand, the administration of them was beneath not only contempt but conception. There was nothing on the British side equal to that caricature of a recruiting system, in which different bounties were offered by Congress, by the States, by the separate towns, so as to make it the interest of the intending soldier to delay enlistment as long as possible in order to sell himself to the highest bidder; to that caricature of a war establishment, the main bulk of which broke up every twelvemonth in front of the enemy, which was only paid, if at all, in worthless paper, and left almost habitually without supplies. To mention one fact only, commissions in British regiments on American soil continued to be sold for large sums, whilst Washington's officers were daily throwing up theirs, many from sheer starvation. On the whole, no better idea can be had of the nature of the struggle on the American side, after the first heat of it had cooled down, than from the words of Count de Rochambeau, writing to Count de Vergennes, July 10, 1780: 'They have neither money nor credit; their means of resistance are only momentary, and called forth when they are attacked in their own homes. They then assemble for the moment of immediate danger and defend themselves.'

A far more important cause in determining the

ultimate failure of the British was the aid afforded by France to America, followed by that of Spain and Holland. It was impossible for England to reconquer a continent, and carry on war at the same time with the three most powerful naval states of Europe. The instincts of race have tended on both the English and the American side to depreciate the value of the aid given by France to the colonists. It may be true that Rochambeau's troops which disembarked on Rhode Island in July 1780 did not march till July 1781,—that they were blockaded soon after their arrival, threatened with attack from New York, and only disengaged by a feint of Washington's on that city. But more than two years before their arrival Washington wrote to a member of Congress, 'France, by her supplies, has saved us from the yoke thus far.' The treaty with France alone was considered to afford a 'certain prospect of success,'—to 'secure' American independence. The arrival of D'Estaing's fleet, although no troops joined the American army, and nothing eventually was done, determined the evacuation of Philadelphia. The discipline of the French troops when they landed in 1780 set an example to the Americans; chickens and pigs walked between the lines without being disturbed. The recruits of 1780 could not have been armed without 50 tons of ammunition supplied by the French. In September of that year, Washington, writing to the French envoy, speaks of the 'inability' of the Americans to expel the British from the south 'unassisted, or perhaps even to stop their career,' and he writes in similar terms to Congress a few days later. To depend 'upon the resources of the country, unassisted by foreign loans,' he writes to a member of Congress two months later, 'will, I am confident, be to lean upon a broken reed.' In January 1781, writing to Colonel Laurens, the American envoy in Paris,

Importance of the foreign aid supplied to America.

he presses for 'an immediate, ample, and efficacious succour in money' from France, for the maintenance on the American coasts of 'a constant naval superiority,' and for 'an additional succour in troops.' And since the assistance so requested was in fact granted in every shape, and the surrender of Yorktown was obtained by the co-operation both of the French army and fleet, we must hold that Washington's words were justified by the event.

The real cause why England yielded in 1782–3 to her revolted colonies was probably this: The English nation at large had never realised the nature of the struggle; when it did, it refused to carry it on. *The war ceased when the English nation thoroughly understood its character.*

Enormous ignorance no doubt prevailed at the beginning of the struggle as to the North American colonies. They had been till then entirely overshadowed by the West Indies, which were perhaps at that time the greatest source of English commercial wealth; and the time was not far past when, *Early popularity of the war the result of ignorance.* it is said, they were supposed like the latter to be chiefly inhabited by negroes. The prominence of the slave-colonies seems to have associated the idea of colonies with that of absolute government. Englishmen did not generally realise the existence in North America of vast countries inhabited by communities of their own race, which enjoyed in general a larger measure of self-government than the mother-country herself. That a colony should resist the mother-country seemed in a manner preposterous. It appears certain, therefore, that when the war at first broke out it was popular, and that the king and Lord North, as has been already stated, were themselves amazed at the loyal addresses which it called forth.

But the early resort to the aid of German mercenaries

showed that this popularity was only skin-deep,—that the heart of the masses was not engaged in the war. The very employment of these mercenaries, as well as of the Indian auxiliaries of the royal forces, tended to lower the character of the war in English eyes. When Chatham, in his scathing invectives, would speak of the ministers' 'traffic and barter with every little pitiful German prince that sells and sends his subjects to the shambles,' or of their sending 'the infidel savage—against whom? against your Protestant brethren, to lay waste their country, to desolate their dwellings, and extirpate their race and name,' he might not carry with him the votes of the House of Lords, but his words would burn their way into English hearts.

That the war with the American colonies themselves was repugnant to the deepest feelings of the nation is proved by contrast through the sudden burst of warlike spirit which followed (1778-9) on the outbreak of war with France and Spain. A few days before the French treaty with America was known, Horace Walpole had written to Mason that the new levies 'don't come, consequently they will not go.' By July of the same year he writes to Sir Horace Mann: 'The country is covered with camps.' In 1776 the king had reviewed the Guards on Wimbledon Common, and pulled off his hat to them before their departure for America. He had now (1779) to review volunteers. The passionate interest which is henceforth taken in so much of the struggle as is carried on with foreign foes, Keppel's scarcely deserved popularity, the riotous popular joy on his acquittal, the outburst of universal rejoicing over Rodney's victories, show a totally different temper to that brought out by either victory or defeat in what was now felt to be a dread civil war with our American kinsmen. Hence it was, no doubt, that after the surrender of Yorktown hostilities were practically at an end with America, whilst the naval warfare with France and Spain was carried on for another twelvemonth, and that the signing of provisional articles of peace with the United States preceded by two months that of similar articles with France and Spain, the armistice with Holland being of still later date. It may even be conjectured that the outbreak of war with France and Spain, instead of incensing the mind of the English people against the Americans, rather gave different objects to their angry passions, and tended to diminish their bitterness towards the colonists. It must have been a kind of relief to Englishmen to find themselves fighting once more against those whom they considered hereditary enemies, against men who did not speak their own mother-tongue; and the wholly unprovoked character of these foreign hostilities would soften men's feelings towards the stubbornness of those colonists of their own blood, who after all asked only to be let alone.

Substantially indeed—although colonial independence would no doubt have been achieved sooner or later—the more we look into the events of the war of 1775–83, the more, perhaps, shall we be convinced that it resolves itself into a duel between two men who never saw each other in the flesh, Washington and George III. *The war in fact a duel between Washington and George III.*

Take Washington out of the history on the American side, and it is impossible to conceive of American success. It is barely possible that under Greene—the one general after Washington's own heart, who wrote to him from his command in the south, 'We fight, get beaten, and fight again'—the army itself might have been commanded with an ability *American success impossible without Washington.*

which would enable it to withstand its British opponents. But neither Greene nor any other general possessed that weight of personal character which fixed the trust of Congress and people on Washington, maintained him in authority through all reverses, and enabled him to criticise with such unflinching frankness the measures of Congress.

Take, on the other hand, George III. out of the history on the British side, and it is beyond question that if the war had ever broken out, it would have been put a stop to long before its ultimate failure. In him alone is to be found the real centre of resistance to American independence.

George III. the centre of English resistance to American independence.

It is now well known that at least from the beginning of 1778, if not from the end of 1775, Lord North was anxious to resign, and desirous of conciliation, and that it was only through the king's constant appeals to his sense of honour not to 'desert' him, that the minister was prevailed upon to remain in office. 'Till I see things change to a more favourable position,' the king wrote to Lord North as late as May 19, 1780, 'I shall not feel at liberty to grant your resignation;' and it was only on March 20, 1781, that Lord North at last compelled his master to accept it. Three ideas were fixed in the king's mind, the first of which was a delusion, the second a mistake, and the third contrary to all principles of constitutional government. 1st. He had persuaded himself that the country was radically opposed to American independence. In January 1778, he opposes conciliatory measures, lest they should 'dissatisfy this country, which so cheerfully and handsomely carries on the contest.' In the autumn of the year he is certain that 'if ministers show that they never will consent to the independence of America, the cry will be strong in their favour.' Two years later, he 'can never suppose this country so far lost to all ideas of self-importance as to be willing to grant American independence.' 2nd. He was convinced (and this conviction, it must be admitted, was shared by some of the strongest opponents of the war), that if the independence of the North American colonies were acknowledged, all the others, as well as Ireland, would be lost. 'If any one branch of the empire is allowed to throw off its dependency, the others will inevitably follow the example.' 'Should America succeed . . . the West Indies must follow, not in independence, but dependence on America. Ireland would soon follow, and this island reduce itself to a poor island indeed.' 3rd. He would not allow the Opposition to rule. 'He would run any personal risk rather than submit to the Opposition . . . rather than be shackled by these desperate men he would lose his crown.' If he authorises the attempt at a coalition (1779), it is 'provided it be understood that every means are to be employed to keep the empire entire, to prosecute the present just and unprovoked war in all its branches with the utmost vigour, and that his Majesty's past measures be treated with proper respect,' *i.e.*, provided the Opposition are ready to stultify themselves, and do all that the king thinks right, and admit that all for which they have contended is wrong. Before the spectacle of such narrow obstinacy, it is difficult not to sympathise with an expression of Fox in one of his letters, 'It is intolerable to think that it should be in the power of one blockhead to do so much mischief.'

Between these two men—it may be conceded, equally sincere, equally resolute—but the one reasoning, like the madman that he was to be, from false premises, self-deluded as to the feelings of his people, anticipating consequences which a century sees yet unrealised, and the other with eyes at all times almost

In such a duel, Washington must win.

morbidly open to all the gloomier features of his cause, void of all self-delusion,—the one conceiving himself justified in imposing the dictates of his own self-will on every minister whom he might employ, entitled alike to chain an unwilling friend to office, and to shut the door of office to opponents except on the terms of surrendering all their principles—the other always ready to accept the inevitable, to make the most use of the least means, to curb himself for the sake of his cause in all things, except fearless plainspeaking—the one, finally, resolved only to hinder the making a nation, the other resolved to make one, if anyhow possible—the issue of the contest could not be doubtful, if both lives were prolonged. From that contest the one emerged as the mad king who threw away a continent from England; the other as the father of the American nation.

The common consent of mankind has ranked Washington among its great men; and although the title may have been fully justified by the course of his civil life, whether in or out of office, after the termination of the War of Independence, it is hardly to be doubted that it would freely have been accorded to him had his career been cut short immediately after the resignation of his military command. Yet of those who have enjoyed the title, few, if any, have ever earned it by actions of less brilliancy. The fame of no conspicuous victory is bound up with Washington's name. His one dashing exploit was the surprise of Trenton; his one victory, that of Monmouth, had no results; his most considerable battle, that of Brandywine, was a severe defeat. His greatness as a general consisted in doing much with little means, never missing an opportunity, rising superior to every disaster. When he had recovered Boston he could say, 'I have been here months together with...

Character of Washington's greatness.

not thirty rounds of musket cartridges to a man, and have been obliged to submit to all the insults of the enemy's cannon for want of powder, keeping what little we had for pistol distance... We have maintained our ground against the enemy under this want of powder, and we have disbanded one army and recruited another, within musket shot of two-and-twenty regiments, the flower of the British army, whilst our force has been but little if any superior to theirs, and at last have beaten them into a shameful and precipitate retreat out of a place the strongest by nature on this continent, and strengthened and fortified at an enormous expense.'

The character of Washington as a commander recalls in various respects that of Wellington. In both we see the same dogged perseverance under all the various phases of fortune; the same strict discipline, hardening readily into sternness, coupled with the same careful consideration for the wants and welfare of the soldier; the same patient, constant attention to every detail of military organisation; the same ability in maintaining a defensive warfare against an enemy superior in force, with the same quickness to strike a blow in any unguarded quarter; the same unflinching frankness in exposing the evils of the military administration of the day. Many of Wellington's despatches from the Peninsula might almost have been written by Washington. The difference between them, while the war lasts, is mainly this, that in Wellington the soldier is all, whilst in Washington the statesman and the patriot are never merged in the soldier. Hence, whilst in after life Wellington had to serve his apprenticeship as a statesman after ceasing to be a soldier, and often bungled over his new craft, Washington's after-life was simply that of a statesman who had

Washington and Wellington compared.

been called to take up arms and **had laid them** down again. In their supreme quality of simple steadfastness **to duty,** both finally met.

In short, though England had never a more successful foe than Washington, **it is** impossible not to **feel,** in studying his character, that no more typical Englishman ever lived; that he belongs **to us as** essentially as our Shakespeare and our Milton.

<small>Washington a thorough Englishman.</small>

CHAPTER VIII.

1783.

<small>State of the world.</small> LET us now cast a final glance at the state of the world at the close of the war.

Except that **an independent state had grown up for the first time since the downfall of the** Aztec and Inca **empires** on the **American** continent, and that England had **been** politically lessened, the balance of power had been little affected by **the war.** France had one West Indian island more, Holland one Indian settlement less. Spain had recovered Minorca and the Floridas. **But** she was irrevocably shut out from one great object of her ambition, the eastern half of the Mississippi basin.

<small>The balance of power but slightly affected by the war.</small>

It might almost be said **that** Europe had stood still **to** watch the past struggle. Among the sovereigns, the only changes had been **the** death of the Empress Maria Theresa in **1780,** leaving her **son** Joseph II. still on the **throne,** and that **of** Joseph I. of Portugal, succeeded by his daughter Maria I. There had been, in the early years of the war, some colonial **warfare** between Spain and

<small>New political events outside of the war.</small>

Portugal (1776-7), and a little later some quarreling in Germany between Austria and Prussia (1777-9), about the succession to the electorate of Bavaria, terminated by the mediation of Russia in favour of the Prussian candidate, Austria receiving some small sop in the way of territory. The Pope (Pius VI.) had astonished the world by a visit to Vienna (1782), whilst in Geneva, where measures taken against Rousseau and his works had led to quarrels between the popular party and the dominant aristocracy, there had been a joint intervention of French, Piedmontese, and Bernese in favour of the latter (1782). Russia was engaged in seizing the Crimea (1783). In the Netherlands, the republican party, encouraged by the success of the Americans, was agitating to curtail the authority of the Stadtholder.

But there had been events which had occupied men's minds far more than the quarrels of princes. Other events.

At the age of 86, Voltaire had been seized with the wish to see Paris again. In February 1778, after many years' absence, he made his appearance, and nothing else was thought of but Voltaire. Crowds stood on the quay all the day outside his door. Voltaire's return to Paris (February 1778). The quasi-regal cry of 'Long live Voltaire!' which greeted him wherever he went, was often mixed with a more ominous one, 'Down with kings! Long live philosophers!' Franklin brought him his grandson to bless, and the great mocker of the age pronounced over the child's head the two great words of heavenly and earthly faith, 'God and freedom.' His greatest triumph was, however, at the theatre (March 30), where one of his latest pieces, 'Irène,' was represented. He was crowned with laurel, almost carried in ladies' arms to his coach, which was drawn by men to his door, amidst such showers of bouquets that he exclaimed, 'My children, do you wish to smother me under roses?'

Two months later he was dead, and the Roman Catholic parochial clergy were refusing to bury him, so that a priest, his nephew, had to carry the body off secretly to be buried in a monastery to which he belonged, and the prior of which was in turn deprived of his office for allowing the ceremony to be performed. So fearfully wide was the gap between the Church and popular feeling.

Voltaire's death, May 30, 1778.

In the same month Rousseau, whose failing sight no longer enabled him to copy music for a livelihood, accepted from the Marquis de Girardin the offer of a cottage at Ermenonville near Paris. A few weeks later he, too, was dead, hoping that 'the Almighty would receive him into His heaven.'

Rousseau's death, July 2, 1778.

Financially France was rushing on to ruin. After five years of seeming financial success, Necker had left office in 1781, as has been said before, leaving behind him a famous report, known as the 'Compte Rendu,' the first balance-sheet of French finance ever yet published, but already out of date, as it applied to the month of January 1778. Necker had himself increased the French debt by over 21,000,000*l.*; his successor added 12,000,000*l.* more. In 1783 the finances were being handed over to the utterly reckless Calonne, who in three years would add 32,000,000*l.*, and whose entire breakdown would bring on successively an Assembly of Notables, the States General, and the Revolution.

Financial ruin of France.

Meanwhile the heroes of the day in France were the young officers who had served in the American war; foremost of all, La Fayette, Washington's friend. But there are already, practising at the bar of country towns, or obscurely at that of Paris itself,—in attorneys' offices, men who in a few years more will come before Europe as the leaders of a

The heroes of the day in France, and then of the future.

French Revolution; and behind them sons of innkeepers, plasterers, labourers, lackeys, and others—a few of them now simple soldiers or non-commissioned officers, who will rise to military fame, become, many of them, the members of a new nobility, and in one or two instances ascend a throne; whilst a single Corsican family will give to Europe an emperor, three kings, and a queen.

The hour of Germany's political wakening is yet far off. But her literature is rising fast to meridian splendour, and her poets and philosophers have mostly been enthusiastic in the American cause. *Germany; sympathy with America.*

In England there is little to be noticed since the opening of the war, beyond what has been already referred to. Dr. Johnson has published his last work (1781), and will have this year that paralytic stroke which will be the forerunner of his death in the next. A new poet, Crabbe, patronised by Burke, has published his first work, the 'Library' (1781), but its success was far surpassed by that of another poem now scarcely known except by name, Darwin's 'Botanic Garden.' Robert Burns has been locally known in Ayrshire for a rhymester, but has published nothing as yet; Walter Scott will go next year to college. *England: the literary world.*

In the political sphere the Prince of Wales has just come of age, and will soon be the patron of the political opposition. Before the year is out (December 19,) Pitt, 24 years of age, will be chancellor of the exchequer and premier, and in him will be typified the spirit of resistance to that coming Revolution which is now casting its shadow before it on the Continent. *The political world.*

America finally, after seeing her independence recognised this year by Sweden, Denmark, Spain, and Russia, all of which will conclude treaties with her as

well as Prussia two years hence, will flounder for four
years more **in the slough** of despond **of** her
Confederation, through repeated mutinies and
a New England **insurrection**, until she reaches firm ground
at last in her Constitution **(September 17,** 1787), under
which **Washington will become the** first President, no
more of Congress, but of the United States.

America.

INDEX.

ACADIANS, their expulsion from Nova Scotia, 62
Adams, John, appointed peace commissioner for France, 165
Adams, Samuel, 69, 80, 84, 104
Africa, slave trade in, 57; colonial power of, 90
Algonquin language, 6
Allen, Ethan, takes Ticonderoga, 105
America, races inhabiting colonies in, 2; commencement of the war of Independence, 103; reception of the proclamation against rebellion in, 114; secretly aided by France and Spain, 118; disasters in Canada, 120; miserable state of the army, 121, 147; enthusiastic reception of the Declaration of Independence, 126; the need of union still scarcely felt in, 127; postponement of the plan of federation, 127; discouragement of the troops, 129; Congress raises a new army, 131; result of the campaign of 1776, 132; Congress adopts the scheme of confederation, 146; treaty with France, 149; rejoicings over the French treaty in, 153; reception of the Conciliatory Bills, 154; neglected state of the army, 172; supineness of, 173; subserviency to France, 194; rejoicings at the surrender of Yorktown in, 198; her weakness, 194-202; preliminary articles of peace with England, 204; discontent of the army, 207; cessation of hostilities, 208; cost of the war, 210; incapacity of politicians in, 220; want of patriotism in, 221; importance of its foreign aid, 226; success of the war due to Washington, 229

America, North, discovery of, 23; permanent settlement of Englishmen in, 23
André, Major, his trial and conviction as a spy, 184
Andros, Sir Edmund, as governor of New England, 54
Arkwright, 101
Arnold, Benedict, attempts to storm Quebec, 115; disastrous results of his expedition to Canada, 120; defeats the British at Stillwater, 143; is found guilty of treason, 183; in Connecticut, 196
Asiento, the, 56
Austria, in 1775, 92; proposes a peace congress at Vienna, 187

BACON'S Rebellion, 30
Bacon, Nathaniel, hostilities of, 30
Baltimore, Lord, promoter of colonisation, 32; as governor of Maryland, 33; his disputes regarding the Virginian Government, 34
Bancroft on the Indians, 4
Baum, Colonel, his defeat at Bennington, 140
Beaumarchais, 119
Bellamont, Lord, governor of New York, 41
Bennington, battle of, 140
Berkeley, Sir William, as governor of Virginia, 29; as governor of New Jersey, 41
Black man, the, 55; effect of the war on, 212; bad treatment by the English, 214
Bonaparte, Napoleon, 103
Boston, riots at, 71; troops sent to, 78 convention at, 78; massacre at, 79;

BOS

destruction of tea at, 81; Port Act, 82; invested by colonists, 105; evacuated by the British troops, 117
Boswell, 101
Braddock, General, his defeat by the French, 61
Bradford, Governor, 47
Brandywine, battle of, 142
Breton, Cape, colonised by the French, 20
Brindley, 102
Bunker's Hill, battle of, 107
Burgoyne, General, commander of an expedition from Canada, 140; is defeated at Stillwater, 142; and surrenders at Saratoga, 143
Burke, 88; his plan of Economic Reform, 178
Burns, Robert, 237
Bute, Lord, 71

CABOT, John, his discoveries, 22
Cabot, Sebastian, his discoveries, 23
Calvert, Sir George, see Baltimore, Lord
Camden, battle of, 180
Campaign of 1776, its results, 132
Canada, population of French in, 21; conquest of, by the English, 63; invasion of, 114; American disasters in, 120; British expedition from, 139, 140
Canonicus, 46
Carleton, Sir Guy, appointed commander-in-chief of the English Army, 221; his conduct regarding the slave question, 207
Carolina, South, invasion of, 161
Carolinas, attempt at colonisation of, by the Spanish, 15; early charters of, 34; peculiar characteristic of their foundation, 35; colonists break up Indian civilisation in Florida, 38; slavery in, 36; become colonies, 37; dissolution of colonial government in 119
Carteret, Sir George, governor of New Jersey, 41
Cartier, Jacques, his discoveries, 17
Charles I., 28, 51
Charleston, taken by the British, 171
Chatham, Earl of, see Pitt, William
Cherokees, 13; defeat of, 167
Choiseul, Duke de, French prime minister, 70, 99

CON

Clark, George Rogers, invades the north-western territory, 167
Clayborne, 33; leader of the republican party, 34
Clinton, Sir H., defeats the Americans at Long Island, 126; evacuates Philadelphia, 156
Coligny, Admiral, 15
Colonies of America, 1; races inhabiting them, 2; Northern and Southern English groups, 23, 24; distinction between these groups, 25 the united colonies of New England, 50, history of from 1748-1764, 58-64; loyalty and disaffection in, 64; sufferings under the Navigation Laws in, 65; coming causes pre-figured, 66; other causes of discontent in, 67; trade discouraged in, 67; mutual complaints between the mother country and the colonies, 68; attempt of English Government to raise a revenue from, 68; protest against the Revenue Act, 69; rejoicings at the Repeal of the Stamp Act, 74; refusal to comply with the requirements of the Quarterly Act, 75; renewed agitation in, 76; troops sent to, 78; spread of non-importation agreements, 79; repressive measures by the English Parliament against, 82; raising of troops in, 86; extension of the prohibition of trade, 88; defence of, 89; colonial powers in 1775, 90; reception of the proclamation against rebellion, 114; dissolution of governments, 119
Committees of correspondence, 80
Commonwealth, the, submission of the colonies to, 52
Conciliatory Bills, 150; their reception, 154
Concord, battle of, 104
Confederation, its first introduction in Congress, 127; its adoption by Congress, 146; signed by several states in 1778, 157; finally signed in 1781, 167
Congress, in New York, 71; continental congress in Philadelphia, 84, 106; attempts at conciliation by, 111; second petition of, 111; important resolutions of, 118; raises a new army, 131; adopts the scheme of confederation, 146; impotency of, 147; reinforces the army, 153; reception of the Conciliatory Bills by, 154; increased impotency of, 157;

Index. 241

CON

solicits French protection, 160; appoints peace commissioners, 165; threatened by mutineers, 208
Connecticut colony, 49
Continental congress, first, 84; second, 106
Convention at Boston, 78
Conway, as inspector of the army, 148
Corn riots of 1775, 96
Cornwallis, Lord, 132; his defeat at Princeton, 136; his victory at Camden against Gates, 180; his march into North Carolina checked, 182; advances into North Carolina, 191; defeats Greene at Guilford Court House, 192; retreats to Wilmington, 192; in Virginia, 194; withdraws to Yorktown, 194; his surrender at Yorktown, 197
Council of Plymouth, 43
Cowpens, the, battle of, 190
Cowper, 101
Crabbe, 237
Creeks, 13
Crown Point, surrender of, 106
Culpeper, Lord, governor of Virginia, 30

DEANE, Silas, 118
Declaration of Independence, proposition of, 119; its adoption by Congress in 1776, 122; its unfairness, 124; looked upon as a declaration of war, 126; its influence on foreign countries, 126; its enthusiastic reception in America, 126; its reception in England, 133
Declaratory Act, 74
De Kalb, 180
Delaware colony, 43
Denmark in 1775, 93
Dickinson, John, 127
Dumouriez, 99
Dunmore, Lord, governor of Virginia, 110, 116
Dunning, his resolutions, 178
Dutch colonies in America, 39

ECONOMIC Reform, 178
Eliot, John, 52
Endicott, John, 48
England, colonies of, in America, 23, 24; its monopoly of the Asiento, 56; its support of slavery, 57; defeats the French, 62; conquest of Canada,

FRE

by the English, 63; complaints of the colonists against, 67; effect of the complaints on, 68; social condition of, before the war, 100-103; at war with Spain, 167; events in 1780, 176; the war everywhere disastrous to, 199; preliminary articles of peace with America, 204; what she gained by the war, 211; success in the war seemingly impossible, 215; its reliance on the loyalists, 217; reasons for its failure, 223; early popularity of the war the result of ignorance, 227; political and literary world after the war, 237
Estaing, Admiral Count d', his engagement with Lord Howe, 157; repulsed before Savannah, 170
Europe, colonial power of, 90; in 1775, 91; war in, in 1871, 185; political events outside the war, 234
Eutaw Springs, battle of, 195

FIVE Nations, the, 13
Flaxman, 102
Florida, discovery of, 14; settlement of, 15
Fox, opposed to the American war, 193
France, colonial power of, 90; in 1775, 91; the only power with Spain directly interested in the American struggle, 93; the intellectual centre of Europe, 94; the new reign a hopeful one, 96; grounds for its sympathy with America, 97; its admiration for England, 97; influence of the partition of Poland on, 99; secretly aids America, 118; ready to treat with America, 147; treaty with America, 149; state of affairs in 1778, 149; war declared against England, 153; its successes against the English, 158, 186; war convention with Spain, 166; anxious for peace, 187; return of the troops to Europe, 206; financial ruin of, 236; its heroes of the future, 236
Franklin, Benjamin, his connection with ' King George's war,' 58; author of the first military organisation in the colonies, 59; in Paris, 133
Free trade in America, 118
French in America, their colonies, 16; early discoveries and settlements of, 17; missionaries and adventurers of, 18; their progress in the Mississippi

FRE

valley, 10; **extension of** colonisation in New York, 20; population of her colonies, 21; defeat of, at Pittsburg, 62; successes in war, 62
French and Indian war, 59
Frobisher, Martin Allen, his attempts to found a settlement in Hudson Straits, 23

GAGE, General, **as governor of** Massachusetts, 86; **defeated at** Lexington, 104; **proclaims martial law**, 106
Gainsborough, 101
'Gaspee,' burning of the, 80
Gates, Horatio, General, defeats Burgoyne, 141 144; is defeated at Camden, 180
George III., his character, 100; his speech at the opening of Parliament in 1782, 205; the centre of English resistance to American Independence, 230
Georgia, the last founded colony, 37; its prosperity, 38; hostilities with Spain, 38
Germain, Lord George, 113, 189; his unpopularity, 200
Germany, in 1775, 91; application for troops from, 111; vote for troops from, 113; its sympathy with America, 236
Gibbon, 101
Gibraltar, siege of, 168, 185
Gilbert, Sir Humphrey, his attempts at colonisation in Virginia, 26
Gloucester, **its** surrender by Cornwallis to the Americans, 198
Goldoni, 74
Gordon, Lord George, 178, riots caused by, 179
Gorges, Sir Ferdinand, 48
Government of the North **American** Indian, 6
Grasse, Admiral Count de, defeated by Rodney in the West Indies, 203
Great Britain, cost of the war to, 211
Greene, appointed commander of the forces south of the Delaware, 182; defeats the English at the Cowpens, 170; in the south, 190; retreats to the Dan river, 191; recovers the greater part of South Carolina, 192; is defeated by Cornwallis at Guilford Court House, 192, whom he defeats at Eutaw Springs, 195

ING

Grenville, George, attempts to raise a revenue from the American colonies, 68
Guilford Court House, battle of, 191

HAARLEM Heights, 131
Hancock, 104
Hargreaves, 101
Henry, Patrick, his resolutions, 70; at the continental congress, 84
Hillsborough, Lord, his policy, 78
Holland, colonial power of, 90
Holland, England's quarrel with, 175, war declared with England, 185; peace with England, 207
House of Burgesses, 27; **dissolution of**, 110
Howe, General, evacuates Boston, 117; his arrival at Sandy Hook, 122; lands at Staten Island, 127; his advance, 131, captures Fort Washington, 131; defeats Washington at Brandywine, 141; inactivity of his army in Philadelphia, 148
Howe, **Lord, his** arrival at Sandy Hook, 122; threatens New York, 127; his fruitless attempts to secure peace, 130; his engagement with D'Estaing, 157
Hudson, Henry, his **discoveries, 39**
Hume, 100
Hunt, 46
Hutchinson, Mrs., 49
Hyder Ali, 152; defeats Colonel Baillie, 185

IBERVILLE, d', 19
Independence, American war of, first period, 183, second period, 149; its results, 211; paradoxes of, and its true character, 215, early popularity of, 227, the war in fact a duel between George III. and Washington, 229; state of the world after the war, 234
Independence, Declaration of, 122 proposition of, 119; its unfairness, 124, its enthusiastic reception in America, 126; looked upon as a declaration of war, 126; its influence on foreign countries, 126; its reception in England, 133
Indian massacres, 108
Indian wars, 28, 37, **52, 185**
Ingersoll, 71

Index. 243

IRE

Ireland, state of, in 1780, 177
Iroquois, 13; devastation of their country by Sullivan, 164
Italy in 1775, 93

JACKSON, Andrew, 180
Jacobite party extinct, 99
Jay, appointed peace commissioner for Spain, 165
Jefferson, Thomas, draws up the Declaration of Independence, 122
Johnson, Dr., 100, 237
Johnstone, Governor, attempts bribery with Joseph Reed, 158
John the Painter attempts to fire Portsmouth dockyard, 133
Jones, Paul, 159; his sea-fight, 169
Junius, 100, 103

KEPPEL, Admiral, 158
Kosciusko, joins the American army, 139

LA FAYETTE, joins the American army, 138
La Salle, Cavalier de, his adventures, 18
Lee, General, capture of, 134; quarrels with Washington, 156
Leisler, Jacob, governor of New York, 41
Lexington, battle of, 104
Lincoln, General, defeated at Briar Arch, 161; surrender of Charleston by, 171
Locke's 'grand model' of Carolina, 35
'London Company,' permanent settlement of Englishmen in the colonies attributed to, 23
London No-Popery riots, 179
Long Island, battle of, 128
Loudoun, Lord, 75

MACPHERSON, 101
Malesherbes, 96
Manhattan, 39
Maryland, formation of, 32; early prosperity, 33
Mason, John, 48
Massachusetts colony, its growth, 48; during the commonwealth, 51; its struggles against restoration, 53; warfare with the French, 54; dis-

NOP

approval of the Navigation Laws, 65; meeting of the House of Assembly of, 77; protests against the Boston Port Bill, 84; provincial congress at, 82; raising of troops in, 86; prepares for war, 89; repeal of the Act for regulating the Government, 150
Massasoit, 46
Miantonomo, his death, 50
Mifflin, General, president of the Congress, 210
Miller, Joaquin, on the Indians, 5, 9
Minorca surrendered to the French, 200
Minuits, Peter, as governor of Manhattan, 39
Mobilian language, 6
Monmouth, battle of, 156
Montcalm, General, 62; his prediction, 64
Montesquieu, 97
Montgomery, Brigadier-General, invasion of Canada by, 114; his difficulties, 115
Morris, Robert, 188, 202
Moultrie Fort, British attack on, 120

NARRAGANSETTS, 49
Natchez, the, destruction of, 20
Navigation laws, the, disapproval and sufferings in the colonies under, 65
Necker, 187
Nelson in Central America, 175
Netherlands in 1775, 93; England's quarrel with the, 175
New Amsterdam, 40
New Brunswick, conquest of, 62
New England, early attempts at settlement in, 43; united colonies of, 50; King Philip's war in, 52; struggles against the Navigation Laws, 65; freedom of, 117
New Hampshire, 48
New Jersey, its history connected with that of Pennsylvania, 41; recovered from the British, 136; ravages of the British in, 137
New Sweden, 40
New York, the centre colony of a subgroup, 39; in the hands of the English, 41; Congress at, 71; suspension of the Assembly, 75; strengthening of its fortifications, 128; evacuation of, by the Americans, 130; evacuation of, by the British, 209
No-Popery riots in London, 179

Norfolk, burning of, 116
North American Indian, what he is, 3;
what he was, 4; his arts, 4; language, 6; government, 6; compared
with the Australian black, 5; inferiority of women, 7; beliefs, 7;
mode of warfare, 8; **absence of the**
pastoral element, 8; his morals and
endurance, 9; general character of
relations between the red and white
man, 11; distinction between the
Latin and Teutonic races in relation 10, 12; success of Roman
Catholic nations in Christianising
him, 12
North, Lord, his policy, 78; attempts
a compromise with America, 71; his
new measures, 88; his Conciliatory
Bills, 150; his policy, 177; fall of his
ministry, 200; his resignation, 201
Nova Scotia, French settlements in,
17; population of French in, 21

OGELTHORPE, James, failure of
his plans, 36; his charter and
government, 37; hostilities with
Spain, 38
Ohio Company, 51
'Olive Branch,' the, 111
Oliver, 71, 72
Opechancanough, 28, 29
Otis, James, 67

PARIS, peace of, 63
Parliament, debates in, 132; support of the ministry respecting
American affairs, 113; proceedings
regarding the war, 194; and the surrender of Cornwallis, 197
Penn, Richard, and the 'Olive Branch,'
111
Penn, William, his proprietary rights, 42
Pennsylvania, the last founded of the
religious colonies, 42; disaffection
in, 124
Penobscot Bay, the British in, 164
Pequod war with the English, 45
Peters, Hugh, 48
Philadelphia, continental congress at,
84; occupied by the British, 142;
rejoicings in England at the news of
its capture, 144; evacuation of, by
the British, 155
Philip, King, his war with the white
men, 52

Pilgrim fathers, 43
Pitt, William (afterwards Earl of Chatham), concurs with the American
resistance of the Stamp Act, 73; his
cabinet, 76; urges conciliation, 87,
129; his inconsistencies, 145; the
King refuses to make him premier,
152; last scene in his political life,
152; his death, 152
Pitt, William, opposed to the American
war, 174
Plymouth colony, 45
Pocahontas, 28
Poland, in 1772, 172; traditional friendship with France, 99
Ponce de Leon, discoverer of Florida, 14
Pontiac's war, 63
Portugal in 1775, 93
Prescott, Colonel, defeated at Bunker's
Hill, 107, 108
Prevost, Colonel, defeats Lincoln at
Briar Arch, 161
Priestley, 102
Princeton, battle of, 136
Protestant Association, 178
Putnam, General, defeated at Long
Island, 128

QUAKERISM in America, 42
Quartery Act, 75
Quebec, storming of, 115

RALEIGH, his attempts at colonisation in Virginia, 26
Rawden, Lord, defeated by Greene
in South Carolina, 193
Rebellions, predecessors of against, 111
Red man, the, 3; his relations with
the white men, 11; distinction between the Latin and Teutonic races
in relation 18, 12; success of the
Roman Catholic nations in Christianising him, 12; effect of the war on, 211
Reed, Colonel Joseph, 102, 126, 134
Restoration, the, 57
Revenue Act, failure of, 80
Revolution of 1688, 54
Reynolds, Sir Joshua, 101
Rhode Island, 48; dissolution of colonial government in, 119; recovered
by the British, 137; evacuation by
the British, 171
Rochambeau, 196
Rockingham cabinet, 73, 201
Rodney, Admiral, his successes at sea,

ROU

174; takes St. Eustace, 186; his defeat of Count de Grasse in the West Indies, 203
Rousseau, 94; his death, 236
Russia, in 1775, 92; its declaration of armed neutrality, 176
Rutledge, 127

ST. AUGUSTINE, 15
St. Eustace is taken by Rodney, 186
Saratoga, battle of, 143; gloomy impression in England produced by its surrender, 145
Savannah, taken by the British, 161; failure of the French and Americans at, 170; evacuated by the British, 204
Scott, Walter, 237
Separatists, 43; emigration of, 44; their compact before landing, 44; early difficulties of, 45; their relation with the Indians, 46
Shaftesbury's 'grand model' of Carolina, 35
Shelburne, appointed manager of American affairs, 201; as prime minister, 203; fall of his ministry, 207
Sheridan, 101
Slavery, in South Carolina, 36; growth of, 56; royal traders in, 56; in Africa, 57; passage in the Declaration of Independence struck out, 124
Slave trade, 118, 209; effect of the war on, 213
Smeaton, 103
Smith, Adam, 101
Smith, John, his adventures, 28
Smith, Lieut.-Colonel, defeated at Lexington, 104
Sons of Liberty organisations, 81
Soto, Ferdinand de, explorations of, 14
Spain, colonies of, in America, 14; position in America after the treaty of Paris, 1763, 16; colonial power of, 90; the only power with France directly interested in the American struggle, 93; in 1775, 93; secretly aids America, 118; her backwardness in going to war, 165; war convention with France, 166; at war with England, 167; negotiations stopped by the no-popery riots, 180; their successes against the English, 186
Spaniards, 14; discoveries by, in America, 14

VIR

Stamp Act, 1765, 69; riots caused by its introduction, 70, 71; cannot be carried into effect, 72; repealed, 1766, 73
Stillwater, battle of, 142
Strachey on the Indians, 4
Strutt, Jeredinh, 101
Stuart, Colonel, defeats Greene at Eutaw Springs, 195
Stuyvesant, governor of New Netherlands, 40
Sullivan, General, joins Washington, 134; devastates the Iroquois country, 164
Sumpter, Colonel, defeated by Tarleton at Camden, 181; and defeats him at Blackstock, 182
Sweden, colonies of, in America, 39; in 1775, 93

TARLETON, defeats Sumpter at Camden, 181; and is defeated by him at Blackstock, 182
Tea, Act of 1770, 79; repeal of Act, 151; destruction of, at Boston, 81
Thackeray, on colonists in America, 24
Thirteen English colonies, 24
Ticonderoga, surrender of, 105
Tippoo Sultan, his peace with England, 207
Tobacco, growth of, in Virginia, 31, 32
Trade Act, general prohibition of, 113
Trenton, surprise of the British at, 135
Turgot, 96, 118
Turkey in 1775, 92
Tryon, General, 163

UNCAS, the Mohegan, 50
Underhill, John, 40
United colonies of New England, 50
United States acknowledged as free, 206

VALLEY FORGE, Washington's winter quarters, 147
Vane, Sir Harry, governor of Massachusetts, 49
Vergennes, Count de, 111, 144, 146
Verrazzani, his discoveries, 17
Virginia, early attempts at colonisation in, 26; colonisation of, 27; first assembly in, 27; effect of the wars on, 28; submits to the Commonwealth, 29; its restoration, 30; its distress,

VOL.

31; effect of the stoppage of the growth of tobacco on, 31; its prosperity, 31; disputes about its government, 34; protests against the Boston Port Bill, 83; a Congress called in, 83; prepares for war, 84; dissolution of the House of Burgesses, 113; ravages in, 193

Voltaire, 94, his return to Paris, 235, his death, 236

W

WALPOLE, Horace, 101
Washington, Fort, surrender of, 132
Washington, George, takes part in the French and Indian war, 57; his proposed congress, 60; his bravery, 61; defeats the French, 62; his feelings respecting the conduct of England, 79; at the continental congress, 84; disclaims the idea of independence, 85; appointed commander-in-chief, 106; his character, 107; his difficulties, 108, 110; at New York, 120; his conduct towards the royal commissioners, 127; wretched state of his army, 107; evacuates New York, 130; his retreat through New Jersey, 132; outcry in America against him, 133; his temporary military dictatorship, 135; attacks Trenton, 135; defeats Cornwallis at Princeton, 136; recovers New Jersey, 136; his winter difficulties, 139; is defeated at Brandywine, 141; his retreat, 142; renewed outcry against, 142; his winter quarters at Valley

YOU

Forge, 137; his army during the winter of 1777–8, 162; his policy, 162; starving state of his army, 172; mutiny in his army, 184; junction with the French, 196; marches to Virginia, 197; defeats Cornwallis at Yorktown, 198; offered the crown, 201; discontent of his officers, 207; is thanked by Congress, 210; character of his greatness, 232; compared with Wellington, 233; success of American war attributed to him, 226; a thorough Englishman, 234

Watt, 102
Wedgwood, 102
Wellesley, Arthur (Duke of Wellington), 103, compared to Washington, 233
White, **Colonel**, ludicrous success of, 170
White man, the, 14; Spaniards, 14; French, 16; English, 22; advancement of in consequence of the war, 212
Whitefield, 38
Wilkes, John, 100
Williams, Roger, founder of Rhode Island, 48
Wyoming massacres, **158**

Y

YORKSHIRE Committee, 177
Yorktown, Cornwallis at, 195; invested by the French and Americans, 197; surrendered by Cornwallis to the Americans, 198
Young, Arthur, 102

MODERN HISTORICAL HANDBOOKS.

————◆◇◆————

In course of publication, each volume in fcp. 8vo. complete in itself.

Epochs of Modern History:

A SERIES OF BOOKS NARRATING THE

HISTORY OF ENGLAND AND EUROPE

At Successive Epochs subsequent to the Christian Era.

EDITED BY

EDWARD E. MORRIS, M.A.

Of Lincoln College, Oxford; Head Master of the Melbourne Grammar School, Australia;

BY

J. SURTEES PHILLPOTTS, B.C.L.

Late Fellow of New College, Oxford; Head Master of the Bedford Grammar School;

AND BY

C. COLBECK, M.A.

Fellow of Trinity College, Cambridge; Assistant Master on the Modern Side at Harrow School.

THE SERIES intitled '*Epochs of Modern History*' had its origin in the conviction that for purposes of Education or Study, a complete picture of any one important period of the World's history, carefully prepared and in an inexpensive form, is of more value than a mere outline of the History of a Nation.

The difficulty in applying this idea to books of history is the risk of spoiling **the** interest by diminishing the detail. But it is generally allowed that the complete picture of any short period is of more value, in an educational point of view, than a mere outline of the history of a nation; and the practice dictated by the course of many public examinations, of reading *periods* of history, seems to suggest a way **in** which it may be possible to secure in handy and cheap volumes that fulness without which history is unprofitable.

For schools the study of elaborate history is, and must remain, an impossibility; and generally, it may be safely said that in school routine time cannot be found for going through the complete continuous history of more than one or two countries at **most**. But it is **not** possible to understand thoroughly the history of even one country, if it be studied alone. A knowledge of the condition of surrounding countries is of at least equal importance with its own **previous** history. This is, so to speak, a horizontal rather than a vertical **study of history.**

It is hoped, therefore, **that** this series of books relating to definite periods of history, may meet a want which cannot be met by continuous histories of any one country. The series is by no means confined to the history of England, but deals also with European history; and where the course of events in England gives to the epoch its name and character, care has been and will be taken to trace the connexion of English history with that of the continental nations, and with the progress of ideas at work among them.

Great as the improvement **has been** in the histories prepared of late years for the use of schools, manuals thoroughly adapted for boys and girls are still required. The memories of the young cannot retain mere names, or retain them only at the cost of efforts which weaken their powers in other directions. In school histories no reference should be made to events of which some clear idea cannot be laid before the reader, and no names mentioned of actors in the history unless enough can be said to exhibit them as living men. To this rule the contributors to the present series will, as far as practicable, strictly adhere.

In short, it is their object, not to recount all the events of any given epoch, but to bring out in the clearest light those incidents and features on which the mind of the young most readily fastens.

Special attention is paid to those characteristics which exhibit the life of a people as well as the policy of their rulers.

With each volume is given a Map or Maps, illustrative of the period of which it treats, a Chronological Analysis, shewing the relation of English and foreign events, and an Index for reference. Foot-notes are avoided as tending to interrupt the reader's interest in the narrative. To bring out the sequence of events a full Marginal Analysis is supplied throughout.

Epochs of Modern History. 3

Eight Volumes now published :—

The ERA of the PROTESTANT REVOLUTION. By F. SEEBOHM, Author of the 'Oxford Reformers—Colet, Erasmus, More.' With 4 Coloured Maps and 12 Diagrams on Wood. Price 2s. 6d.

The CRUSADES. By the Rev. G. W. COX, M.A. late Scholar of Trinity College, Oxford; Author of the 'Aryan Mythology' &c. With a Coloured Map. Price 2s. 6d.

The THIRTY YEARS' WAR, 1618-1648. By SAMUEL RAWSON GARDINER, late Student of Ch. Ch. Author of 'History of England from the Accession of James I. to the Disgrace of Chief Justice Coke' &c. With a Coloured Map. Price 2s. 6d.

The HOUSES of LANCASTER and YORK; with the CONQUEST and LOSS of FRANCE. By JAMES GAIRDNER, of the Public Record Office, Editor of 'The Paston Letters' &c. With 5 Coloured Maps. Price 2s. 6d.

EDWARD the THIRD. By the Rev. W. WARBURTON, M.A. late Fellow of All Souls' College, Oxford; Her Majesty's Senior Inspector of Schools. With 3 Coloured Maps and 2 Genealogical Tables. Price 2s. 6d.

The AGE of ELIZABETH. By the Rev. M. CREIGHTON, M.A. late Fellow and Tutor of Merton College, Oxford. With 5 Maps and 4 Genealogical Tables. Price 2s. 6d.

The FALL of the STUARTS; and WESTERN EUROPE from 1678 to 1697. By the Rev. EDWARD HALE, M.A. Assistant Master at Eton. With Maps. Price 2s. 6d.

The PURITAN REVOLUTION. By SAMUEL RAWSON GARDINER, late Student of Ch. Ch. Author of 'The Thirty Years' War, 1618-1648,' in the same Series. With Maps. Price 2s. 6d.

From the ATHENÆUM, *May,* 8, 1875.

'The value of a set of little books on different epochs of history will probably be appreciated more as time goes on. At present the idea is a new one, and the work before us is only the fifth volume that has appeared. The design of the whole series is, however, one that must recommend itself

Volumes, in continuation of the Series, in various stages of preparation:—

The NORMANS in EUROPE. By Rev. A. H. Johnson, M.A. Fellow of All Souls' College, Oxford.

FREDERICK the GREAT and the SEVEN YEARS' WAR. By F. W. Longman, of Balliol College, Oxford.

The AGE of ANNE. By E. E. Morris, M.A. original Editor of the Series.

The FRENCH REVOLUTION to the BATTLE of WATERLOO, 1789-1815. By B. Merivale Cordery, Author of 'King and Commonwealth.'

The WAR of AMERICAN INDEPENDENCE. By J. M. Ludlow, Barrister-at-Law, Author of 'A Sketch of the History of the United States from Independence to Secession' &c.

The BEGINNING of the MIDDLE AGES: Charles the Great and Alfred—the History of England in its connexion with that of Europe in the Ninth Century. By the Very Rev. R. W. Church, M.A. Dean of St. Paul's.

The EARLY PLANTAGENETS and their RELATION to the HISTORY of EUROPE; the Foundation and growth of Constitutional Government. By the Rev. W. Stubbs, M.A. Professor of Modern History in the University of Oxford.

London, LONGMANS & CO.

www.ingramcontent.com/pod-product-compliance
Lightning Source LLC
Chambersburg PA
CBHW031936230426
43672CB00010B/1943